THE MODERN WOMAN'S

FIX IT
YOURSELF

HANDBOOK OF HOME REPAIR

THE Betty Crocker HOME LIBRARY

THE MODERN WOMAN'S
FIX IT
YOURSELF
HANDBOOK OF HOME REPAIR

BY HARRY ZARCHY

GOLDEN PRESS · NEW YORK
Western Publishing Company, Inc.
Racine, Wisconsin

Photographs by Bruce J. Roggeri

Dear Friend,

If your sink has been known to back up just when a dinner party is in the making, this book is for you. If the design of your kitchen wallpaper frustrates you and the cost of a decorator frustrates you even more, this book is for you. If you've waited days or weeks for someone to splice, sand, or service, this book is most certainly for you!

The Modern Woman's Fix It Yourself Handbook of Home Repair won't turn you into an expert overnight. But it should give you the confidence and the know-how to tackle a myriad of minor everyday jobs, and to help you avoid some of the headaches and repair bills that plague every householder. As a dividend, you may be encouraged to try some of the easy decorating fix-ups that will make your home more attractive both inside and out.

The author, Harry Zarchy, is not only skilled in both doing and teaching, but he is a prolific writer as well. You can count on him to take some of the mystery out of the complicated conveniences around the house that are so comforting when they work, so annoying when they don't. And because it's equally important to know when *not* to do it yourself, Mr. Zarchy is careful to caution you at these times as well.

There is money to be saved and satisfaction to be gained in learning how to fix and finish, renovate and repair. With these incentives, you will want to start right away!

Betty Crocker

Contents

3 FURNITURE   41

4 WALLS   71

5 WINDOWS 103

6 DOORS 117

7 FLOORS 127

8 HOUSE PAINTING 139

9 OUTDOORS 149

10 TOOLS, MATERIALS, AND EQUIPMENT 161

Index 209

Some Tips Before You Start

You don't have to be a mechanical genius to fix most things around the house. If you can drive an automobile, operate a vacuum cleaner, use a sewing machine, wield an electric carving knife, and cope with other sophisticated household appliances, you can certainly handle minor home repairs.

There are dozens of small, odd jobs that should be done to keep your home shipshape. You needn't call a professional for these because (1) they aren't important enough to warrant the services of a skilled mechanic; (2) the services of a professional are expensive; and (3) *you can fix most things yourself.* Many of these jobs are surprisingly simple; all it takes is a couple of turns of a screwdriver to tighten a loose doorknob, and you don't need any tools to replace a blown electrical fuse.

In addition to fixing things, you can make all kinds of useful and interesting improvements in your home. Why not install decorative tiles on the blank stretch of wall above the kitchen sink? Or lay colorful carpet tiles to glamorize a dull-looking bathroom floor? Or transform a worn piece of furniture with a new finish or a bit of fresh upholstery?

Evaluate your skills, but don't underestimate yourself. Just because you have never done something before doesn't necessarily mean that you can't do it. If you can follow a cookbook recipe, you can follow fix-it directions. It's much easier to repair a leaky faucet than it is to put a good meal together. Start with small jobs you are certain you can handle; then after doing a few minor repairs, you can make a fairly accurate estimate of your abilities. You may discover skills you never suspected you had.

Take Your Time

When you make up your mind to do a home repair job, try to choose a time when you won't be interrupted. Give yourself the chance to concentrate on what you are doing. Remember, no matter how insignificant a job may seem, it cannot be done right if you are in a hectic rush to get finished. Unless it is an emergency, do only part of the job, if necessary, but do it well. Then finish it the next day or whenever you can devote adequate time to it. In the long run, working unhurriedly will save time because you won't have to do things over again to undo mistakes, and there will be fewer spills, less frustration, and less chance of accidents.

Work Carefully

Good work habits will make any home repair job easier and safer. Read all labels and directions carefully, and analyze each step before you start, no matter how small the job may be. Get someone to work with you on big projects, such as taking down a door or putting up wall panels. Pay particular attention to cautionary notices on all containers. And use your common sense about routine safety measures—never smoke when you are working with paint or other flammable materials, make sure a ladder is steady before climbing on it, and work in a well-ventilated room or outdoors when you are using spray paints, varnishes, or other toxic substances. One more tip: before you start, gather all the tools and materials you will need; there's nothing more exasperating than getting well into a project only to find that an essential tool or part is missing.

Tools

You need good tools to do any job successfully. Forget about using Junior's Toy Tool Set, or anything like it; such sets just won't do. Instead, buy good tools of professional quality, the best you can afford.

How can you tell a good tool from one that is poorly made? First, ask questions. If you know any good mechanics or tool hobbyists, get their opinions about which tools to buy. Also, enlist the aid of your hardware dealer; he knows which brands craftsmen prefer.

Next, pick up a tool and handle it. Examine its finish—there should be no rough edges, and metal surfaces should be polished or chrome-plated. Jaws of pliers must work smoothly and fit together neatly when closed. A hammer handle, whether wood, metal, or plastic, should be shaped properly; it should be thin at the neck where it fits the head, then gradually become thicker so that you can grip the other end comfortably. Wooden handles should be hickory, coated with varnish or lacquer. A hammer must not only *feel* good in your hand, it should also look good.

Compare prices. You can expect to find price differences among brands, but be suspicious of tools that cost far less than any of the others. Stay away from bargain tools. Because they are usually inferior in design and construction, such tools perform poorly.

Which Tools Do You Need?

Although you can't become a functioning fix-it-yourselfer without a set of essential tools, don't rush out to buy every tool in sight; chances are you won't use most of them. Start with the basic tools and equipment listed here. Then get the specialized tools when the need arises.

Basic Home Repair Tools:
- **Hammer**
- **Assorted nails**
- **Screwdrivers:**
  - **three slotted drivers (small, medium, large)**
  - **three Phillips drivers (small, medium, large)**
- **Assorted wood screws**
- **Slip-joint pliers**
- **Hand or electric drill**
- **Assorted twist drills**
- **Crosscut saw**
- **Smooth plane, block plane, or rasp plane**
- **Adjustable-end wrench**
- **Utility knife**
- **Single-edged razor blades and holder**

Basic Equipment:
- **Steel tape measure**
- **Can of oil (any light machine oil)**
- **Assorted abrasive papers**
- **Pipe clamp**
- **Rubber plunger, or force cup**
- **Assorted plumbing washers**
- **Spare fuses (if your home has a fuse box)**
- **Electrician's plastic tape**
- **Silicone cement**
- **Silicone spray**
- **Contact cement**
- **White glue**
- **Epoxy glue**

Familiarize yourself with any tools and materials called for before you start working with them. In Chapter 10 (page 162) you will find a glossary of tools listed alphabetically for easy reference. Advice on where to buy tools and equipment is also provided (page 161). As you come across each new tool, turn to these pages to find out what it is, what it is used for, and how to use it. In a separate section in the same chapter, a list of terms and definitions will tell you what you need to know about the materials and equipment mentioned in the projects in this book.

Once you start doing your own home repair jobs, you will find that you are not only saving money, but that you are enjoying the sense of pride and accomplishment that comes when you "fix-it yourself!"

1

ELECTRICAL FIX-ITS

Because we depend on electricity to such a great extent, a power failure can virtually paralyze a modern home. Most people think that a breakdown in anything electrical is far too complicated for the average person to tackle. Nonsense! Although you can't do anything about a large-scale blackout, you can learn how to cope with everyday home emergencies.

You can also take care of many small nuisance problems which occur with electricity and electrical appliances. For example, you don't need special talent to change a fuse or reset a circuit breaker, install a new plug on an appliance cord, make an extension cord, install a room light dimmer, or rewire a lamp.

However, there are some jobs you should not attempt—*do not install new outlets or make any changes in the basic wiring in your home.* These jobs *must* be done by a licensed electrician who will observe national and local safety codes. Should a fire occur as the result of an unapproved electrical wiring change, you may have difficulty collecting fire insurance. In many areas, it is illegal for unlicensed people to do any electrical wiring.

CIRCUITS, FUSES, VOLTS, AMPERES, AND WATTS

Electrical Circuits and Fuses

You can easily understand all you need to know about electrical circuits, if you go about it logically. Begin with the idea that electrical power lines are brought in from outside to a *control panel*, usually located in a garage or basement. In apartments, panels are usually found in closets or hallways.

In a house, the control panel contains a main switch which can be used to turn off all the electrical current. The panel is also a terminal for *branch circuits*, which spread throughout different parts of the house. A branch circuit may supply current to a single appliance, such as an electric range, or to a single room or several rooms.

The panel also contains a *fuse* or *circuit breaker* for the main line, and one for each branch circuit. Fuses and circuit breakers are safety devices. A fuse (Figure 1) is screwed into

Figure 1. Fuse

a socket on the control panel, and is part of one circuit. Should a short circuit occur, a wire in the fuse will heat up and melt, creating an "open" circuit through which current cannot flow. A fuse can also "blow" when too many lights or other appliances are plugged into any one circuit (more about this later). Figure 2 shows a typical fuse-panel control board.

Many modern homes use panel-mounted circuit breakers instead of fuses. Excessive current in a circuit will trip a circuit breaker, so that current can no longer flow; as a result, the circuit-breaker handle will flip over to the "off" position. After you find and remedy the trouble,

Figure 2. Typical fuse-panel control board

push the handle to its "on" position to restore the current (Figure 3).

Figure 3. Circuit-breaker control panel

You can update a fuse board by replacing each fuse with a screw-in type circuit breaker (Figure 4). Should an overload trip one, reset it by simply pressing the little button on top.

Figure 4. Screw-in circuit breaker

To shut off the current on a fuse-panel control board, pull the handle on the section marked "Main," to remove the main fuse. If there is no main fuse, unscrew each fuse.

Figure 5. Main circuit breaker on control panel

To shut off all the current on a circuit-breaker control panel, flip the main circuit breaker to "off" (Figure 5). It's easy to find because it's larger than the other circuit breakers.

Volts

Every appliance—even the tiniest light bulb—is supposed to work at a specific *voltage*, or electrical pressure, and is so marked. Should you try to operate one on the wrong voltage, you'll run into trouble. Too little voltage will cause it to run inefficiently or not at all. Too much voltage can burn it out. However, these are things you

really don't have to worry about. House voltages in the United States are standardized at an average of 115 volts. Consequently, no matter what part of the country you live in, you can safely plug in a home appliance.

On the other hand, a 220-volt supply is standard in many European countries, and if you plan to travel abroad, you should buy a special *transformer*. This handy little gadget, which is plugged into a 220-volt outlet, reduces voltage to 115 volts, allowing you to use a hair dryer, electric shaver, heating pad, or any other appliance without burning it out.

Amperes

Amperes, or *amps*, refer to the amount of current flowing in a circuit. Every fuse or circuit breaker is marked to show how much current (how many amperes) it can safely handle. Circuits which supply current for home lighting usually require 15-amp fuses. Special circuits for heavy-duty appliances, such as laundry dryers and electric ranges, require 20 to 60-amp fuses.

Watts

Every electrical appliance is marked to show how many *watts* (how much power) it consumes. The more power an appliance needs to make it run, the more watts it uses up.

Overloaded Circuits

Have you ever plugged in an appliance, only to find that all the lights go out? You have probably overloaded the circuit, and a fuse or circuit breaker has let go.

To check for an overload, you must first determine how much current is being drawn, or is flowing, in the circuit. *Examine every appliance in the circuit*, including all light bulbs, and add up the watts they use up. Your list might look something like this:

Lights (adding all together)	400 watts
Blender	900 watts
Toaster	1000 watts
	TOTAL 2300 watts

To convert watts to amps, simply strike the last two zeros from the total wattage. In the example above, this would give you 23 amps, which, in a 15-amp circuit, would represent an overload of 8 amps. Under such conditions, the fuse or circuit breaker will pop. The solution is easy: simply reduce the amount of current being drawn through the circuit. Disconnect either the blender or the toaster, and plug them into a less-used circuit. Then replace the fuse or reset the circuit breaker.

But, you may ask, why not simply install a larger fuse which can pass more current? Wouldn't the circuit then be able to handle both the blender and the toaster? No! Most house circuits use No. 14 wire, designed to carry 15 amps safely. If too much current flowed through, the wires could heat up to a dangerous degree, enough to start a fire. Remember: a fuse is *supposed* to burn out, and a circuit breaker is *supposed* to pop open in case of an overload. *Never bypass a fuse!* Little tricks like placing a copper coin behind a fuse in order to "cure" an overload and prevent the fuse from burning out can be extremely dangerous.

Modernizing an Electrical System

Many homes are seriously underpowered. Those built before the 1940s are likely to have woefully inadequate electrical systems, some of which supply as little as 30 amps to an entire house. This doesn't begin to approach the requirements of a modern home, which may use an electric range, dishwasher, washing machine, clothes dryer, and air conditioners. An all-electric home needs a service line of at least 200 amps.

If you live in an older home, check to see whether your electrical service is adequate. It is *not* adequate if:

1. Fuses or circuit breakers are constantly popping.
2. Your TV picture shrinks when another appliance goes on (color TV sets may lose their color).
3. Lights dim when an oil burner, dishwasher, or other major appliance starts up.

Should these conditions exist, get a licensed electrician to look things over and make recom-

mendations. He may separate existing circuits for more efficient use, install a new control panel with more circuits, or even pull in a heavier service line from outside. In any case, this is not a fix-it-yourself operation, but must be done according to local and national safety codes.

THINGS EVERY MEMBER OF THE FAMILY SHOULD KNOW

Locate the control panel in your home and learn how to pull the main switch or circuit breaker to shut off all the current.

Find out which fuses or circuit breakers control the different circuits in your home. To do this, first turn on all the lights. Then disconnect one circuit by removing a fuse or flipping off a circuit breaker. Make a note of which lights go out. Do this with each fuse or breaker. In each room, check unused outlets and those normally used for your various appliances by plugging in a small lamp. You may end up with notations such as: Fuse No. 1—hall and rear bedroom lights and outlets; No. 2—outlets over kitchen counter; No. 3—living room and dining room lights, No. 4—washer-dryer, etc.

If the inside of your control-panel door does not already have a printed form for this information, make a written or typed list and paste it there. Should you ever have to cut off a circuit for any reason, you can isolate it by turning off the proper fuse or circuit breaker, leaving power in the rest of the house.

Never do any work on circuit wiring unless you first remove the fuse from that circuit or turn off the circuit breaker.

Never stand in a wet area while you turn on an electrical appliance. Even touching one that has not been properly installed can give you a severe shock. Have an electrician check out all basement-situated appliances to see that they are properly grounded.

In the event of a power failure, reach for a flashlight. (It is a good idea to keep a flashlight stored where everyone can get at it easily. A good place might be a kitchen cabinet or drawer. Be sure it is kept in good working order by checking the batteries once in a while.) After locating the flashlight, find the control panel and *pull the main switch*. Next, disconnect all portable appliances and turn off all lights. When current is restored, there won't be a tremendous surge that could blow the fuses or breakers.

WHAT TO DO IF AN APPLIANCE DOESN'T WORK

A simple check will often reveal the reason for a small electrical difficulty. You may save yourself lots of exasperation, as well as the cost of a service call, if you can remedy the problem yourself.

Many appliances don't work simply because they aren't plugged in or because they are plugged into overloaded circuits. Others may be defective.

Electrical Appliance Checklist

Follow as many steps as necessary in order to find out why the appliance doesn't work:

Is the appliance plugged into a wall outlet?

Is the outlet alive? Check it by plugging in either a lamp, or an electrical-circuit tester (Figure 6, and page 196).

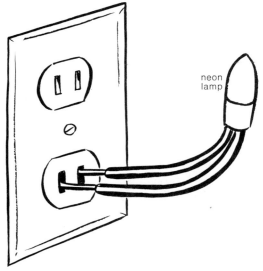

neon lamp

Figure 6. Circuit tester

If the outlet is dead, pull out all the plugs connected to that circuit, and check the fuse or circuit breaker.

After restoring the fuse or circuit breaker, plug the appliance back into the same outlet. If the appliance works properly, either the circuit has been overloaded or another appliance in the circuit is faulty.

If the fuse or circuit breaker pops when you plug in the appliance, something is wrong with the appliance. Don't use it again until it has been repaired. A defective cord or plug may be at fault. If you replace both, and it still doesn't work, turn it over to a professional for repair.

Other Possible Sources of Trouble

Motor may need oiling. Many appliances have motors. Some are permanently sealed and lubricated and require no maintenance; among these are washing machines, dryers, and dishwashers which do not have to be oiled for the life of the appliance. Others, such as sewing machines and electric fans, and pump motors which circulate hot water in your heating system, should be lubricated once a year. Some motors have oiling instructions printed on them; follow these instructions exactly. Circulator motors are equipped with oil cups, into which you squirt a few drops of lubricating oil. Motors of electric fans usually do not have oil cups; to lubricate a fan motor, apply two or three drops of oil to the motor shaft at the point where it enters the motor.

Use oil sparingly! Don't assume that if a little oil is good, a lot of oil must be better. You can ruin a motor by overoiling it.

Setting may need adjusting. Servicemen are often summoned to "emergencies," only to find that an appliance has not been set or adjusted properly. Washing machines and dishwashers, for example, can be set for different operating cycles. If a machine does not perform properly, don't automatically assume that it's defective; you may have set it for the wrong cycle. As a case in point, a dishwasher that leaves dishes dirty and sopping wet may have been set for a simple rinse instead of a complete wash.

Filter may need cleaning. A clogged filter places a strain on a motor, causing it to work too hard, overheat, and possibly burn out. Washing machines, dryers, vacuum cleaners, and air conditioners all have dust or lint filters that must be replaced or cleaned at regular intervals. Be sure to read the instructions that come with your appliance to see if it has a filter.

If your vacuum cleaner seems to be slowly dying, runs very hot, and doesn't clean very well, it may need a new filter bag, or else the hose may be clogged. To unclog a hose, remove it from the motorized cleaning unit and examine it to see if you can remove any clogged material with your fingers. If not, *slowly* push a broom handle through the hose. If it meets a solid obstruction, reverse the hose and push the handle through from the other side. This should dislodge whatever it is that is causing the trouble.

Dishwashers employ filters to prevent food particles from causing clogged drains. Clean them at regular intervals.

Warm-air furnaces use filters. Some are disposable, while others can be either vacuumed or washed clean. Most filters are simply slipped into a slot behind the furnace and can be replaced without using tools.

The filters in air conditioners are usually easy to get at, and they can be vacuumed or washed. Some air-conditioner filters can be removed and replaced by pulling them out of the top of the machine, then pushing them back in. Sometimes it is necessary to remove the front panel in order to get at the filter. In any case, consult the manual which came with your unit. In ordinary use, clean the filter at the beginning of each air-conditioning season. If you live in a dusty or smoggy area, clean it once a month.

The hood over your kitchen range uses a filter, too. This is usually a permanent type and should be cleaned. Immerse it in hot water and household detergent, and scrub off all accumulated grease. Allow it to dry before you replace it.

Your washing machine probably has a lint filter. Clean it each time you use the machine. The hoses which go to the hot and cold water-supply faucets also contain filters—finely meshed metal screens that trap and hold particles carried in with the water. Disconnect the hoses, remove the screens, flush them under running water, then replace them. Do this once a year.

Clean the lint filter in your clothes dryer each time you finish using the machine. If you don't, lint will build up inside the filter, forming a thick felt which will prevent the dryer from exhausting hot air properly.

Other Maintenance Hints

If you live in a particularly dusty area, it's a good idea to cover the outside of your air conditioner during the winter. Covers are available in all sizes. You can vacuum the insides of some air conditioners by removing the front panel. Others are sealed, so that no parts of the mechanism can be reached.

If you can move your refrigerator away from its accustomed nook (some have rollers, which make moving easy), vacuum the condenser on the back. This looks like a network of tubing, covered with metal fins. Since the condenser gives off heat, a layer of dust will prevent it from operating efficiently.

Many electric heaters have polished metal reflectors. Keep them polished so that heat is properly dispersed. Unplug the heater and remove the metal guard from the front. If the guard does not slip off easily, loosen one or two screws in order to remove it. Wipe the reflector with a damp, soapy cloth, then dry it with a clean soft cloth. If it is badly tarnished, use metal polish to shine it up.

Keep TV sets free and unencumbered. Don't set plants or knickknacks on top of them. Like other electronic devices, a TV set must radiate heat in order to remain cool, and if you cover the top, you may damage the set by preventing the heat from escaping.

Handle sink dishwashers with care. These are hand-held units connected to the water supply by means of a pliable hose. Don't bend the hose sharply; it may break. For the same reason, avoid twisting the hose by always replacing it in exactly the same position it was in before you picked it up. A twisted hose may become kinked; this causes breakage, and replacing a hose is a messy job which calls for a special wrench, a plumber's skill, and an even temper.

REPLACING A WALL RECEPTACLE

Do appliance plugs keep falling out of an outlet? If the plug is in good condition, this may mean you need a new receptacle.

You will need:

> **Duplex receptacle**
> **Screwdriver**
> **Needle-nose pliers**
> **Electrical circuit tester**

What to do:

1. Disconnect the fuse or circuit breaker so that the circuit with which you are working is dead. Or pull the main switch on the control panel, cutting off all the current (see Figure 5).

2. Check the circuit to make certain it's dead by plugging in either an electrical tester (see page 196), or a small lamp. If no lights show, proceed with the next step.

3. Use a screwdriver to remove the wall plate from the old outlet (Figure 7).

Figure 7. Removing wall plate from receptacle

4. Remove the two screws which hold the receptacle to the wall box (Figure 8).

Figure 8. Removing screws holding receptacle to wall box

5. Pull the old outlet, or receptacle, out of the wall box. Unscrew and release the wires attached to it . Discard the old receptacle.

6. Use needle-nose pliers to wrap the wires clockwise around the screws of the new receptacle. Connect the white wire to the screw on the silvery side of the receptacle and the black wire to the screw on the brass side (Figure 9). It is important that this be done to avoid the possibility of shocks.

Figure 9. New receptacle with wiring attached

7. Fasten the new outlet to the wall box. New outlets are equipped with machine screws held in place with fiber washers.

8. Replace the wall plate. Tighten the screws so that the plate is held firmly.

9. Turn on the current. Check the outlet with your electrical tester to make certain the outlet is alive.

Hints

Two types of wall receptacles are used with 115-volt circuits. One has two holes in its face and accepts plugs with two prongs. The other has three holes, for plugs with three prongs. The third prong is attached to a ground wire. Should an appliance develop a short circuit, the ground wire would safely bypass the current. Since 3-wire receptacles require 3-wire circuits, they cannot replace older, 2-wire receptacles. Replace your old receptacle with one that is the same type as the one you are discarding.

REPLACING A WALL TOGGLE SWITCH

Wall switches seldom break down. However, old types are noisy and can easily be replaced by new, silent ones.

You will need:

> **Toggle switch**
> **Screwdriver**
> **Needle-nose pliers**
> **Electrical circuit tester**

What to do:

1. Disconnect the current from the circuit you are working on. Remove the wall plate. Test the switch to see whether it is alive by touching the test prods of the electrical tester to the two switch terminals. If the tester lights up, there's current in the circuit. If no light shows, the circuit is dead.

2. Remove the two screws which hold the switch in place (Figure 10) and pull the switch out of the wall box. Unscrew and release the wires attached to it. Discard the old switch.

Figure 10. Removing wall switch

3. Use needle-nose pliers to wrap the wires clockwise around the two screw terminals of the new switch. (Either wire can be wrapped around either screw.) Turn the screws down tight.

4. Push the new switch into the wall box. *Important:* Be sure the switch is positioned properly. The toggle should point down, with the word *off* clearly visible.

5. Fasten the switch to the wall box. New switches usually have two machine screws attached, held in place with fiber washers.

6. Replace the wall plate. Tighten the screws so that the plate is held firmly.

7. Restore current in the circuit, then test the new switch by flipping it on and off a few times.

INSTALLING A ROOM LIGHT DIMMER

There are times when you'd like to cut down on the amount of light in a room. It's pleasant to be able to eliminate glare and to control the light in a dining room chandelier or bedroom fixture.

You can easily install a *dimmer* to take the place of a wall toggle switch.

You will need:

> **Dimmer unit**
> **Screwdriver**
> **Needle-nose pliers**
> **Two solderless wire connectors**
> **Electrical circuit tester**

What to do:

1. Turn off the current.

2. Use a screwdriver to remove the toggle-switch wall plate. Check the circuit with the electrical tester to be sure it's dead.

3. Remove the two screws which hold the switch in place and pull it out of the wall box.

4. Unscrew and release the wires attached to the switch and discard the old switch.

5. With pliers, straighten the ends of the wires which were attached to the switch.

6. Using solderless wire connectors, connect these two wires to the two wires leading from the dimmer. Place the ends of two wires together, insert them into the opening of a wire connector, and twist the connector clockwise as far is it will go (Figure 11).

7. Push the wires into the wall box, tucking them into the corners to make room for the dimmer.

8. Fit the dimmer into the box, and secure it with two machine screws. Finally, install the wall plate.

Figure 11. Installing dimmer

FIXING A FLUORESCENT LIGHT

What Makes Lights Work?

Current flowing through the filament of an incandescent light bulb causes it to glow, giving off light. A fluorescent lamp, or tube, has no filaments. It requires high voltage, which is supplied by a ballast; this causes a coating of phosphorus on the inside of the tube to glow. You can't see the ballast because it's tucked away inside the light fixture (Figure 12).

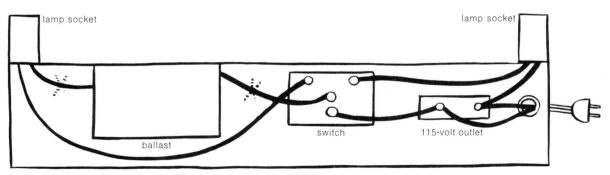

Figure 12. Inner components of a fluorescent lamp

All you can see on a modern fluorescent fixture is the tube and the sockets into which it fits. Older fixtures also use a *starter*, a small, metal cylinder that projects from the fixture underneath one end of the fluorescent lamp. It triggers the lamp into giving off light.

Troubleshooting Fluorescent Lights

If you flip the wall switch and a fluorescent light doesn't go on, don't immediately blame the fixture. First check the circuit; you may have a popped fuse or circuit breaker.

If the circuit is alive, check the condition of the tube. Do this by replacing it with one you know to be good. This could be a new one or one that works in another fixture.

Older Fixtures (with starters)

If the good tube fails to light, replace the starter. To remove it, press in and give it a half turn to the left.

Sometimes nothing seems to help: you have a live circuit, a new tube and starter, and still the light does not go on. Don't give up; try this instead: grasp the tube firmly with both hands and rotate it toward you, and then away from you, alternately tightening and loosening the tube in its sockets. (*Don't* twist the tube or it may break.) This movement will often wear away a thin coating of oxide which may be preventing the pins at the ends of the tube from making contact with the socket. Do this with each tube in the fixture. *Caution:* Don't let go of a tube until you are certain it is seated in the socket and can't fall out.

New Fixtures (no starters)

Replace the defective tube with one you know to be good. If it doesn't light at once, try turning the tube as previously described.

With all types of fixtures, discard any tube that glows weakly, flickers, burns brighter at one end than the other, or gives off a reddish light.

Although it doesn't happen too often, a ballast can go bad. It will simply stop operating, and the tubes won't light no matter what you do. You can detect a short-circuited ballast immediately, for it usually gives off the sharp, acrid smell of burning insulation. It may also smoke. Should this happen, switch off the current at once. Have the ballast replaced by an electrician or buy a new fixture.

Hint

Turning fluorescent lights on and off at frequent intervals will shorten their life. It is better to let them burn for a while; the cost of electricity used will be less than that of a new tube.

MAKING A LIGHT-DUTY EXTENSION CORD

There are times when you desperately need an extension cord. You may want to move an electric fan to a better location; rig up a temporary light on a porch or patio; hook up an electric shaver, radio, electric toothbrush; or use a cord for any number of other reasons.

You will need:

> No. 18 lamp cord (zip cord)
> Diagonal-cutting pliers
> Solderless male plug
> Solderless female receptacle

There are several different types of solderless plugs and receptacles on the market that you can attach to a lamp cord in seconds with no difficulty. They may differ slightly in appearance, but they all operate on the same principle: when you press down a lever, a set of sharp teeth engages the wire and holds it firmly in the plug.

What to do:

1. Use the pliers to cut through about ½ inch of insulation between wires at one end of the cord (see page 178).

2. Raise the lever at the top of the plug to a vertical position. (Some plugs have a lever at the side instead of the top.) Push the cut end of the wire into the slot in the side of the male plug (Figure 13).

3. Press the lever down (Figure 14), securing the cord. Install the female receptacle at the

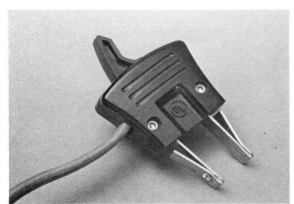

Figure 13. Male plug with lever up and wire inserted

other end of the cord, following the same directions.

Figure 14. Male plug with lever down

MAKING A HEAVY-DUTY EXTENSION CORD

It may become necessary to temporarily relocate a heavy-duty appliance. For example, you may find a better place for an electric heater or large ventilating fan. If the cord won't reach the outlet, you'll need a heavy-duty extension cord which can easily pass the current required. You'll also need such a cord when operating electric tools, such as drills and sanders. If the outlets in your home have only two slots in them, use 2-conductor wire to make the cord.

You will need:

> **No. 14 2-conductor extension wire of the length required**

> **2-piece heavy-duty male plug, 2-wire**
> **2-piece heavy-duty female extension cord receptacle for 2-pronged male plug**
> **Cutting pliers**
> **Screwdriver**
> **Utility knife or single-edged razor blade in holder**
> **Insulation stripper, penknife, or single-edged razor blade in holder**

Attaching a 2-Conductor Male Plug
What to do:

There are several different types of 2-piece male plugs. They are all hooked up in essentially the same way, although you may find minor differences in the amount of insulation you must strip away before attaching the extension cord wires to the plug. The directions given here apply only to those plugs which can be clamped to the extension wire.

1. Using the razor blade or knife, cut through about 1 inch of outer insulation at one end of the cord. Be careful not to cut into the wires inside. Pull off the outer insulation and trim away the twisted paper to expose the two insulated wires beneath.

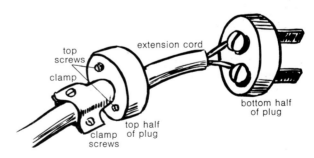

Figure 15. Heavy-duty extension-cord wires attached to 2-piece male plug

2. Take the plug apart by removing the top screws. Loosen the clamp screws so that you can pass the extension cord through the clamp to the plug (see Figure 15).

3. Now use the insulation stripper to remove about ¾ inch of inner insulation from the end

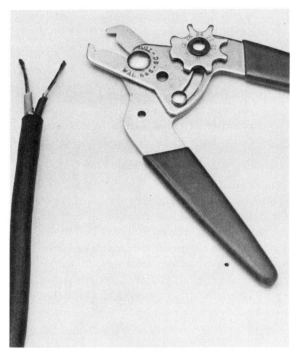

Figure 16. Wire ends stripped to ¾ inch and insulation stripper

of each wire on the cord (Figure 16). Twist the bared wire ends clockwise with your fingers as much as you can, and shape each end into a loop.

4. Loosen the screws and U-shaped metal pieces under the screws on the bottom part of the plug. Around each screw, under the U-shaped pieces (Figure 15), wrap one of the loops of the extension cord wires (it doesn't matter which wire goes around which screw). The end of each wire loop should point in the direction the screw must be turned in order to tighten it. Tighten both screws.

5. Reassemble the plug by fitting the top and bottom parts together, then tighten the screws which hold both halves together.

6. Tighten the screws that secure the clamp and one end of the extension cord is complete.

Attaching a Female Receptacle

The other end of the heavy-duty extension cord is attached to the female receptacle. The procedure is the same as that used to attach a male plug. Again, specific directions will vary slightly with different makes of receptacles.

What to do:

1. With any receptacle, first take the two halves apart by loosening the screws in its top.

2. Pass the end of the extension cord through the top half of the receptacle. Cut away about 1½ inches of outer insulation, then bare about ¾ inch of the ends of each wire. Twist the wire ends clockwise, then attach them to the bottom half of the receptacle, exactly as you did with the male plug.

3. Reassemble the receptacle by screwing the two halves together.

4. With some receptacles, you must attach the wires to the *top half.* In that case, strip away enough outer insulation to allow you to bring each wire end around a prong and a screw.

MAKING A HEAVY-DUTY, GROUNDED, 3-WIRE EXTENSION CORD

If your home has 3-wire, grounded outlets, you should use extension cords which contain three wires. Each end of the cord is attached to three screw terminals at the plug and receptacle.

Three-wire circuits lessen, and can eliminate, the possibility of electric shock. Should an appliance or power tool develop a short circuit while you are using it, current will be bypassed through the *ground wire,* instead of through you.

You will need:

    No. 14 3-conductor extension wire
    2-piece, 3-wire, heavy-duty male plug
      (clamp type)
    2-piece, 3-wire, heavy-duty female
      receptacle (clamp type)
    Cutting pliers
    Screwdriver
    Utility knife, or single-edged razor blade
      in holder
    Insulation stripper, penknife, or single-
      edged razor blade in holder

What to do:

1. Prepare the ends of the wire as you would if you were making a 2-wire extension cord. The only difference is that the wires in a 3-conductor cord are connected to three screws at each end.

2. Take the plug apart. Loosen the clamp screws. Strip about 1½ inches of outer insulation from each end of the cord. Use the stripper to remove about ¾ inch of insulation from the end of each wire.

3. Connect the bared wire ends to screws in both the plug and the receptacle, following this nationally standard code:

> The *green* (ground wire) is connected to a green or hexagonal screw.
> The *white* (neutral) wire is connected to a silvery-colored screw.
> The *black* (hot) wire is connected to a brass-colored screw.
> (The term "hot" has nothing to do with temperature; it simply means that the wire is electrically alive when the current is turned on.)

Figure 17. One end of 3-wire extension cord, showing 2-piece male plug assembled

4. Reassemble the plug (Figure 17) and the receptacle. Tighten the screw clamps so that the cord is held firmly.

REWIRING A LAMP

Check your lamps. Many old lamps were originally wired with cotton-covered, rubber-insulated lamp cord. Often the rubber hardens and cracks, and the cotton covering frays. Short circuits can easily occur in cords in this condition. Rewire such lamps with modern, plastic-insulated cord.

You will need:

> Screwdriver
> Insulation stripper, penknife, or single-edged razor blade in holder
> Cutting pliers
> Utility knife
> Lamp cord (also known as zip cord)

What to do:

1. Unplug the lamp, remove the shade and lamp bulb. Take the socket apart by squeezing the shell where it is marked "press," and pulling it at the same time. If necessary, pry the shell from its base with a screwdriver after it has been loosened (Figure 18).

2. Remove the brass outer shell and the inner fiber sleeve. This exposes the core, or socket, to which the lamp cord is connected.

3. Loosen the two screws on the socket core, and remove the wires. Put the core aside.

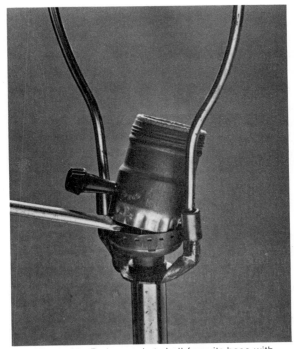

Figure 18. Prying socket shell from its base with screwdriver

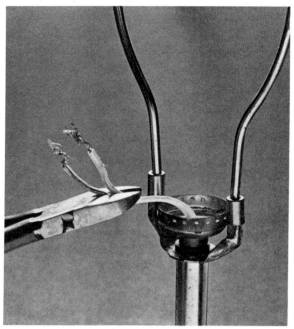

Figure 19. Cutting through ends of wires with side-cutting pliers

4. With the cutting pliers, cut through both wires, removing the twisted ends, as in Figure 19. This makes it easier to remove the old wire. Just pull it out through the bottom of the lamp (Figure 20).

Figure 20. Pulling old wire from bottom of lamp

5. Measure and cut off the length of cord you need in order to rewire the lamp. Push one end of the wire through the bottom of the lamp until it emerges from the base of the socket (Figure 21).

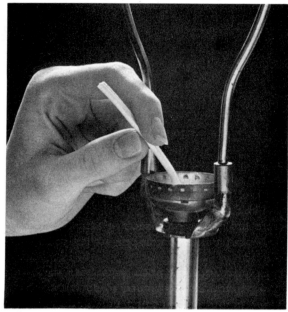

Figure 21. New wire brought through base of socket

6. Use cutting pliers or a utility knife to slit about 1 inch of the insulation between the ends of the double wire (Figure 22).

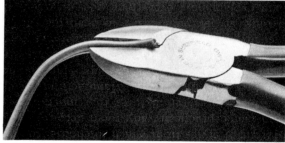

Figure 22. Slitting insulation between ends of double wire

7. Separate the wires so that you have two ends about 3 inches long. Use the insulation stripper to remove 1 inch of insulation from the end of each wire. Twist the bared ends of the wires clockwise so that individual strands are held together.

8. Examine the socket core. If it's broken, or if you'd like to replace it with one that has a different type of switch, discard it. Some stores sell socket cores separately. You can probably use the brass shell from the old socket. If necessary, buy a whole new socket, and just use the core and fiber sleeve.

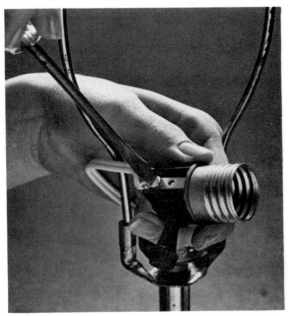

Figure 23. Fastening wire to terminals in socket

9. Wrap the ends of the bared wires clockwise around the screw terminals on the socket core and tighten the screws (Figure 23).

Figure 24. Replacing socket shell

10. Slip the fiber sleeve and brass shell over the core, and replace them in the socket base. Push down until you hear the shell click solidly into place (Figure 24).

WIRING A MALE PLUG

After you have rewired the socket core of the lamp, you can fasten a solderless plug to the other end of the wire (as described on page 12); or you can attach a 1-piece, screw-type male plug. This widely used type of male plug, of rubber or plastic, is molded in one piece. Wires are attached by means of screws.

You will need:

    Insulation stripper
    Screwdriver
    Male plug

What to do:

1. Push the end of the lamp cord through the bottom of the plug and up through the top.

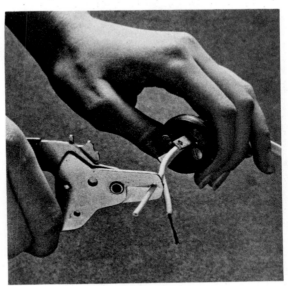

Figure 25. Stripping ends of wires

Make a small cut between the two insulated wires. Pull the wires apart so that you have two single, insulated wires about 3 inches long. Strip about ¾ inch of insulation from the end of each wire, as in Figure 25.

2. Make an *Underwriters' Knot* in the two wires (Figure 26). Pull it tight, then draw it down into the body of the plug. If anyone should yank the cord to remove it from an outlet, the knot would prevent it from pulling loose.

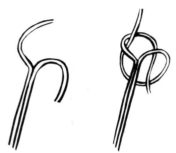

Figure 26. Underwriters' Knot

3. Wrap each bare wire around a prong, then clockwise under the head of a screw. Tighten the screws (Figure 27). Replace the fiber shield over the prongs of the plug.

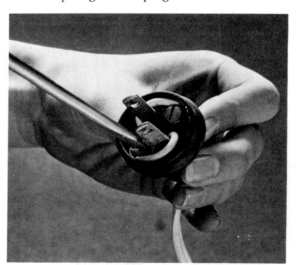

Figure 27. Tightening screw in 1-piece male plug

REPLACING A HEAVY-DUTY PLUG ON AN APPLIANCE CORD

You may have to replace the plug on appliance cords that get lots of use and abuse, such as those attached to toasters and electric irons. Since these appliances draw an appreciable amount of current (which tends to heat up cords), they are usually attached to asbestos-insulated wire cords.

You will need:

> Heavy-duty, 2-piece male plug, clamp-to-cord type
> Cutting pliers
> Screwdriver
> Insulation stripper
> Utility knife or single-edged razor blade in holder
> Plastic electrician's tape

What to do:

1. Remove the old defective plug by snipping it off with cutting pliers.

2. Take the new plug apart by loosening the screws at its top. Pass the end of the appliance cord through the bottom of the lower half of the plug.

3. Heavy-duty appliance wires are often covered with cotton wrapping. Use the knife or razor blade to slit the cotton wrapping back 2 inches from the end.

4. Cut away the cotton covering and any loose insulation to expose 2 inches of the two insulated wires (Figure 28).

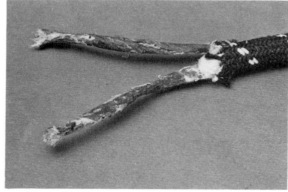

Figure 28. Wire ends with 2 inches of insulation exposed

5. Wrap a couple of turns of plastic electrician's tape around the end of the cotton covering, to prevent it from unraveling (Figure 29).

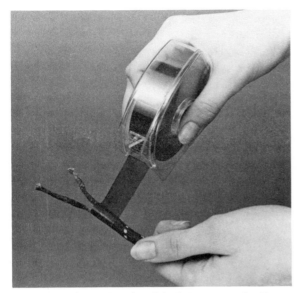

Figure 29. Wrapping electrician's tape around cotton covering of wire

6. Cut the stripped wire ends, leaving them just long enough to go around a prong and a terminal screw. With the insulation stripper, bare about ¾ inch of each wire end. Twist the ends clockwise so that the separate strands are held together.

7. Wrap each wire clockwise, under the head of a screw. Tighten the screws to hold the wires securely.

8. Assemble the two halves of the plug. Tighten the clamp screws so that the wire is held securely. *Important:* Clamps must be tight, otherwise someone pulling the wire to unplug it might rip the cord out of the plug. A tight clamp takes the place of an Underwriters' Knot (see Figure 26).

REDUCING APPLIANCE CLUTTER

Some appliances such as toasters, juicers, can openers, blenders, and broilers are usually kept in one place on a kitchen counter causing two problems: (1) they can't all be plugged into one outlet, and (2) they all have wires which can cause clutter.

You can easily plug in a multiple outlet plate which simply fits into your present outlet—no

alterations are needed. Some multiple outlets will allow you to plug in up to four appliances at once. Or use a multiple outlet strip, which is also plugged into your wall outlet. This allows you to plug in up to six light appliances. Again, be careful not to overload the circuit by using too many appliances at once.

You can eliminate cluttered wires by shortening them, then fitting them with either their original male plugs or new ones, if the old plugs are molded to the wire.

REPLACING A DOORBELL PUSH BUTTON

Since push buttons are located outside the house, they are exposed to all kinds of weather. Eventually the switch contacts inside may corrode or oxidize, and the button will not work.

You can replace it with a simple push button, or one that lights up and has a slot for your name. Lighted push buttons use very little current, and are good for use in dark areas. Figure 30 shows a simple doorbell hook-up. When

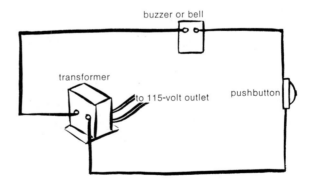

Figure 30. Buzzer or bell circuit

you push the button you close the circuit, causing the buzzer or bell to sound.

You will need:

    Screwdriver
    New push button
    Utility knife

What to do:

1. Remove the screws that hold the old push button in place and pull the button away from the wall. If it is the type that is pressed into a hole in the door frame, pry it loose with a screwdriver.

2. Unscrew and remove the two wires attached to the push button. Discard the old push button. Using a knife blade, scrape the ends of the wires until they are bright and shiny.

3. Connect the wires to the new push button by bending them clockwise around the screws; then tighten the screws.

4. Press the push button to test it. If it works, install it.

If your new push button doesn't work, it may not be the fault of the button. You can perform a few simple tests to determine where the fault lies. It may be the bell or the bell transformer. Test each one and you will find the defect by the process of elimination.

Testing the push button

If the push button doesn't work, "short" the two wires by bridging them with a knife or screwdriver. You should see a spark and hear the doorbell ring. If this happens, tighten the wire connections and try the push button again. If it still doesn't work, the push button is defective.

Testing the bell

If you don't see a spark and the bell doesn't work when you "short" the wires, disconnect one wire from the bell. Disconnect the two push button wires and twist them together. Touch the disconnected bell wire to the other bell wire. If there is a spark, the bell circuit is alive but the bell is defective.

Testing the bell transformer

If there is no spark when the bell wires are shorted, check the fuse or circuit breaker to see whether the circuit is alive. Short the wires again. If there is still no spark, the transformer is defective. (The transformer is a device which changes 115 volts to the 10 or 15 volts needed to operate bells and chimes.) Get an electrician to replace it.

With a new transformer installed, hook up the bell and push button. Press the button. If the bell still doesn't work, replace it.

RECONDITIONING CHIMES

When you press a doorbell push button, an electromagnet in the chime unit causes a plunger to slide over and strike a metal bar; this produces a tone. If no tone is heard when you press the push button, the chimes may need reconditioning. Chime plungers often become sluggish and stop working. This may be caused by accumulated dirt or rust.

You will need:

    Screwdriver
    Fine steel wool
    Lighter fluid

What to do:

1. To clean a plunger, remove it from its sleeve. To do this, it is necessary to remove the tonal bar, which is held by two screws (Figure 31).

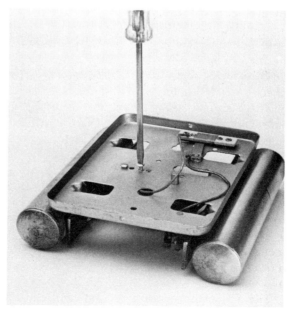

Figure 31. Removing screws which hold tonal bar

2. If the plunger is rusted, polish it with fine steel wool, then wipe it clean with a cloth moistened with lighter fluid. *Caution:* Lighter fluid is highly flammable. Use it out-of-doors or near an open window. And, of course, don't smoke while using it.

3. Clean the inside of the plunger sleeve with steel wool, and wipe it with a cloth and lighter fluid.

4. Replace the plunger in its sleeve, and replace the tonal bar. Don't lubricate the plunger in any way; oil would eventually gum it up. Work the plunger back and forth a few times by hand. It should now move freely.

REPLACING A CEILING FIXTURE

Does your home have an old-fashioned ceiling fixture that's ready for retirement? You can easily replace it with a modern one. There are dozens of styles from which to choose, so you can match practically any room decor.

Most stores sell fixtures that must be assembled by the buyer. Manufacturers save time, money, and space by supplying all the parts in a carton. Assembly instructions are usually included but they are sometimes confusing, so ask your dealer to open the carton and explain how everything goes together. If you look properly baffled by his explanation, he may even assemble the fixture for you. In any case, this will give you an opportunity to check for missing parts.

There are several basic things you ought to know before you install a new fixture.

All fixtures are fastened to an *outlet box,* a steel box with an open face, located in the ceiling.

Wires from the outlet box are joined to wires from the fixture by means of screw-on *solderless connectors.*

Every fixture has a *canopy,* a decorative metal shell that fits against the ceiling and hides the outlet box. The canopy may be part of a fixture or a separate piece.

There are various simple systems used to hold fixtures. If you are replacing an old fixture

with another of the same type, use the same system that held the old fixture.

REPLACING A KEYHOLE-SLOT MOUNTED FIXTURE

Kitchen ceiling fixtures, particularly those which use glass globes, are the easiest to install.

You will need:

> **New fixture**
> **Screwdriver**
> **2 solderless connectors**
> **Stepladder**

What to do:

1. Turn off the current, either at the wall switch or the control panel.

2. Remove the globe and bulb from the fixture.

3. Figure 32 shows how the fixture is held in place. The canopy has two slotted holes that fit

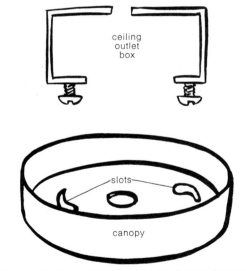

Figure 32. *Top:* Ceiling outlet box. *Below:* Canopy, showing slots

over screws driven into holes in the outlet box.

Loosen the two screws by giving them a few turns counterclockwise, but don't remove them completely. Grasp the fixture and rotate it slightly to the left so that the screw heads are under the large parts of the slotted openings. You can now lower the fixture from the ceiling.

4. Disconnect both wires which join the fixture to the wires in the outlet box. Turn the solderless connectors counterclockwise, until they come off the wires.

5. Hook up the new fixture. Connect its wires to the outlet wires, using either the old solderless connectors or those supplied with your fixture. Place the two wire ends together and twist them slightly. Place a solderless connector over the ends, and turn it clockwise until it is tight.

6. Connect the white wire on the fixture to the white wire in the outlet box. Connect the black or red wire on the fixture to the black wire in the outlet.

7. The new fixture may have one solid white wire and another white wire with a colored tracer thread running through it. If so, connect the colored tracer wire on the fixture to the white outlet wire.

8. Push the new fixture against the ceiling. Adjust it so that the screw heads in the outlet box poke down through the slotted openings in the canopy. Rotate the fixture clockwise so that the screw heads are shifted to a narrow part of each slot, and thus hold up the fixture. Tighten each screw.

Mounting a fixture with screws

The fixture you have removed may have been fastened to the outlet box with two screws; these go through the canopy and into threaded holes in the outlet box. If the screws that go through the canopy aren't the same distance apart as the holes in the outlet box, first screw a *mounting strap* to the box. A mounting strap is a strip of metal which has threaded holes in it (Figure 33). Then screw the canopy to the strap.

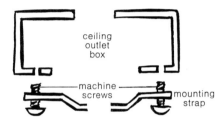

Figure 33. *Top:* Ceiling outlet box. *Below:* Mounting strap with machine screws

2

PLUMBING PROBLEMS

Every family has to cope with plumbing emergencies at one time or another. A home with children runs into plumbing problems every so often because children seem to enjoy throwing assorted objects into toilet bowls.

Even if there are no playful children to cause problems, plumbing can go awry for no apparent reason. What can you do? Depending on the nature of the problem, you can either fix it yourself or take the proper emergency measures until the plumber arrives.

Most minor, everyday plumbing problems are easily remedied. It's not necessary to be able to replace pipes, but you should know how to fix a leak. It takes only a few minutes to stop a dripping faucet or shower head, and not much longer to fix a running toilet.

Water pipes often present other problems as well. When subjected to intense cold, they can freeze and must be defrosted very carefully. During damp, muggy weather, exposed cold-water pipes become covered with moisture. Such pipes should be insulated.

Should your house heating system suddenly stop working, you can conduct a few simple checks before calling the serviceman.

Does your family have a summer house? It's important to winterize it to protect drains and pipes from the cold.

If you know how, you can handle many of these problems yourself.

Shutting Off The Water

The first thing to do when you discover a leak is to *shut off the water*. Every member of the family should know how to do this.

Water is supplied to most houses through a *water main*, a pipe which usually comes in through a basement wall. A simple *shutoff valve* is connected to the pipe at this point; sometimes it is next to a water meter. To shut off all the water in the house, turn the valve handle clockwise (Figure 1).

In nearly all homes, each sink has its own shutoff valves. Look underneath and you'll see them in the hot- and cold-water supply pipes. You can shut off the water to any one faucet without interrupting the water supply to the rest of the house.

Don't look for a water main in an apartment; there isn't any. However, you will find individual shutoffs at each sink.

Figure 1. Shutting off water supply

Faucets

Although there are many different types of faucets, they all contain basically the same parts (Figure 2): handle screw, handle, pack-

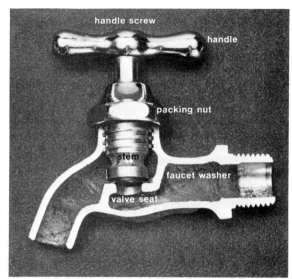

Figure 2. Inner construction of a typical faucet

ing nut, packing material and/or packing washer (see Figure 6), stem, faucet washer (held by a screw), and valve seat.

Most faucet leaks are caused by worn washers or defective packing material.

Fixing a Leaky Faucet

If water drips from the faucet spout, it probably needs a new *faucet washer* or else the *valve seat* may be worn. Buy a package of assorted washers and screws so that you can take care of any faucet in your home should the need arise. Kits containing an assortment of washers, screws, and packing are available at hardware and variety stores.

A smooth-jawed, adjustable-end wrench is best for this job because it won't mar plated surfaces. If the only wrench you have is one that has teeth, protect the surface by covering it with two or three turns of adhesive or masking tape.

REPLACING A FAUCET WASHER

You will need:

    Adjustable-end wrench
    Masking or adhesive tape (if necessary)
    Screwdriver
    Assorted faucet washers and screws

What to do:

1. Turn off the water either at the fixture or at the main supply valve.

2. Remove the screw in the faucet handle. Tap the underside of the handle with the handle of your screwdriver, and at the same time, pull it up to remove it.

3. Loosen and remove the *packing nut* by turning it counterclockwise with an adjustable-end wrench.

4. Remove the stem by twisting it in the direction used to turn on the water.

5. Remove the screw which holds the faucet washer at the end of the stem. Be careful! Screws often corrode and fall apart as they are being removed. (If the screw head breaks off, remove the washer, grasp what's left of the screw with a pair of pliers and twist it out by turning counterclockwise. Even if it comes out in one piece, discard it and replace it with a new one.)

6. Pry out the old washer and select a new one that matches exactly. It should be made of the same material and have the same shape; some are flat, and others are beveled. Some washers can be installed without screws; ask your dealer about them.

7. Install the screw that holds the washer. Don't leave it loose, or you may end up with a "singing" faucet. Every time you turn on the water, the loose, vibrating washer will produce a buzz, or a tone. On the other hand, don't use brute force when tightening the screw or you'll break it off.

8. Replace the stem in the faucet body. Turn it as far as you can by hand, in the direction used to shut it off.

9. Screw the packing nut back into place. Make it as tight as you can by hand, then tighten it a bit more with a wrench.

10. Turn on the water and open the faucet. Allow it to run for a few moments, so that all the air in the pipe can escape. Now shut the faucet. If it no longer leaks, your job is a success!

REPLACING A VALVE SEAT

If the faucet still leaks at the spout after you have replaced a worn washer, you will either have to *replace* or *ream* the valve seat. Valve seats can become rough as a result of corrosion or after long use. This prevents them from making a waterproof seal when pressed against the faucet washer.

Removable valve seats have a square or hexagonal opening into which a special wrench fits. You may be able to borrow one from your hardware dealer.

You will need:

    Adjustable-end wrench
    Valve-seat wrench
    Replacement valve seat

What to do:

1. Turn off the water. Remove the screw in the faucet handle. Tap the underside of the handle with the handle of your screwdriver, and at the same time, pull it up to remove it.

2. Use the adjustable-end wrench to remove the packing nut. Twist out the stem, turning in the direction you would if you were turning on the water.

3. Slip the end of the valve-seat wrench into the opening in the valve seat. Turn counterclockwise, and the seat will come out. Bring it to your dealer, and get an exact replacement.

4. Install the new valve seat by turning it clockwise; make it tight. Reassemble the faucet and turn on the water.

REAMING A VALVE SEAT

Your faucet may not have a removable valve seat, or it may not be possible for you to borrow the special wrench. In that case, you can buy a special *valve-seat reamer* (Figure 3) at any hardware or plumbing supply store. This is an inexpensive tool used to smooth the rough valve seat.

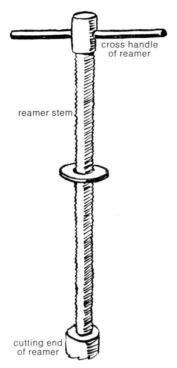

Figure 3. Valve-seat reamer

You will need:

> Adjustable-end wrench
> Screwdriver
> Valve-seat reamer

What to do:

1. Turn off the water. Remove the screw in the faucet handle. Tap the underside of the handle with the handle of your screwdriver, and at the same time, pull it up to remove it.

2. Use the adjustable-end wrench to loosen the packing nut; remove it. Pull and twist out the stem.

3. Remove the cross handle of the reamer. Slide the packing nut down over the stem of the reamer, over the adjusting nut and packing washer. Before you put the packing nut in place, set the adjusting nut by turning it up or down on the reamer stem until the cutting end of the reamer presses against the valve seat (Figure 4).

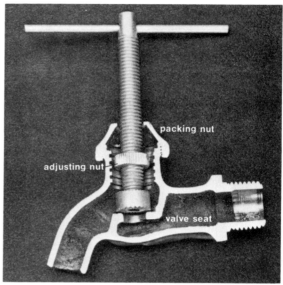

Figure 4. Valve-seat reamer in faucet

4. Reinsert the cross handle. Turn the reamer clockwise; at the same time, tighten the packing nut by hand. Don't press down on the reamer; the nut will exert downward pressure as you tighten it. Three or four turns should be enough to smooth the valve seat.

5. Remove the reamer cross handle, the packing nut (with packing washer), and the reamer. Reassemble the faucet, then turn on the water to test it.

REPACKING A FAUCET

Packing fits snugly under the packing nut. When the nut is screwed down tight, the packing is compressed against the stem, preventing water from leaking out. In time, both stem and packing wear, and the faucet may leak at the stem. Try tightening the packing nut by turning it just a bit, clockwise. If this doesn't stop the leak, you will have to repack the faucet.

Packing may consist of loose, fibrous material that has been compressed under the nut and/or a dome-shaped washer. The new type faucets use an easy-to-install O-ring instead of packing (Figure 5). This is a rubber ring that fits into a groove in the packing nut and presses against the stem.

You will need:

Screwdriver
Adjustable-end wrench
Graphite or teflon stem packing,
  new packing washer, or O-ring

What to do:

1. Turn off the water.

2. Remove the screw in the faucet handle. Tap the underside of the handle with the handle of your screwdriver, and at the same time, pull it up to remove it. Use the adjustable-end wrench to loosen the packing nut.

3. Slide the packing nut up on the faucet stem, but don't remove it. Use a screwdriver to push down the packing washer that rests under the packing. Cut just enough packing to fit once around the stem, between the packing washer and the packing nut (Figure 6). Push the washer and packing under the packing nut.

4. Turn the packing nut back onto the faucet stem *by hand*, until it engages the threads properly. Then tighten it with a wrench. Be sure the faucet stem is all the way down.

5. Replace the handle and turn it to "off." Turn on the water. If water still oozes at the stem, tighten the packing nut slowly, until it stops. Although the handle may now be hard to turn, a couple of drops of oil applied to the stem will make turning easier.

If stem packing doesn't stop the leak, take the packing nut, complete with its original packing, to your hardware or plumbing-supply dealer, and get a replacement packing washer.

Pry out the old washer. Slide the new packing washer, and packing nut over the faucet stem, in that order. Turn the packing nut back into place.

Replace the handle, and test the faucet for a leak. If it leaks at the stem, tighten the packing nut until it stops.

Figure 6. Packing fits between packing washer and packing nut.

REPLACING AN O-RING

It's easy to stop a stem leak in a faucet that uses an O-ring. Your hardware or plumbing-supply dealer can match an O-ring exactly.

You will need:

Adjustable-end wrench
Screwdriver
New O-ring

What to do:

1. Turn off the water. Remove the screw in the faucet handle. Tap the underside of the handle with the handle of your screwdriver, and at the same time pull it up to remove it.

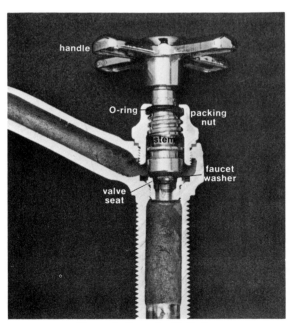

Figure 5. Faucet with O-ring

Use the adjustable-end wrench to loosen the packing nut.

2. Pry the O-ring out from inside the packing nut (see Figure 5). Take it to your dealer and get an *exact replacement.*

3. Push the new O-ring into the packing nut. Use a screwdriver, wood sliver, or strong toothpick to position it in its slot.

4. Replace the packing nut and faucet handle. Turn on the water.

Single-Stem Faucets

Single-stem faucets, in which one lever is used to adjust both the temperature and the flow of the water, are not too difficult to repair. Since there are many types, it is not feasible to give directions here for repairing them. You can buy a kit of repair parts for your particular faucet. The directions on the package are easy to follow.

Faucet Aerators

An aerator is screwed to the end of a faucet. It eliminates splashing by breaking up the direct flow of water from the nozzle.

Aerators work by introducing millions of tiny bubbles into the stream of water. This is done by forcing the water through a number of fine screens. When the screens become clogged with sediment, the units fail to work. Remove an inoperative aerator, and take it apart. Clean each screen under running water, then reassemble the aerator and screw it back onto the faucet. If it still doesn't work, you may want to replace it.

REPLACING A FAUCET AERATOR

Two types of aerators are generally used as replacements. One is a standard, fixed unit. The other has a swivel arrangement which will enable you to direct a jet of water to any portion of the sink. Both are attached in the same way.

You will need:

> Replacement aerator
> Slip-joint pliers

What to do:

1. Use slip-joint pliers in their open position (see page 177) to remove the old aerator from the faucet. Turn to the left.

2. Screw in the new aerator. Start by hand, turning it with your fingers as far as you can. Then tighten it with the slip-joint pliers.

3. Turn on the water. If there is a leak at the joint where the unit is screwed into the faucet, tighten it with the pliers until it stops.

FIXING A DRIPPING SHOWER HEAD

Does your shower head drip? Believe it or not, it's a faucet repair problem. (Figure 7 shows a typical shower installation.) The handles which control the flow of water to the shower head are exactly the same as faucet handles, and they operate valves that are constructed like faucets.

You will need:

> Screwdriver
> Adjustable-end wrench
> Replacement faucet washer

What to do:

1. First determine whether the hot or cold water valve is leaking.

2. Next turn off the water supply to the shower. In a private house, if you can't find separate controls for each pipe, cut off the water at the main valve (see page 24).

3. Remove the screw which holds the valve handle to its stem. You may have to pry out or unscrew a covering tab, which reads "hot" or "cold." Pull off the handle.

4. Remove the *bell,* the decorative, dome-shaped piece of ceramic or metal which covers the area where the pipe comes from the wall. You may be able to unscrew it by turning it counterclockwise. If the bell is held in place by a screw fitting, unscrew to remove.

5. Use the adjustable-end wrench to remove

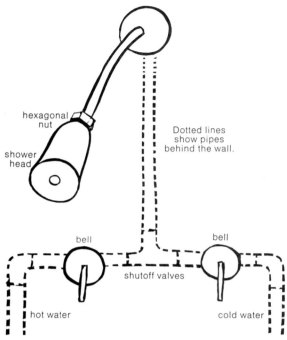

hexagonal nut

shower head

Dotted lines show pipes behind the wall.

bell   bell

shutoff valves

hot water   cold water

Figure 7. Typical shower installation

the *packing nut*; turn to the left to loosen and remove it.

6. Remove the *stem* by turning it either to the right or left, depending on the type of valve you have in your shower.

7. Unscrew and discard both the washer and the screw at the end of the stem. Replace them with exact duplicates. Screw the stem back into the valve housing.

8. Replace, and tighten the packing nut. Turn on the water to test the valve and see whether it still leaks. If it doesn't, replace the bell and the handle. If it still leaks, follow procedures outlined on pages 25–26. You may have to ream the valve seat.

REPLACING A SHOWER HEAD

You will need:

    Adjustable-end wrench
    New shower head
    Plumber's joint compound or
       plastic joint tape

What to do:

1. Adjust the wrench to fit the hexagonal nut that joins the shower head to the water pipe (Figure 8). Hold the pipe firmly with one hand to prevent it from twisting. With the other, slowly turn the hex nut counterclockwise to loosen it. Don't lean on the wrench or use too much force; you may break the pipe. Remove the old shower head.

Figure 8. Adjusting wrench to fit hexagonal nut on shower head

2. Thread the new shower head onto the pipe. Give it one full turn, then coat the exposed threads with joint compound, or wrap on one turn of plastic joint tape.

3. By hand, continue to thread the shower head on the pipe, as far as you can. Then tighten it with the wrench. It need only be tight enough to prevent leakage.

Cleaning a shower head

Most modern shower heads are self-cleaning. Older types sometimes have perforated front sections which you can remove by turning them counterclockwise.

Use a toothpick to clean all the holes, then reassemble the head.

Pipes

Stopping a Pipe Leak

Before attempting to repair a pipe leak, you must shut off the water and drain all the water pipes. Somewhere in your basement you will find a *drain cock* in a water-supply pipe. It looks like the fitting to which you attach a garden hose (Figure 9). To open it, turn the drain-cock handle to the left. Catch the water in a bucket or attach a garden hose and let the water drain outside. Opening all the faucets in the house will help to drain the pipes more quickly.

If you have a hidden leak, evidenced only by a wet area on a ceiling or wall or by dripping from an unknown source, call the plumber.

Or the leak may be one you can see at a joint or on a straight section of pipe. This kind of leak you can fix!

Figure 9. Drain cock

FIXING A LEAK AT A FITTING OR JOINT

You will need:

> **Epoxy cement (see page 194)**
> **String**
> **Plastic electrician's tape**

What to do:

1. Dry the pipe. Wipe it with a cloth, apply a heat lamp, or *warm* it gently with a propane torch.

2. Mix up epoxy cement and apply a liberal coat to the entire joint.

3. Wrap string tightly around the pipe giving it three or four turns at the joint. Coat the string with a layer of epoxy cement.

4. Wrap the joint with stretchy plastic electrician's tape, as though you were applying a bandage. Consult the epoxy cement container to determine the time it takes for the cement to harden; don't disturb the repaired area during that time.

FIXING A LEAK IN A STRAIGHT SECTION OF PIPE

You will need:

> **Pipe clamp**
> **Adjustable-end wrench**

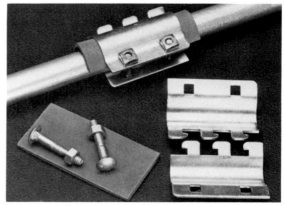

Figure 10. *Top:* Assembled pipe clamp. *Below:* Rubber gasket, nuts and bolts, and unassembled clamp

What to do:

1. Unhinge the two halves of the pipe clamp and assemble the clamp over the pipe, with the rubber gasket directly over the leak (Figure 10).

2. Fasten the two halves together with two nuts and bolts, which are provided with the clamp. Use the adjustable-end wrench to tighten the nuts.

Hints

Leaks often occur in horizontal pipes that run through the basement, particularly in older homes that have galvanized iron pipes and fittings. Measure the diameter of the pipes in your basement, buy a pipe clamp to fit, and keep it for emergency use.

It is a good idea to label all the shutoff valves in your basement so that anyone can quickly turn off the water in any part of the house. Look for shutoff valves in pipes (Figure 11).

Figure 11. Shutoff valve

To locate the valves in your basement, turn on all the faucets in the kitchen and bathrooms. Go to the basement and turn the valves off, one by one. As you do so, have someone upstairs tell you which faucets stop running, and label each valve accordingly. If you can't find any valves, use the main shutoff.

If a hot-water heater develops a leak, shut off the water at once. Drain the tank into a bucket or a garden hose. You'll find a drain cock at the bottom of the tank. If the leak occurs in a hot-water storage tank, it may be possible to plug it. (A plumber should do this.) If it's in an automatic hot-water heater, you may have to get a new one.

FROZEN PIPES

If you live in a northern climate, you may occasionally have to deal with a frozen water pipe or drain. This is usually the result of poor construction, where a pipe runs along an outside wall or in an uninsulated space under a house.

The best way to combat a frozen pipe is by preventing it from freezing in the first place. Pipes in cold basements or crawl spaces should be insulated by wrapping them with tape made of fiberglass, cork, or other suitable material. You can buy kits of pipe-insulating tape.

Or wrap such pipes with an electrical *pipe-heating cable*. After wrapping, plug the cable into an outlet and forget about it. A built-in thermostat will heat the cable when the temperature drops near freezing.

Suppose you don't have an electrical cable installation, and a pipe freezes? If you aren't in a hurry, buy a cable, wrap it around the pipe, plug it in, and wait until it thaws.

If you don't have access to a cable, boil some water. Wrap rags around a few feet of pipe, and saturate them with the hot water. This may take a little time, as you will have to keep the rags hot.

Other de-icing sources of heat include hair dryers, clothes irons, or heat lamps. Or, wrap a heating pad around the pipe, turn it to "high," and move it slowly along the pipe.

Open the faucet nearest the frozen area before you employ any thawing measures. This will give thawing water a chance to flow. As a rule, start at a faucet, and continue defrosting the pipe toward the source of blockage.

For information on how to thaw frozen drains, see page 35.

ELIMINATING CONDENSATION ON COLD-WATER PIPES

During the summer, cold-water pipes may sweat. Hot, moisture-laden air comes into contact with an exposed cold pipe, and water condenses on its surface and drips off. In order to prevent condensation, such pipes should be insulated. You can buy an insulation kit made for use on pipes. It contains a length of porous insulating material, such as fiberglass, and a similar length of waterproof plastic.

You will need:

> Pipe-insulation kit
> Masking or adhesive tape
> Scissors

What to do:

1. Wait for a dry day when the pipes are not wet.

2. Starting at one end of the exposed pipe, anchor the end of the strip of insulation with a strip of masking or adhesive tape.

3. Wrap the insulation around the pipe as though you were applying a bandage. It should be one layer thick, overlapping slightly at the edges.

4. Anchor the end of the insulation by wrapping it with a strip of tape.

5. Cover the insulated area with the waterproof plastic. Apply it the same way you did the insulation—by wrapping and overlapping.

Hints

There are several types of pipe insulation on the market. Some are self-adhering; all you need do is simply wrap them around a pipe.

To cut down your fuel bill, also insulate hot water pipes that run through cold areas.

Drains

Clearing a Clogged Drain

Kitchen drains usually become clogged with grease deposits, and lavatory drains are often blocked by soap curds and wads of hair. But you can cope with these common household problems quickly and easily.

Before doing anything else, try to remove any obstructions by sticking your fingers down into the drain. A long pair of tweezers will help. If your drain has a strainer, this can be removed by turning it to the left.

USING A PLUNGER

If a drain is completely blocked so that no water runs down, first try clearing it with a plunger (Figure 12). This handy device, also known as a force cup or plumber's friend, should be part of every home-emergency repair kit.

You will need:

> Rubber plunger
> Petroleum jelly (optional)

What to do:

1. Smear a thick coat of petroleum jelly on the bottom rim of the plunger. Although you can operate the plunger without it, it may help to maintain an airtight seal while it is being used.

2. Hold the plunger vertically, covering the drain opening. Push down *hard*. Run some water into the drain and keep pumping up and down until the drain clears.

Hints

If you are clearing a double sink, have someone hold a wet cloth over the drain opening of the other sink. It's also important to plug up overflow openings in sinks with a rag or a sponge when using a plunger; if you don't,

Figure 12. Plunger, or force cup

pressure can't built up in the drain to clear the obstruction and you may get squirted.

If the plunger fails to clear the obstruction, you will have to use a clean-out auger. This is a long coil spring with a sliding, adjustable crank handle used for cleaning out drains (Figure 13).

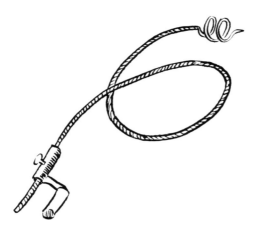

Figure 13. Clean-out auger

USING A CLEAN-OUT AUGER

You will need:

    Clean-out auger
    Adjustable-end wrench

What to do:

1. Loosen the thumbscrew on the crank handle of the auger, pull out about three feet of coil, and then tighten the screw.

2. Insert the auger into the clogged drain, feeding it in slowly and carefully.

3. When you reach an obstruction, loosen the screw in the handle, and slide it down the

coil to within about one foot of the drain. Tighten the screw.

4. Crank the handle clockwise (to the right), at the same time maintaining firm pressure against the obstruction.

5. Move the auger in and out of the drain as you crank until you can feel the obstruction give way.

6. Run water into the drain, and remove the auger.

If the auger will not go around the trap:

1. Place a pail or other container under the sink trap.

2. Using an adjustable-end wrench, remove the *clean-out plug* at the bottom of the trap by turning it counterclockwise (Figure 14). Allow water from the trap to run into the pail.

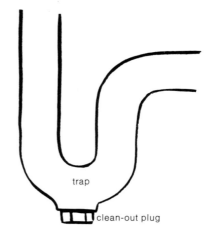

trap

clean-out plug

Figure 14. Clean-out plug in sink trap

3. Clean out as much of the trap as you can reach with a piece of wire coat hanger or any other stiff wire.

4. Insert the clean-out auger into the plug opening and push it as far as it will go (Figure 15). Sometimes simply moving it back and forth will remove an obstruction.

5. When you feel an obstruction, maintain pressure against it and crank the handle of the auger to the right.

6. After the obstruction has been cleared away, remove the auger and replace the clean-out plug.

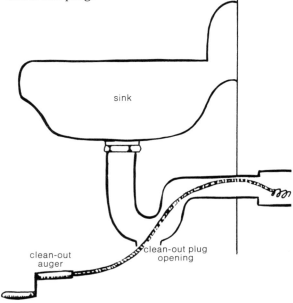

Figure 15. Clean-out auger inserted through plug opening in sink trap

REMOVING THE TRAP

If your sink does not have a clean-out plug, you will have to remove the trap. This is not as difficult as it sounds.

You will need:

    Large pipe wrench
    Bucket
    Clean-out auger

What to do:

1. Place the bucket under the trap so that water which has accumulated will not spill all over when you remove the trap.

2. Loosen the two nuts that hold the trap (Figure 16) and remove the trap.

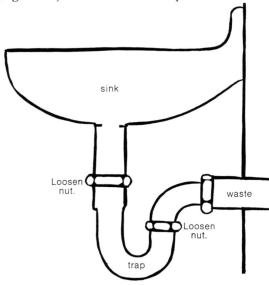

Figure 16. Location of trap-removal nuts

3. If the trap is clogged, clear it with a piece of wire coat hanger. If not, there may be a stoppage between the sink and the trap (very unusual) or, more likely, in the drain between the trap and the cesspool or sewer. Insert the auger as far as it will go into the drainpipe leading into the wall. If you encounter an obstruction, clear it.

4. Hook up the trap by tightening the two nuts and run some water into the sink as a test.

5. If the auger is too short to reach the obstruction, it will have to be cleared with a plumber's rod or *snake*. This is similar to an auger, but stronger and heavier. Snakes come in lengths up to 100 feet. If you don't happen to have a snake around, call a plumber.

Hints

If you do use a snake, be careful when you withdraw it from the drain. Keep a supply of rags handy and wipe the snake as it comes out. If you don't, you'll have a rusty, smelly mess all over your floor.

CLEARING A DRAIN CHEMICALLY

You will need:

Chemical drain cleaner

Do not expect a chemical drain cleaner to clear a completely blocked drain. Use one only when water drains out, no matter how sluggishly, after the blockage has been broken with an auger.

Read the directions on the container, and *follow them to the letter.* If your house has a cesspool or septic tank, be sure to choose a drain cleaner that will not damage your disposal system.

Many chemical cleaners contain lye. They remove grease by turning it into a water-soluble soap. However, they can cause serious burns if used carelessly. Wear rubber or plastic gloves, and pour lye-type cleaners directly into drains through a funnel. Keep them off porcelain sink surfaces.

All containers should be shut tight and stored out of the reach of children.

FROZEN DRAINS

You may be working hard to clear a clogged drain which proves to be frozen. Ice can plug a drain as effectively as anything else. Pour in two pounds of salt, followed by two quarts of boiling water. It works! All you have to do is wait about an hour.

ODORS FROM DRAINS

A trap in a drain is always filled with water, trapping sewer and septic-tank gases and preventing them from coming up into the house. Occasionally, during the heating season when the humidity is very low, water will evaporate from an unused trap, permitting odors to come up through a drain. Check household drains from time to time to see that they aren't dry. If they are, simply run the water briefly. Flush toilets to refill dry drains.

Toilets

If a toilet problem does exist, it's probably caused by either stoppage in the toilet drain or a malfunction in the flush-tank mechanism.

Stoppages can be caused by children throwing things into toilets, or by wadded paper. First try to clear the clogged drain with your trusty plumber's friend. If that doesn't work, then resort to a drain auger (see page 33).

One of the most common ailments is a toilet that runs continuously. You can often fix a running toilet simply by bending the float arm inside the flush tank (see below). Or you may need a new float. For a complete flush-tank overhaul, you would also replace a couple of washers and install a new ball cock.

Repairing a Flush-Tank Mechanism

Figure 17 shows a typical flush-tank mechanism. Yours may not look exactly the same, but it has comparable parts which serve the same purpose.

If water continues to run after the tank is flushed, it may be due to one of the following:

—the float rod may have to be repositioned
—you may need a new float
—the valve may need a new set of washers
—you may need a new ball cock

REPOSITIONING A FLOAT ARM

What to do:

1. Remove the cover from the flush tank.

2. If water is running into the overflow tube, lift the float arm. If this stops the water from running, all you need do is to readjust the position of the arm.

3. Flush the tank. While the water flows out, use your fingers to bend the float arm near the center, so that the float will be about

½ inch lower (see Figure 17). Do this very carefully; old rods become brittle and may break if handled roughly.

4. Allow the tank to fill and check the water level. It should be about ½ inch below the top of the overflow tube.

5. If water continues to flow into the overflow tube after you have bent the rod, examine the float for leaks. Unscrew it and shake it. If there's water inside, you'll hear it sloshing around. Get a new float.

6. If necessary, bend the arm again to reposition it.

7. If raising the float arm does not stop the water from running, replace the valve washers.

INSTALLING VALVE WASHERS

You will need:

> **Pliers**
> **New valve washers**

What to do:

1. Shut off the water supply to the flush tank. Flush the toilet to empty the tank.

2. Remove the two thumb screws which hold the float arm in place. Slide the entire float-arm unit out of the slot in the top of the plunger (see Figure 17).

3. Lift the plunger (Figure 18) out of the valve body. Pry out the old washer at the bottom of the valve and simply push the new one into place; it is not held with a screw.

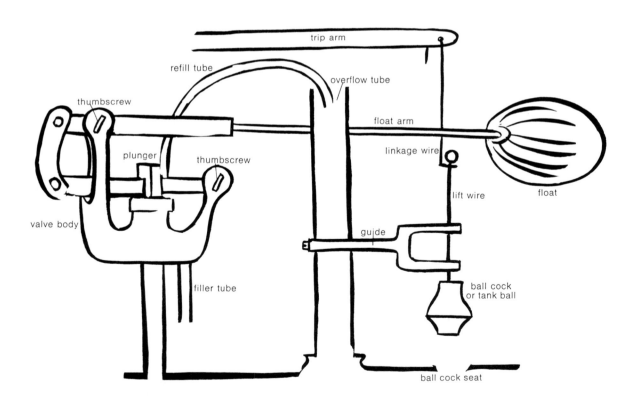

Figure 17. Toilet flush-tank mechanism

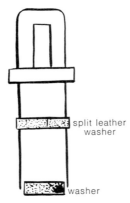

split leather
washer

washer

Figure 18. Plunger, showing washers

4. Replace the leather washer that fits into a groove in the side of the plunger. This is a split washer which slides into place very easily.

5. Replace the plunger in the valve body, reassemble the float-arm unit, and replace the two thumb screws.

6. Turn on the water, and allow the tank to fill. If the water still rises above the top of the overflow pipe, lift the float arm again; the water should stop running.

7. If you have replaced the float and the valve washers, and water is still running into the toilet bowl, replace the ball cock.

REPLACING A BALL COCK

Ball cocks are made of rubber which hardens in time; as a result, the ball cock can't seat itself to prevent the water from leaking out of the tank.

You will need:

> Pliers
> New ball cock
> Steel wool

What to do:

1. Shut off the water. Disengage the linkage wire from the trip arm (see Figure 17). Hold the top of the lift wire with pliers and unscrew the ball cock.

2. Scour the seat with steel wool and wipe it clean.

3. Thread a new ball cock into place, and replace the linkage wire in the trip arm.

4. Flush the toilet. The ball cock should remain raised after it is picked up by the lift wire and drop into its seat after the water has left the tank.

5. If it falls too soon, allowing only part of the water in the tank to flush the toilet, shorten the linkage wire that connects the trip arm to the lift wire.

Hints

Get valve washers to fit your particular flush-tank unit. Bring an old one to your hardware store in order to match it.

Conventional floats have traditionally been made of sheet copper. You can also buy floats made of hollow plastic and solid foam plastic. Foam floats have one advantage over other types; they never develop leaks.

The linkage made up of the trip arm, linkage wire, and lift wire must operate without binding anywhere. Check to see that it moves freely in the guide. If the ball cock does not drop directly onto the seat, reposition the guide. Loosen the screw which holds it to the overflow tube, shift its position, and retighten the screw.

Heating

Everyone knows that a heating system goes on during the winter and shuts down during the summer. However, that isn't all you should know. For example, do you know how to cut off all electrical power to the heating system? Do you know how your heating system works? What should you do if you have no heat on a sub-zero morning?

Many heating problems are not serious and can be solved by simple adjustments you can make yourself.

Thermostats

A thermostat is a heat-sensitive switch. Turn it up when you want more heat; lower the setting if the house is too warm.

Unless it is properly located, a thermostat can make your heating system work erratically. It should never be on an outside wall, or near a window; the best location is an inside wall, away from front-door drafts. Nor should it be near a radiator or any other source of heat. For the same reason, don't place floor or table lamps too close to a thermostat. Ask your serviceman to check on the location of your thermostat, and have him move it elsewhere if necessary.

Steam Heating

In a steam-heating system, steam is generated in a boiler, usually located in a basement, and flows through pipes to different parts of the house. The steam heats up radiators which in turn heat up the rooms in which they are located.

If radiator remains cold

Should a radiator fail to heat up, the cure may be very simple, for the radiator is probably *airbound*. Each radiator has a shutoff

Figure 19. Typical steam-radiator vent

valve that controls the steam going into it and an *air vent* (Figure 19) that permits air to escape. If the air vent is stuck, clogged, corroded, or otherwise out of action, steam will not be able to enter the radiator because it is filled with air. The solution is to replace the air vent.

REPLACING AN AIR VENT IN A STEAM-HEATED RADIATOR

You will need:

> Steam-heating air vent
> Adjustable-end wrench
> Plumber's joint compound or plastic
>   joint tape

What to do:

1. Turn off the steam entering the radiator by turning the large-handled shutoff valve clockwise. This is the valve that controls the steam just before it enters the radiator.

2. Wait until the steam has stopped coming up from the boiler and the radiator has cooled. *Caution: Never work on a hot steam radiator; always wait until it has cooled.* A hot radiator may be filled with water or steam under pressure, and if you remove the air vent, hot, rusty water or steam—or both— may be sprayed over the room.

3. Grasp the air vent with both hands and turn it to the left to remove it. If you can't budge it, use the adjustable-end wrench to get it started, then remove it manually. Be careful not to break it off.

4. Insert the new air vent in the threaded hole and give it one full turn to the right by hand. Apply plumber's joint compound to the exposed threads or wrap them with a layer of plastic joint-sealing tape. Turn the vent to the right by hand as much as you can.

5. Use the adjustable-end wrench to bring the vent to an upright position; it won't work upside down.

6. Open the shutoff valve.

Hints

Do you have a problem radiator that remains cold long after other radiators in the house have warmed up? Solve the problem by replacing the old air vent with an adjustable, quick-venting type. You will also have to experiment with the vent setting (controlled by a screw). Adjust it until you find a setting at which the problem radiator will heat up at the same time as all the others.

Do you have a radiator that knocks and gurgles and heats up only partially, or not at all? It may be slanted, and as a consequence, the end in which the vent is installed is lower than the other. It should be just the other way around: the vent side should be very slightly higher, or else the radiator should be perfectly level. Slip a checker or a square of plywood under each radiator foot on the vent side, raising it so that water trapped in the radiator can run back down the pipe to the boiler. If this doesn't help, your steam-supply pipe may have been installed incorrectly; this is a job for your plumber.

Hot-Water Heating

In a hot-water heating system, water is heated in a boiler and circulated through pipes and radiators that give off heat. If a radiator becomes airbound (filled with air that can't escape), hot water will not be able to enter and the radiator will remain cold. Each hot-water radiator is therefore equipped with an *air vent* which allows air to escape from the radiator but retains the hot water.

The vent in Figure 20 is the screw type which

Figure 20. Screw-type hot-water radiator vent

is self-venting. Your hot-water system may have old-style vents which must be bled every year soon after the heat goes on. Bleeding means opening the vent with a special key (Figure 21) to allow air to escape and then

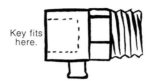

Key fits here.

Figure 21. Key insert on old-style hot-water radiator vent

closing it again. (A pan must be placed under the vent to catch any water that drips out.) You can replace these old style vents with automatic, self-bleeding types. Once in place they need no further adjustment.

REPLACING A HOT-WATER RADIATOR VENT

You will need:

> **Adjustable-end wrench**
> **Plumber's joint compound or**
>   **plastic joint tape**
> **Automatic vent for hot water**

What to do:

1. Close the radiator shutoff valve. This is located on one of the pipes that goes into the radiator. *Wait until the radiator cools before you start to work on it.*

2. Use an adjustable-end wrench to unscrew the air vent. Work quickly, and have your replacement vent at hand, for water may squirt out of the vent hole. It's a good idea to spread a few old towels on the floor, just in case.

3. Thread the new vent into place. Give it one or two full turns, then apply joint compound to the exposed threads or wrap them with one turn of plastic joint tape.

4. Turn the vent up tight, as much as you can by hand. Give it an extra turn with the adjustable-end wrench.

5. Open the shutoff valve.

What to Check if Heat Supply is Inadequate

Your house has a wall switch with a red plate that controls your heating system. To prevent children from playing with the switch and turning it off, put a strip of masking tape over the toggle leaving it in the "on" position. If your heat suddenly goes off, check the switch first.

Check the thermostat setting; it may be too low.

Next look into your fuel supply—you may need oil. If you have a supply of oil, press the button on the *stack switch*, a squarish metal box attached to the sheet-metal duct which goes from the furnace to the chimney. Push the switch (or twist it, depending on the type you have) only once. If the furnace doesn't go on, call your serviceman.

If you have a gas-fired system, check the pilot light; it may be out, in which case the gas supply is automatically cut off. Call your serviceman to relight it.

WINTERIZING A SUMMER HOUSE

You may have a great cabin up in the woods, where the family goes to get away from it all; but, unless you take a few simple precautions, you will encounter more problems with it than you do with your permanent home.

If you intend to use your hideaway during the winter, *keep it heated.* If you have auto-matic heat, adjust it for about 50°. This isn't exactly the temperature you would choose for comfortable living, but it will prevent pipes and drains from freezing solid.

But suppose you only use the place for summer vacations? It doesn't make sense to heat it all winter if it isn't going to be used. The solution? Winterize it.

What to do:

1. First turn off the water supply. If you have a well, turn off the valve that is closest to the well.

2. Next drain the water out of each water-supply pipe. Open all sink faucets. Open the drain cock in your water-supply pipes.

3. Flush the toilets so that the tanks are dry. Use a sponge to sop up any water in the tanks.

4. Using a rubber plunger, force as much water as you can out of every toilet bowl. Then sponge out as much water as you can.

5. Into each toilet bowl, pour one gallon of kerosene to take the place of the water. Pour the same amount into each sink, so that drain traps are free of water and filled instead with kerosene.

6. If your house has a fireplace, be sure to close the flue.

7. Put up shutters or storm windows.

8. Pull the main electrical switch, and your summer home is ready for winter.

3

FURNITURE
Refinishing and Repair

Refinishing and restoring furniture is really more than a fix-it job—it also involves interior decorating decisions. You start with something quite ordinary and transform it into a thing of beauty. This transformation is the exciting part.

In order to refinish furniture, however, you must first learn how to remove old finishes and how to apply paint, lacquer, stain, and varnish. You can also learn to refinish wicker and metal furniture as well as old wooden pieces.

Why not apply an antique finish? Or antique kitchen cabinets and woodwork? You can even mix your own antiquing finishing materials.

If you have a perfectly sound table with a damaged top, try covering it with decorative, colorful ceramic tile. It is easy to apply and makes a waterproof, stainproof, heatproof surface that is perfect for informal use either indoors or on a patio.

Once you become a confirmed do-it-yourselfer, you won't have to put up with wobbly tables and chairs any longer. With a little glue and a clamp, you can make such furniture stable again. And wouldn't you like to spruce up those old kitchen or side chairs? Re-covering slip seats with colorful vinyl or fabric is a simple thing to do.

There is so much you can do easily and inexpensively to make your furniture look better and work more efficiently. Once you get started, you will find many small jobs that will be both rewarding and useful to you and your family.

Refinishing Furniture

Finishing Materials

Finishing materials are usually either transparent or opaque liquids which are applied over raw wood, metal, or old finishes.

Some finishes, such as stains, are purely decorative. They are absorbed by wood and serve only to bring out interesting wood-grain patterns. Other finishes, such as lacquer and varnish, are transparent. They not only accentuate the stain patterns, but also form protective coats on wooden furniture. Enamels provide both color and "cover-up" for furniture; they may be used on both wood and metal.

Application of Finishing Materials

Finishing materials may be brushed, sprayed, or wiped on. Figure 1 lists the ways in which commonly used finishing materials are applied.

	BRUSHED	SPRAYED	WIPED
Linseed oil	●		●
Varnish	●	●	
Lacquer	●	●	
Enamel	●	●	
Plastic	●	●	
Stain	●	●	●
Wax			●

Figure 1. How finishes are applied

Basic Procedures:

Two basic steps are involved in refinishing a piece of furniture: (1) the surface is properly prepared, and (2) the finish is applied as directed. Finishing materials are always applied in a definite, logical order:

On bare wood:

1. Stain (optional)
2. Clear varnish, plastic, lacquer, or wax

Or if you wish to cover the wood grain and finish a piece of furniture in a color:

1. Enamel undercoat, or primer
2. Enamel

Over old varnish, plastic, or clear-lacquer finishes:

1. Clear varnish or plastic
2. When dry, apply second coat

Or paint over an old finish:

1. Enamel undercoat
2. Enamel

On bare or painted metal:

1. Rust-inhibiting metal primer
2. Enamel

On natural wicker, raffia, reed, or bamboo:

1. Clear varnish, plastic, or lacquer
2. When dry, apply second coat over dull spots.

On painted wicker, reed, or bamboo (or painting over natural finish):

1. Enamel undercoat
2. Enamel

Or:

1. Lacquer undercoat
2. Colored lacquer

Finishing materials should only be applied over compatible surfaces. For example, you can use enamel over lacquer, but you can't apply lacquer over enamel. The thinner in the lacquer would act as a paint remover, softening and wrinkling the enamel underneath.

Some combinations are not used even though no damage would result. It would be pointless to apply wood stain over varnish or plastic, for the latter seal the wood and prevent the stain from being absorbed.

Figure 2 illustrates whether or not specified finishing materials can be used over one another.

Preparing Furniture for Refinishing

Remove all hardware (see page 58).

All surfaces to be refinished must be clean and smooth. If the old finish is badly scarred, scratched, cracked, or flaking, remove it completely, right down to the wood. Otherwise, simply smooth it lightly with sandpaper, and apply a new finish over the old one.

To remove an old finish completely, either sandpaper it off or use paint remover.

Sanding

Use a sandpaper block (see page 192), or an electric sander (see page 180).

To smooth an old finish, go over the entire surface with medium sandpaper (60 to 100 grit, or 1/2 to 2/0), followed by fine sandpaper (120 to 180 grit, or 3/0 to 5/0). Be sure to sand *with* the grain when working over old varnish or lacquer. Direction makes no difference if you are sanding an old painted surface. Give the piece a final rub with fine steel wool and you should have a satin-smooth finish.

To remove a finish completely, sand with medium sandpaper until the wood shows underneath. Discard the paper when it becomes clogged, and use a fresh sheet. After the entire finish has been removed, smooth the wood with fine sandpaper, followed by fine steel wool.

Using paint remover

You can't always remove an old finish with sandpaper. If the piece you are refinishing contains carvings or fine moldings, you need paint remover.

Paint remover is used either to strip an entire piece of its old finish or to remove selected

FINISHING MATERIAL:	VARNISH	PLASTIC	ENAMEL	ENAMEL UNDERCOAT	LACQUER	WAX	LINSEED OIL	WOOD STAIN
● Can be used over finishing material at left ○ Cannot be used over finishing material at left								
Varnish	●	●	●	●	○	●	○	○
Plastic	●	●	●	●	○	●	○	○
Enamel	○	○	●	●	○	○	○	○
Enamel Undercoat	○	○	●	●	○	○	○	○
Lacquer	●	●	●	●	●	●	○	○
Wax	○	○	○	○	○	●	○	○
Linseed Oil	●	●	●	●	○	●	●	○
Wood Stain	●	●	○	○	●	●	●	●
Bare Wood	●	●	●	●	●	●	●	●

Figure 2. Chart shows which finishing materials can be applied over others.

portions of its finish. For example, you may wish to refinish a tabletop without touching the legs.

There are two types of paint remover: one is water-soluble, and the other is soluble in alcohol or turpentine. Do not use water-soluble removers on veneered furniture. Veneers are thin slices of fine wood glued to cores of common wood. The moisture in water-soluble removers may soften the glue that holds the veneers, causing them to separate.

Paint-remover hints

First read directions on the paint-remover container.

Always work in a well-ventilated area. If possible, work out-of-doors. If you can't do this, shut the doors and open the windows of the room in which you are working.

Never use flammable paint remover near an open flame, such as a pilot light for a gas stove or a space-heating furnace.

Always wear plastic or rubber gloves when handling paint remover. It is a powerful chemical that can injure your skin.

Spread five or six thicknesses of newspaper to protect the floor. Obviously, if paint remover can dissolve a furniture finish, it can also ruin the finish on your floor.

Remove any knobs or drawer pulls from the piece you are refinishing. These are usually held by one or two screws, so they should give you no trouble.

HOW TO REMOVE AN OLD FINISH

You will need:

> **Paint remover**
> **Solvent for paint remover (consult**
> **container)**
> **Old brush, about 2 inches wide**
> **Putty knife or paint scraper**
> **Coarse steel wool**
> **Fine steel wool**
> **Rags**
> **Rubber gloves**

What to do:

1. Before doing anything else, put on the rubber gloves.

2. Use the brush to flow on a thick layer of paint remover, but do not brush it out (Figure 3).

Figure 3. Flowing on paint remover with a brush

3. Allow the remover to remain untouched until it becomes thick and wrinkled. This shows that the finish underneath has become soft.

4. Carefully scrape a small area with the putty knife or paint scraper (Figure 4). If the old finish comes off easily, remove it completely. If not, remove the softened portions and apply a fresh layer of paint remover. Wait until this becomes wrinkled, then scrape it off. The thicker the old finish underneath, the more remover you will need, and the longer it will take for it to soften up.

5. Remove the old finish entirely. Clean up corners, carvings, and moldings with the corner of a putty knife and coarse steel wool.

6. Saturate a clean cloth with the recommended solvent, and wash away all traces of paint remover. Use another cloth to wipe the piece dry. Discard all used cloths by placing them outdoors in a metal container.

Figure 4. Scraping off softened paint

7. Allow the piece to dry completely, then rub it down with fine steel wool.

8. Clean the brush (see page 46).

HOW TO APPLY A NEW FINISH: BRUSHING

This is the old, tried-and-true method of applying paints, varnishes, and other finishing materials. It seems easy enough: dip the brush into the finish, and apply the finish to whatever you're working on. It's not quite that simple, however.

You will need:

> Finishing material (enamel, varnish, etc.)
> Paint thinner (this varies with the type
>   of finish used)
> Flat brush, 2 or 3 inches wide
> Mixing stick

What to do:

1. Use a large coin or nail to twist open the cover of the can. Stir the contents with a stick, mixing everything thoroughly, including any pigment which may have settled to the bottom of the can.

2. Dip the brush no more than halfway into the contents of the can. Make a stroke with

the loaded brush. Most of the material on the brush will be deposited at the beginning of the stroke. Distribute it in a thin, even coat by brushing outward from this area (Figure 5).

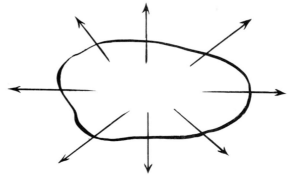

Figure 5. Brush finishing material out from center of initial brush stroke.

3. Make another brush stroke near the first one. Brush out the finishing material, overlapping and blending it with the previously coated area.

Hints

If you keep the brush handle pointing up, paint will not run down over your hand. Hold the brush at right angles to the surface you are finishing. Use very little pressure. Work with the tip of the brush, not the side, so that the natural springiness of the brush hairs will help to spread the finishing material (Figure 6).

Figure 6. Hold brush almost vertically.

After you have covered a complete area, remove visible brush marks by going over it lightly with the tip of the brush. Do not press against the coated surface. Make all strokes in the same direction.

You may have to apply more than one coat in order to cover a surface completely. In this case, the first coat must be dry before you apply a second; *never* apply a new coat over a partially dry surface. Consult the container to determine drying time.

How to clean a brush

Pour about two inches of thinner into a clean jar or can. This may be mineral spirits, turpentine, lacquer thinner, or even water, depending on the type of finishing material you are using. Rinse the brush. Discard the used thinner and rinse the brush a second time in clean thinner. Wipe the brush on a cloth or paper towel.

Using warm (not hot) water, work up a lather by rubbing the brush against a bar of soap, then against your palm. Or apply either liquid or powdered household detergent to the wet brush. (Do not use dishwasher detergents, as they may ruin natural bristles.) Rinse the brush. Keep soaping and rinsing the brush until no traces of finishing material can be seen.

How to store a clean brush

Take a piece of wrapping paper (or part of a paper bag) and wrap it two or three times

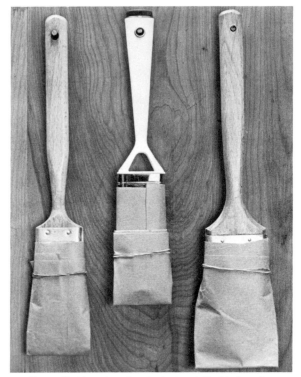

Figure 7. Hang brushes by holes drilled in handles.

around the wet brush. Fold the paper just below the tip of the brush. Bend it upward and secure it with a rubber band (see Figure 7). This will keep the brush in shape.

If you drill a hole in the handle, you can hang the brush on a nail or on a peforated-hardboard hook, or fitting (Figure 7).

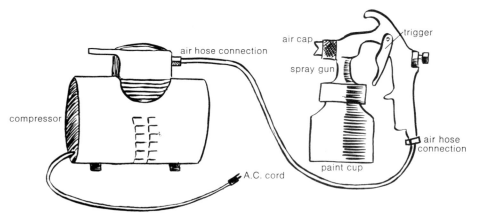

Figure 8. Paint sprayer, compressor, and gun

HOW TO APPLY A NEW FINISH: SPRAYING

Almost every kind of finishing material is available in pressurized spray cans. These self-contained spray bombs are excellent for finishing small articles and single pieces of furniture.

If you intend to do a good deal of painting or refinishing, a power-spray outfit may be a worthwhile investment, for it will help you obtain really professional-looking finishes. The simplest spray outfit consists of an electrically powered compressor and a spray gun. The finishing material is held in a metal cup, which is screwed to the gun; the gun, in turn, has a trigger that controls the spray. Figure 8 shows a small, portable power-spray outfit.

Preparing to Spray

No matter what kind of spray equipment you use, follow the same general preparation procedures:

Prepare the surface you are going to spray (see page 43).

Read the instructions on the container of finishing material. Some finishing materials contain pigments, and if they are in pressurized cans they must be well shaken; if in ordinary cans, they should be stirred before use.

Place the piece you are spraying on a clean surface which has been covered with newspapers. For spraying small articles, an old table makes a perfect work surface. Or work on a clean, newspaper-covered garage or porch floor. Better yet, work outdoors. If you spray indoors, every horizontal surface will be covered with a fine layer of dried spray material. Although you can clean it up easily, it's a messy job.

Avoid inhaling the spray. Wear a face mask,

HOW TO SPRAY

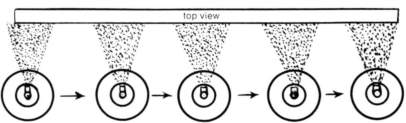

Figure 9. Move spray can parallel to work in one continuous stroke.

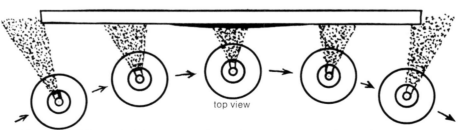

Figure 10. When only the wrist is used to make a spray pass, paint builds up in center.

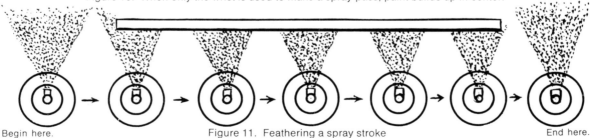

Begin here.   Figure 11. Feathering a spray stroke   End here.

or respirator (see Figure 116, page 200), which can be purchased at little cost at almost any hardware store. It is also a good idea to cover your hair.

If you must spray indoors, be sure to work in a well-ventilated area and never spray in the presence of an open flame, such as a gas-stove pilot light.

USING A PRESSURIZED SPRAY CAN

Read the directions on the can to determine whether the contents should be shaken and how far from the work the can should be held while spraying.

Practice on a piece of scrap wood by making several spray passes, moving the can parallel to the wood (Figure 9). This will deposit an even layer of finishing material on the wood surface. Be sure to move your whole arm as you spray. If you flex your wrist and spray in an arc, a thick coat of material will build up at the center, leaving the sides only thinly covered (Figure 10).

Keep the spray can moving at all times. Maintain even pressure on the spray-release button; don't jiggle it as you work.

Feather each stroke. In order to do this, don't aim the spray directly at the spot you intend to cover; instead begin each spray pass about 6 inches to one side of the piece you are working on. As you move the can, gently depress the spray button so that you are spraying *before* you reach the piece. Then keep spraying for another 6 inches *after* you reach the end (Figure 11).

Spray thin coats. Two or three thin coats will give much better results than one thick one. Allow each coat to dry thoroughly before applying the next. Spray succeeding coats at right angles to each other.

After you have finished spraying, clean the spray-can nozzle by turning the can upside down and pressing the spray-release button until no more material comes out. This takes only a few seconds.

USING A POWER SPRAYER

You will need:
> **Power-spray outfit**
> **Nylon stocking or paint strainer**
> **Mixing stick**
> **Finishing material**
> **Thinner for finishing material**
> **Adjustable-end wrench**

What to do:

1. Check power sprayer to see that the air hose is installed properly. One end should be connected to the compressor and the other to the spray gun (see Figure 8). Tighten these connections by hand.

2. Turn on the compressor and check the air-hose connections for air seepage. If air is escaping from any connection, tighten it further with the adjustable-end wrench (Figure 12).

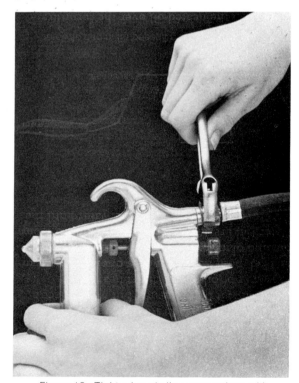

Figure 12. Tightening air-line connections with adjustable-end wrench

6. Screw the paint cup to the spray gun (Figure 14), turn on the compressor, and test the spray. Hold the gun about 6 inches from a piece of cardboard or spread-out newspaper, and press the trigger. At the same time, move the gun. You should get a smooth, even deposit. If the gun spits and delivers thick drops, the material is too thick. Dilute it with thinner.

Figure 13. Straining paint

3. Use a large coin or nail to pry open the cover of the can of finishing material. Stir the material thoroughly with the mixing stick, breaking up any lumps of pigment which may have settled to the bottom of the can.

4. Strain the finishing material by pouring it through a nylon stocking stretched across the the top of the spray cup. Or use a commercially prepared paint strainer (Figure 13). Straining removes particles which could clog the spray gun.

5. Check the thickness of the strained material by dipping your mixing stick into it, then raising the stick so that the finishing material drips down into the cup. It should be just thin enough to run off smoothly. If it falls from the stick in large globs, it is too thick and must be diluted with the proper thinner.

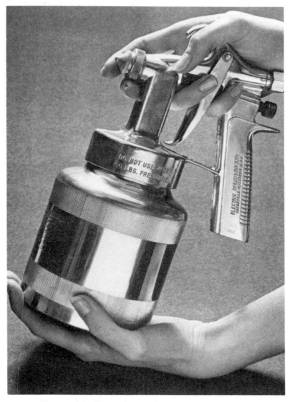

Figure 14. Screwing paint cup to spray gun

7. Spray cans and power sprayers are used in exactly the same manner, which means that you should feather each stroke as described on page 48. To spray a horizontal surface, first make a pass with the spray gun (or can), covering the edge nearest you. The second spray pass should overlap about half of the top edge of the first one. Continue to spray in long, even strokes, each one overlapping the preceding one, until the entire surface has been covered (Figure 15).

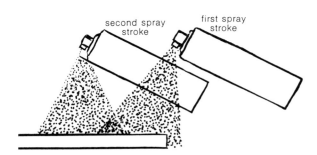

Figure 15. On horizontal surfaces, overlap half of top edge of preceding spray stroke.

8. When spraying a vertical surface, start at the top with your first pass. The second pass should overlap half of the bottom edge of the first one, the third should overlap the second, etc. (Figure 16).

Spray thin coats. Thick deposits of finishing material are likely to sag or run. If it is necessary to spray on a second coat, wait until the first coat has dried thoroughly. Spray succeeding coats at right angles to each other.

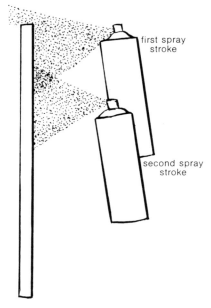

Figure 16. On vertical surfaces, overlap half of bottom edge of each preceding stroke.

To clean a spray gun

Disconnect the spray gun from the spray cup and empty the cup by pouring any unused material back into its original container. Use a cloth dipped in thinner to wipe the inside of the spray can and then rinse the inside of the can with thinner.

Fill the can about halfway with thinner; connect it to the spray gun. Spray thinner into a bunched rag, from a distance of about one inch.

Figure 17. Removing air cap from spray gun

Use the rag to wipe the outside of the gun. Shake the gun and can while spraying so that all material inside both the can and the gun is dissolved. When you have used all the thinner in the can, repeat this procedure with clean thinner.

Remove the air cap from the spray gun by turning it counterclockwise (Figure 17). You should be able to remove it easily; if not, use slip-joint pliers. Use a rag dipped in thinner to wipe the inside of the cap. Clean out airholes with a toothpick or wood sliver; never use a nail or any other metal object.

Apply light, general-purpose lubricating oil to all moving parts, but use the oil sparingly.

REFINISHING LACQUERED OR VARNISHED SURFACES

The following finish can be used for furniture with undamaged wood surfaces that are only lightly scratched or stained.

You will need:

> Fine sandpaper, 120 to 180 grit, or
>   3/0 to 5/0
> Sandpaper block (scrap wood, about
>   2 x 4 inches)
> Fine steel wool
> Polyurethane finish
> Thinner (mineral spirits)
> Flat varnish brush, 2 inches wide
> Cheesecloth, about 2 square feet

What to do:

1. Wash the surface with soap (or mild household detergent) and warm water to remove old wax and grime. Dry with a clean cloth.

2. Smooth the piece with fine sandpaper. Wrap the sandpaper around the scrap wood and sand with the grain, using very little pressure (see page 43). The idea is to smooth the old finish, not to remove it. Then rub the surface with fine steel wool to remove any fine scratches left by the sandpaper.

3. Wipe the piece with a *slightly* damp cloth; this leaves a cleaner surface than a dry cloth.

4. Make a *tack cloth* by folding the cheesecloth into a pad about 4 inches square. Use the brush to dab a few drops of the polyurethane finish on one side of the pad. Work the finish into the cloth so that it becomes slightly sticky. Wipe the furniture with the sticky side of the tack cloth. This leaves a dustless surface.

5. Brush on an even coat of polyurethane, just as it comes from the can. Do not dilute it. Allow the finish to dry (consult the container to find out how long to wait between coats).

6. To prevent the brush from drying out while the first coat is drying, stand it in a can of thinner. Better still, pass a wire through a

hole in the handle, and suspend the brush from the top edge of a container of thinner, with the hairs immersed (Figure 18).

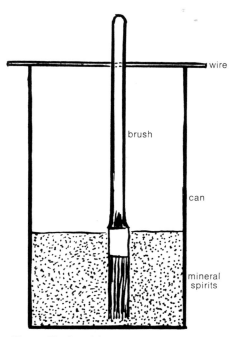

Figure 18. Brush immersed in thinner

7. When the first coat of finish has dried, brush on a second coat.

8. Clean the brush (see page 46).

Hints

Polyurethane is available in either glossy or satin finishes; both are waterproof and highly resistant to heat, alcohol, and food stains.

Some polyurethane products are called *varnishes* while others are referred to as *plastic finishes*. They are not necessarily the same; some are formulated for outdoor use. Ask your paint dealer for further information.

It's a good idea to prepare a piece of furniture for refinishing, then wait to do the actual varnishing until the children have gone to school or to bed. Then you can be sure no one will suddenly open a door, inadvertently admitting a gust of dust-ridden air that will settle on your work.

Be sure the work area is well-ventilated.

A polyurethane finish may be sprayed as well as painted.

To put a waterproof finish on a tabletop

First wipe tabletop with a cloth soaked in mineral spirits. Then wash it with soap (or mild household detergent) and warm water, and dry. Brush on two coats of polyurethane, and you're done.

REFINISHING BADLY SCRATCHED VARNISHED FURNITURE

You will need:

> Penetrating wood stain
> Cabinet varnish
> Polyurethane finish
> Thinner (mineral spirits)
> Flat 2-inch brush for stain
> Flat varnish brush, 2 inches wide
> Clean rags
> Fine steel wool
> Cheesecloth, about 2 square feet
> Plastic or rubber gloves
> Materials for removing the old finish
>   (sandpaper or paint remover; see pages
>   193 and 199).

What to do:

1. Remove the old finish from the piece of furniture (see pages 43–44).

2. Open the can of stain and stir it thoroughly; mix up any material that may have settled to the bottom.

3. Apply the stain by brushing it on liberally; then allow it to dry for about an hour.

4. If you have not already done so, put on your protective gloves. Wipe the stained area with a clean rag. Darken too-light areas by applying more stain; lighten too-dark areas by wiping with a cloth wet with mineral spirits.

5. Allow the stain to dry overnight, then rub the furniture with fine steel wool to obtain a satin-smooth finish. Wipe with a clean rag.

6. Pour a small amount of cabinet varnish into a clean can. Add about 20 percent thinner and stir well. Brush on a coat of this diluted varnish and let it dry overnight.

7. Rinse the brush in thinner, and wrap it in paper. Or suspend it in a can of thinner.

8. Rub the dry varnished surface lightly with fine steel wool. Then make a tack cloth (see page 51) and wipe the surface clean.

9. Brush on an undiluted coat of polyurethane finish. Let it dry for the recommended time (consult the container).

10. Brush on a second, final coat of polyurethane finish. Pour any unused finishing material back into its container.

11. Clean the brush, and wrap it for storage (page 46).

Hints

The coat of cabinet varnish serves as a *sealer* that prevents the polyurethane from acting like paint remover and dissolving the stain. If you use a stain specially formulated for use under polyurethane, you can omit the cabinet varnish and apply the finish coat right over the stain.

You can always apply a dark stain over a light one, but you can't lighten dark wood by applying a light stain.

APPLYING A LINSEED-OIL FINISH

If you are in no great hurry to get the job done, you can refinish a piece of furniture with linseed oil. This will give you a soft, satiny, waterproof finish. An oil finish works best on hardwoods such as oak, maple, mahogany, cherry, or walnut. It shouldn't be used on soft-woods such as pine, cedar, redwood, or fir.

You will need:

> Boiled linseed oil
> Penetrating wood stain
> Flat 2-inch brush for stain
> Flat 2-inch brush for linseed oil
> Clean, lintless cloths

Plastic or rubber gloves
Materials for removing old finish
(sandpaper or paint remover; see pages
193 and 199).

What to do:

1. Remove the old finish.

2. Open the can of stain and stir the contents thoroughly.

3. Apply the stain by brushing it on liberally; allow it to dry for about an hour. Put on protective gloves, and wipe the stained areas with a clean cloth.

4. Allow the stain to dry overnight, then rub the furniture with fine steel wool. Wipe it with a clean rag.

5. To make the linseed oil flow more freely and thus better penetrate the pores of the wood, heat it before using. But *never* place a container of oil over a direct heat source. Instead, pour about 2 inches of oil into a clean can and place the can in a saucepan of hot water (Figure 19) that has been removed from the stove. Leave the can in the water until the oil is lukewarm.

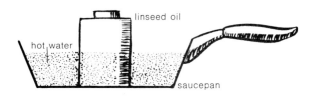

linseed oil

hot water

saucepan

Figure 19. Warming linseed oil in pan of water

6. Brush the heated oil over the furniture, applying more to those areas that soak it up quickly.

7. Polish the piece with a clean, wadded cloth. As soon as you have finished, dispose of the oily rags in a metal container, outdoors.

8. Reapply warm oil at weekly intervals, polishing each application. As the wood becomes saturated with oil, a soft patina will result. At this point, apply less oil and more

elbow grease. Finish by rubbing with the palm of your hand.

It is impossible to predict the exact number of applications needed to acquire a good oil finish. Just stick with it until you get the finish you want. You may need as few as three or as many as ten applications and rubbings.

Hints

Be sure to buy linseed oil labeled "boiled." Ordinary linseed oil should not be used because it takes too long to dry.

You can speed up the drying action of the linseed oil by adding about ten drops of Japan drier to each ounce of oil. Drier can be purchased at most hardware and paint stores.

PAINTING WOOD FURNITURE

You will need:

Fine sandpaper, 120 to 180 grit,
or 3/0 to 5/0
Sandpaper block (scrap wood about
2 x 4 inches)
Enamel undercoat (spray or brush-on)
Enamel in desired color (spray or
brush-on)
Flat 2-inch brush
Thinner (mineral spirits)
Clean rags
Powdered wood putty or prepared spackle
Putty knife or paint scraper

What to do:

1. Scrape off any loose paint with the putty knife or scraper. Wrap a piece of sandpaper around the sandpaper block, and go over the entire piece of furniture. Don't try to remove all the old paint; simply sand it smooth.

2. Mix the wood putty with water, according to directions on the container. Using the putty knife or scraper, fill in any irregularities such as deep scratches, dents, or tears in the wood (Figure 20). Or use prepared spackle (a type of patching compound) directly from its container.

Allow the putty or spackle to dry. Sand the filled-in area with the sandpaper block. If the putty has shrunk, apply a second layer. Allow the second layer to dry, then sand lightly until it feels smooth, and wipe with a cloth dampened with thinner.

Figure 20. Filling irregularities in tabletop with wood putty

3. Brush or spray on enamel undercoat. Allow it to dry, then sand lightly with the sandpaper alone—don't use the block.

4. Brush or spray on a coat of enamel. If you find dull spots after the enamel has dried, apply a second coat.

5. Clean the brush or spray equipment (see pages 46 and 50).

Hints

Use exactly the same procedure when painting over a previously lacquered or varnished piece or when painting unfinished furniture.

When sanding the undercoat, be careful not to remove too much from the corners and edges; if you do, you'll expose the old finish.

PAINTING METAL FURNITURE

You will need:
>   Wire brush
>   Paint scraper or putty knife
>   Emery cloth, medium grade
>   Rust-inhibiting metal primer
>   Rust-inhibiting enamel
>   (Rust-inhibiting finishes are available in either brush-on or spray form.)
>   Flat 2-inch brush
>   Thinner (mineral spirits)
>   Clean rags

What to do:
1. Use the putty knife, scraper, or wire brush to remove all loose paint and rust from the piece. Smooth the surface with the emery cloth, then wipe it clean with a soft rag so that no loose particles remain.

2. Spray or brush the piece with rust-inhibiting metal primer. Allow it to dry.

3. Then spray or brush on a coat of rust-inhibiting enamel. If one thin coat does not cover the undercoat completely, apply a second coat after the first has dried thoroughly.

4. Clean the brush or spray equipment (see pages 46 and 50).

Hint

Use rust-inhibiting materials to refinish other metalwork around the house. For example, you can repaint a rusty barbecue grill, a metal fence, or a just-beginning-to-rust decorative grill (Figure 21).

REFINISHING WICKER FURNITURE

The easiest way to refinish wicker and other woven furniture is to spray it. If you are able to, buy polyurethane finish in pressurized cans, or try to get access to a portable power sprayer. If neither is possible, you will simply have to take the necessary time and trouble to refinish your furniture with a brush.

Natural Finish

You will need:

> Fine sandpaper, 120 grit, or 3/0
> Putty knife or paint scraper
> Polyurethane finish, clear, glossy
> Thinner (mineral spirits)
> Flat 2-inch brush
> Clean rag

What to do:

1. Use the putty knife or scraper to remove all loose finish or built-up dirt. Sand all rough or worn spots; armrests usually show more signs of wear than other areas. Dampen a rag with thinner and wipe the piece clean. Allow to dry.

2. Brush or spray on a coat of polyurethane finish. Allow it to dry the necessary length of time; consult the container for directions.

3. Apply a second coat of polyurethane.

4. Clean the brush or spray equipment (see pages 46 and 50).

Colored Finish

You will need:

> Fine sandpaper, 120 grit, or 3/0
> Putty knife or paint scraper
> Enamel undercoat (spray or brush-on)
> Quick-drying enamel (spray or brush-on)
> Thinner (mineral spirits)
> Flat 2-inch brush
> Clean rags

What to do:

1. Use the putty knife or scraper to remove any loose finish. Sand all rough areas until they are smooth. Dampen a rag with thinner and wipe the piece clean.

2. Brush or spray on a coat of enamel undercoat. Allow to dry.

3. Then brush or spray on a coat of quick-drying enamel. Allow to dry. Examine the finish—if there are dull areas, touch them up with a little more enamel. Or apply another complete coat.

4. Clean the brush or spray equipment (see pages 46 and 50).

Hints

You can apply enamel directly over wicker that is in good condition without using an undercoat. However, if there are worn or rough surfaces, an undercoat is needed to furnish a smooth base for the enamel.

Dingy-looking wicker may not require painting at all; it may simply be dirty. Don't be afraid to wash wicker pieces. Scrub with a stiff brush and plenty of soap and warm water (or a mild detergent solution). Rinse thoroughly.

Figure 21. Spraying decorative grill

HOW TO ANTIQUE FURNITURE

There are many kits on the market that contain everything needed to antique furniture. If you are planning to antique only one piece of furniture, it may be more convenient to buy a kit. However, if you have several pieces to do or would like to develop your own unusual color finishes, you will find it more practical to mix your own antiquing glazes.

You will need:

    Shellac
    Shellac thinner (alcohol)
    Paint thinner (mineral spirits)
    Latex paint for base coat (see text below)
    Antiquing glaze (see text below)
    Satin-finish varnish or polyurethane finish
    Flat 2-inch brush
    Sandpaper, 120 grit, or 3/0
    Sandpaper, 220 grit, or 6/0
    Screwdriver
    Clean rags

What to do:

1. Remove all drawer pulls, knobs, and ornamental metalwork. It is not necessary to remove doors.

2. Wash the piece with mineral spirits to remove old polish and wax. Go over the piece lightly with 3/0 sandpaper. Don't try to remove the finish; just sand it enough to remove the gloss.

3. If you are *antiquing a stained, varnished piece,* you will have to give it a *sealer* coat of shellac. Many old pieces were finished with aniline stains which will "bleed" through finishing materials applied over them. Shellac stops bleeding.

Pour about two inches of shellac into a clean can. Mix it with an equal amount of shellac thinner. Brush a coat of the thinned shellac over the entire piece. Allow it to dry overnight, then sand it lightly with 3/0 sandpaper to remove its glossy finish.

If you are *antiquing unfinished furniture,* shellac sealer is not needed.

4. Brush on a *base coat* of flat latex wall or ceiling paint. This should be a medium tint of the same general color you want the finished piece to be. Make long strokes, following the grain of the wood. To get the "antique" effect you want, don't smooth out the brush strokes, but allow each brush mark to show as a series of sharp ridges. The thicker the paint, the easier it will be to leave sharply defined brush marks (Figure 22).

5. Allow the base coat to dry for at least four hours. In the meantime, paint a few scraps of wood to use later for testing the color of your glaze.

Figure 22. Brushing on a thick coat of paint to show brush marks

HOW TO MAKE ANTIQUING GLAZE

You will need:

    2 ounces raw linseed oil
    2 ounces varnish or polyurethane finish
    ¼ teaspoon Japan drier
    About 1 teaspoon oil color, same as base color
    About ½ teaspoon black oil color
    About 1 teaspoon burnt umber oil color
    3 ounces turpentine

What to do:

1. The oil colors can be the kind used by artists or those obtainable in tubes or cans from your local paint store. Mix the colors with the linseed oil so that there are no lumps. Add the varnish or polyurethane, drier, and turpentine, and stir well.

2. Brush some of the resultant glaze on one of your test pieces of scrap wood. It should be considerably darker than the base coat; if it isn't, add more oil color.

Figure 24. Wipe the glaze while it is still wet.

4. Allow the glaze to dry thoroughly; this should take at least two hours. During this time, clean the brush you used for glazing by rinsing it in thinner until it is clean. Wipe it dry on a rag.

Figure 23. Brushing on glaze

3. When you have obtained the color you want, brush a thin coat of the antiquing glaze over the furniture (Figure 23). Do one side at a time, for the glaze sets rapidly. While the glaze is still wet, wipe it gently with a clean cloth to make it lighter and even in tone (Figure 24). Allow the glaze to remain in dents, scratches, and other surface irregularities to enhance the antique effect. Wipe it from the tops of carvings and moldings, but allow it to remain darker in crevices (Figure 25).

Figure 25. Wiping antiquing glaze from molding

5. Sand the dry piece lightly with 6/0 sandpaper. Stroke with the grain, in the same direction as the brush marks. This will remove the glaze from the tops of the brush marks, exposing the base coat underneath and leaving

Figure 26. Sanding glazed surface

the darker, glazed areas in between (Figure 26). Wipe the piece with a clean cloth.

6. Brush on a thin coat of satin-finish varnish or polyurethane.

7. Clean the brush. Dispose of all rags by placing them in a metal container outside.

8. Replace hardware after the final coat of glaze has dried.

Hints

Use any colors you like. There are no rules, so experiment. You can obtain interesting effects by using a white base coat instead of a colored one. Cover the white with colored antiquing glazes.

For a brighter effect, use less black oil color when mixing the glaze.

You needn't limit yourself to antiquing furniture. You can use the same technique on kitchen cabinets, and doors and woodwork throughout the house.

Articles such as picture frames, which aren't likely to be handled much, need not be varnished. However, don't fail to varnish all furniture tops.

To give furniture an even more worn, antique look, "distress" it before you apply the first coat. Anything that will leave marks on the wood will do the trick; you can even drop rocks on it or beat it with chains! Then smooth all rough spots with sandpaper to make them look well worn.

Furniture Hardware

Distinctive hardware can lend character to furniture, but it is important to coordinate hardware and furniture styles.

As a general rule, all hardware should be removed before refinishing or antiquing a piece of furniture. Either refinish and replace it, or install new hardware when the new surface of the furniture is completely dry.

REFINISHING OLD BRASS HARDWARE

Bright Finish

You will need:

> **Steel wool, fine grade**
> **Paint remover, brush (optional)**
> **Fine wire**
> **Clear metal lacquer or clear plastic spray**

What to do:

1. Clean any dried paint or varnish from the hardware with paint remover (see page 43). Use newspaper to protect the work surface.

2. Rub the entire piece with steel wool (rub in only one direction). The finer the steel wool, the higher the polish will be. For a duller polish, use coarse steel wool.

3. Suspend the piece from fine wire, and dip it into a container of clear lacquer. Allow the excess lacquer to drip back into the can. Or, instead of using clear metal lacquer, spray the hardware with clear plastic spray.

4. Then hang the hardware up to dry.

Antique Finish

You will need:

> **Metallic spray paint**
> **Paint remover, brush (optional)**
> **Wood stain**
> **Steel wool**
> **Clear varnish or clear plastic spray**
> **Cloth**

What to do:

1. If necessary, use paint remover to clean off all old paint and varnish (see page 43). Use a pad of old newspaper to protect the work surface.

2. Smooth the hardware by rubbing it in one direction with steel wool.

3. Apply an even coat of metallic spray paint and allow it to dry.

4. Next apply a coat of wood stain over the metallic finish. Wait until the stain has almost dried, then wipe the piece with a cloth. Don't remove all the stain; leave enough to give a slightly streaky—or if you prefer—an even-textured finish. Allow the stain to dry overnight.

5. Brush on a coat of clear varnish, or spray on a coat of clear plastic.

6. Clean and store the brush (see page 46).

Hints

Hardware stores and large lumberyards often carry replacement hardware for furniture and cabinets. Investigate these places; you may prefer new hardware for a piece of refinished furniture.

For a wrought-iron look, spray hardware with flat black lacquer.

If you do not care for the dead-black wrought-iron look, try this: spray with flat black lacquer; then apply a coat of white or lightly tinted paint. Wipe it off, leaving enough to give a textured effect.

REMOVING FINE SCRATCHES FROM FURNITURE

Scratch-removing polish contains stain as well as polishing agents. Use it only on medium-to-dark furniture.

You will need:

　Scratch-removing furniture polish
　Cotton swab
　Clean, soft cloth

What to do:

1. Apply scratch-removing polish directly to scratches with a cotton swab or brush (Figure 27).

2. Polish the entire section and rub it down with a soft cloth until it feels dry.

Figure 27. Applying scratch-removing polish with brush

REMOVING WHITE SPOTS AND RINGS

White spots and rings are usually caused by placing wet or hot dishes on a varnished surface. They can be easily removed.

You will need:

　Soft flannel
　Spirits of camphor or household ammonia
　Furniture wax

What to do:

1. Dampen a soft flannel pad with either spirits of camphor or ammonia, and rub lightly with a circular motion.

2. Go over the entire surface with a good furniture wax. (NOTE: Do not use wax or furniture polish on teak or oiled walnut. Instead, use a few drops of lemon oil and buff with a soft cloth.)

FILLING DEEP SCRATCHES, DENTS, AND NICKS

You will need:

    Putty stick, of a color to match the
      furniture finish
    Furniture polish that contains oil
    Single-edged razor blade in holder
    Putty knife
    Soft cloth

What to do:

1. Polish the entire surface, rubbing it until it is dry.

Figure 28. Rubbing putty stick over dent

2. Then rub the putty stick across the scratch or dent, turning it at the same time. Build up the rubbed material in the dent until it is higher than the surrounding surface (Figure 28). Use

Figure 29. Pressing filler into dent with putty knife

the putty knife to press the filler into the dent (Figure 29).

3. Scrape away excess filler material with the razor blade, leaving it even with the furniture surface. Be careful not to scrape the furniture finish.

4. Repolish the surface.

Hints

Putty sticks are made of hard wax in color assortments to match most standard furniture finishes. In an emergency, if you can't get a putty stick, use ordinary hard crayons.

If you can't fill a deep dent by rubbing across it, apply a match to the putty stick and allow the melting material to pile up in the dent until it is slightly higher than the surrounding surface. Then proceed as outlined above.

Use your ingenuity. An occasional scratch can be removed by carefully applying tincture of iodine, alcohol, or even shoe polish with a toothpick to darken the scratch. Apply alcohol sparingly so it covers only the scratch. Use furniture wax to brighten the surface after the scratch removers are dry.

The best time to fill a deep dent is when a surface is being refinished, just before the final coat of finish is applied.

REFINISHING A TABLETOP WITH ADHESIVE-BACKED VINYL

You will need:

    Fine sandpaper, 120 to 180 grit,
      or 3/0 to 5/0
    Sandpaper block (scrap wood, about
      2 x 4 inches)
    Powdered wood putty, or ready-mixed
      spackling putty
    Putty knife or paint scraper
    Flat 2-inch brush
    Shellac
    Shellac thinner (alcohol)
    Adhesive backed vinyl
    Clean rags
    Single-edged razor blade in holder

What to do:

1. Sand the tabletop until it is smooth. It is not necessary to remove the old finish. Wipe it thoroughly with a clean rag.

2. Fill all holes, deep scratches, or dents with putty; work it into each damaged area with the paint scraper or putty knife (see pages 185–186). Allow the putty to dry.

3. Wrap a piece of sandpaper around the wood block, and sand lightly over all filled areas. You may find that the putty has shrunk; if so, apply a second layer. After the second layer of putty has dried, sand the entire top lightly so that all filled areas are level with the table surface.

4. Wipe the top clean and brush on a coat of shellac, allowing it to dry overnight.

5. Rinse the brush in two changes of alcohol, then wash it clean (see page 46).

Figure 31. Work from center to smooth second half of vinyl sheet into place.

the end, smooth one half of the sheet into place. At the same time, force out air bubbles. Smooth down the other half (Figures 31 and 32).

Figure 30. Center of self-adhesive vinyl sheet in contact with tabletop

6. Cut a sheet of vinyl slightly larger than the tabletop and peel off the backing. Hold the ends of the sheet in both hands so that just the center portion makes contact with the tabletop (Figure 30). Rubbing from the center toward

Figure 32. Smoothing whole vinyl sheet on tabletop

7. Trim around the edges with a single-edged razor blade.

Hints

Adhesive-backed vinyls are made to match almost every wood grain. Others are imprinted with designs, and still others are produced in solid colors.

Get rid of air bubbles by pricking them with a pin, then rubbing them down until they disappear.

Don't apply vinyl sheets over rough surfaces; for best results, surfaces should be as smooth as possible.

Use adhesive-backed vinyl to recover worn or damaged kitchen cabinets, too.

TILING A TABLETOP

You will need:

> Sheet tile or single tiles to cover
>   the tabletop
> Mastic tile adhesive
> Paint thinner (mineral spirits)
> Notched trowel
> Tile nippers (only if tile must be cut to fit)
> Plastic tile edging to fit around edges of
>   the tabletop
> Scissors or sharp knife
> Common nails, ¾-inch
> Grout
> 8-ounce paper cup
> Grout spreader (see Hints, page 63)
> Tongue depressor, ice cream stick, or
>   wood scrap
> Soft cloths

What to do:

1. Prepare the tabletop for tiling by filling in and smoothing any dents, nicks, or deep scratches (see page 61).

2. Use scissors or knife to cut strips of plastic edging; these will fit around the edges of the tabletop framing the tile. Cut the corners at a 45-degree angle so that they will fit snugly together.

3. Use a tongue depressor, ice cream stick, or wood scrap to apply a *thin* layer of mastic tile adhesive to the bottom of each plastic strip,

Figure 33. Plastic edging stapled all around tabletop

and apply the strips to the table's edges, making sure the corners fit snugly together. Once the strips are in place, insert staples or nails about two inches apart (Figure 33).

4. Lay the tile on the tabletop, right up against the outer lip of the edging. If necessary, cut tiles to fit so that the entire top is covered.

5. If you are using single tiles, distribute them so that they cover the entire top with no more than a ¼-inch space around each one. If you are using sheet tiles (tiles cemented to a mesh backing), you can remove the tiles from the backing in order to adjust the spaces between them.

6. If you cannot cover the tabletop by rearranging the tiles with no more than a ¼-inch space between each one, it will be necessary to place the tiles close together, and cut narrow pieces of tile to fill vacant end areas.

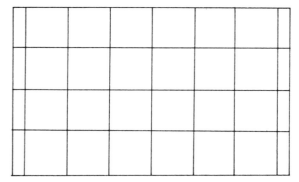

Figure 34. Tiles centered, with end pieces cut to fit

7. Center the tiles and cut pieces to fit the end spaces as in Figure 34.

8. Now that you've determined how the tiles are to fit, remove them and use the notched trowel to spread a thin, even layer of adhesive over the tabletop; be sure to include the portion of the edging that will lie flush against the edges of the tiles (Figure 35). Do not use too much adhesive. If it oozes up between the tiles, it is difficult to remove.

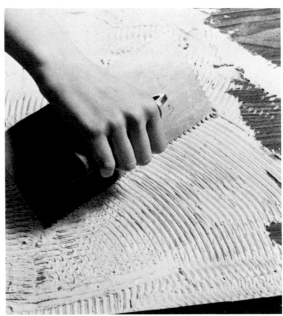

Figure 35. Use notched trowel to spread adhesive on tabletop.

9. Reassemble the tiles on the tabletop. Press them straight down onto the adhesive. Don't slide them from side to side, this will squeeze the adhesive up between the tiles. There should be even spaces between the tiles.

10. Allow the adhesive to dry for at least twenty-four hours before applying grout to the joints. Otherwise, it will remain tacky for a long time, causing the grout to crack and fall out.

11. Pour about one inch of water into a paper cup. Sift dry grout into the water until it seems as though the water cannot hold any more. Stir it, then pick it up on a tongue

depressor and tap it to test its consistency. What you need is a thin, putty-like mixture—about the consistency of yogurt or sour cream; if necessary, add more water or grout to get the mixture just right.

12. Use the tongue depressor to transfer a gob of grout to the tile. With the grouter, force it into the spaces between tiles (Figure 36).

Figure 36. Applying grout with grouter

13. With a damp cloth, wipe the surplus grout from the tiles. Wipe off the remaining haze with clean, dry cloths.

Hints

Paper cups are recommended for mixing grout because they can be discarded; there isn't any messy cleanup.

Grouters are rubber pads with handles, specially made for applying grout. You can do just as well with a piece of stiff cardboard or a rubber window-cleaning squeegee. Don't use a metal tool for grouting—it may scratch the tile.

You can retile an unattractive fireplace hearth. Use mastic adhesive to cement plastic strips around the front and side edges of the hearth, then cement new tiles right over the old surface.

Furniture Repair

FIXING A WOBBLY CHAIR

The directions below are for a chair with a slip seat.

You will need:

>Large screwdriver
>White glue
>Clean rags
>Cabinet clamps, or rope (about 4 feet), or large rubber bands (about 15)
>Stick
>Scrap wood

What to do:

1. Remove the slip seat. Screws that hold the seat in place are located on its underside (Figure 37).

Figure 37. Loosening screws that hold slip seat

2. Spread the loose joints only enough to permit you to coat them with glue. Some joints can be spread with a large screwdriver; others can be easily spread by hand.

Figure 38. Cabinet clamp on chair

3. Clamp the glued joints together. Use a *cabinet clamp* (Figure 38), if you have one. Be sure to protect the furniture finish by placing pieces of soft scrap wood between the clamp and the chair. Or improvise a clamp from a loose loop of rope. Slip the loop around the chair. Insert a stick in the loop and twist it; this shortens the loop, bringing the chair joints

Figure 39. Rope clamp on chair

together. Place one end of the stick against the inside of one chair leg to prevent the rope from loosening and unwinding. Place folded rags or cardboard under the rope to prevent damage to the furniture finish (Figure 39).

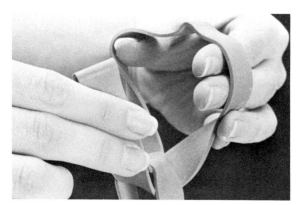

Figure 40. Lacing rubber bands together

You may also improvise a clamp from large, thick rubber bands. Lace them together as in Figure 40 so that their combined length is about two feet shorter than the circumference

Figure 41. Rubber-band clamp around chair

of the chair. Place the rubber-band loop around the chair and pull the ends together. Pull one end through the loop in the other end and secure it with a stick (Figure 41).

4. After you have clamped the glued joint, use a damp cloth to wipe off any glue that may have been squeezed out. Then rub with a dry cloth.

5. Allow the glue to harden thoroughly before you remove the clamp.

Hints

For a strong repair job, scrape away all old glue before you apply fresh glue.

You can make an effective clamp from strips of automobile tire inner tubing. Use heavy scissors or tin snips to cut 1-inch wide loops; this will give you a set of extremely strong rubber bands.

To repair a wobbly table, use the same system as that used to reglue a chair: separate the joint, apply glue, clamp it together, and allow the glue to harden.

RE-COVERING A SLIP SEAT

You will need:

> Upholstery material for new seat cover
> Thin fabric for underside of chair seat
>   (cotton, percale, cambric, muslin, etc.)
> Tack remover or small screwdriver
> Large screwdriver
> Magnetic hammer and No. 2 tacks,
>   or staple gun and staples

What to do:

1. Turn the chair upside down and remove the screws that hold the seat in place; these are found on the underside of the chair (see page 64).

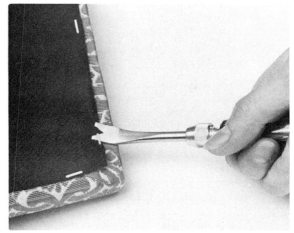

Figure 42. Removing staples from underside of seat

2. Use the tack remover or small screwdriver to remove the tacks or staples which hold the cover material to the underside of the seat (Figure 42).

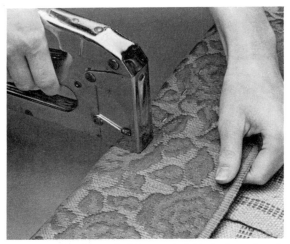

Figure 43. Stapling upholstery material to bottom of seat

3. To replace the old cover with the new, spread the new material right side down on a clean surface. Place the seat over it, top down. Fold the new material up over each side, and tack or staple it to the seat bottom (Figure 43). Stretch it slightly to take out wrinkles.

Figure 44. Thin fabric stapled to chair underside

4. Tack or staple the thin fabric to the underside of the seat (Figure 44). (If the fabric you removed from the underside of the old seat is in good condition, you can use that instead of new material.) Fold edge under before fastening it down.

5. Put the seat back into the chair frame and replace the screws that hold the seat in place.

RE-COVERING AN UPHOLSTERED SIDE-CHAIR SEAT

You will need:

> Upholstery fabric for recovering the seat
> Pliers
> Tack remover or small screwdriver
> Tack hammer
> No. 2 tacks
> Single-edged razor blade in holder
> Gimp tape to go around the edge
>   of the seat
> White glue

What to do:

Figure 45. Removing old gimp tape from chair

1. Remove the old gimp tape from the chair by prying it loose with a screwdriver blade or tack remover, or by pulling it loose with pliers (Figure 45).

Figure 46. Removing tacks that hold old fabric to chair

2. Remove all tacks that hold the old fabric cover in place. However, if there is a muslin covering underneath the upholstery fabric, do not disturb the tacks that hold it—remove only the old fabric (Figure 46).

Figure 47. Fabric tacked on centers of front, back, and sides of chair seat

3. Arrange the new fabric cover on the seat so that it hangs down evenly on all sides and is long enough to cover the places where the old fabric was tacked. Secure the fabric to the center of the back edge of the chair with two tacks placed about ½ inch apart. Stretch the fabric just enough to remove all wrinkles and use two more tacks to hold it in the center of the front edge. Do the same on the centers of the left and right sides (Figure 47).

Figure 48. Fabric tacked to edge of chair from center to corner

4. Now secure the fabric more firmly by first tacking it down over the center of each front corner and then working around to each side. (Figure 48). Place the tacks as close together as is necessary to eliminate wrinkles.

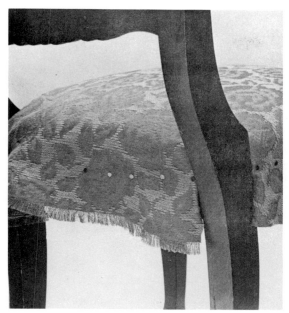

Figure 49. Fabric cut and folded around back support

5. When you reach the back supports, cut and fold the fabric (with the raw edges turned under) so that it fits snugly around these pieces (Figure 49).

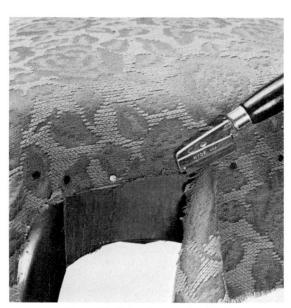

Figure 50. Trimming surplus fabric

6. Cut away surplus material with the single-edged razor blade, as in Figure 50.

Figure 51. Gimp tape tacked between back supports

7. Now cut a piece of gimp tape just long enough to fit between the two back supports. Coat the back of the tape with a thin layer of white glue, and glue and tack the tape lightly into place so that it covers the heads of the tacks that hold the upholstery fabric in place (Figure 51).

Figure 52. Gimp tape tacked around front of chair

8. Cut a piece of gimp tape to fit around the rest of the chair. Again, coat the back with a thin layer of glue and glue and tack the tape lightly in place (Figure 52). After the glue has dried, remove the tacks that hold the gimp tape in place (Figure 53).

Figure 53. Finished chair

Installing Chair Glides

Glides are fastened to the bottoms of chair legs to prevent the legs from splintering and to make it easier to slide chairs on smooth floors.

There are several types of glides, the most common of which is a shallow metal dome with

Figure 54. Domed chair glide

three teeth around the top edge (Figure 54). To install one, simply center it on the bottom of a chair leg and tap it into place with a hammer.

Figure 55. Hammering glide into bottom of chair leg

Another type is made of a plastic or metal disk from which a nail-like spike protrudes. To install it, first drill a pilot hole (see page 167) slightly smaller than the diameter of the spike, then tap it into place with a hammer (Figure 55).

Other glides are designed to fit *over* the ends of chair legs (Figure 56); these are used primarily on metal legs. To install one, slip it over the end of the leg and hammer it gently into place.

Figure 56. Chair glide fitted over end of chair leg

Hint

If your floor is becoming marked with dark streaks, examine the bottoms of your chair legs; they probably have metal glides. If so, replace them with glides made of plastic.

TO LOOSEN STICKING WOODEN DRAWERS

You will need:

> **Smooth or block plane**
> **Fine abrasive paper, 3/0 to 6/0**
> **Fine steel wool**
> **Shellac**
> **Small brush**
> **Silicone spray**

What to do:

1. After removing the drawer and emptying it, plane down the top edge of each side (Figure 57). Remove enough wood to enable the drawer to slide freely in its track without binding.

Figure 57. Planing down top edge of drawer side

2. Sandpaper the areas you have just planed, rounding them as you work (Figure 58).

Figure 58. Sandpapering and rounding top edge of drawer side

3. Dust sanded areas and apply a coat of shellac to them. Shellac acts as a sealer that keeps out moisture and prevents the wood from swelling. Allow the shellac to dry, then smooth lightly with fine steel wool.

4. Spray a light coating of silicone (see page 203) on the tops and bottoms of the drawer sides.

Tightening a Wooden Drawer Handle

Hold the handle firmly. Open the drawer and tighten the screw that holds the handle by turning it clockwise. If the screw keeps on turning, remove it. Push a piece of a wooden matchstick into the screw hole, and replace the screw.

Tightening a Metal Drawer Handle

Use the method outlined above to tighten a metal drawer handle. However, a matchstick may be too thick to use in the screw hole, so use part of a flat toothpick instead.

Adjusting a Kitchen-Cabinet Door Latch

If a cabinet door does not remain shut, ex- amine the catch; it may be loose. Tighten the screws that hold it. If the screws don't hold, remove them, plug the holes with pieces of a wooden matchstick, and replace them.

A friction catch may break. If it does, replace it with a magnetic catch. This consists of two parts: a magnetic unit which is screwed to the door, and an iron or steel plate which is fastened inside the cabinet.

To adjust a magnetic catch, loosen the screws that hold the plate. Shift the position of the plate as desired, then tighten the screws. The magnet on the door should touch the plate when the door is shut.

4

WALLS
Decorating Without Paint

The quickest and easiest way to make a wall interesting and visually exciting is to cover it. Wall coverings are available everywhere in just about every color, texture, and pattern imaginable. Use renewable coverings like wallpaper, or permanent types like wood paneling or tiles. You can choose from dozens of different wall panels, some faced with beautiful, exotic wood veneers and others made of plastic-covered wallboards. All are prefinished; just put them up.

Plastic wall coverings can last indefinitely without losing their color or texture. A wall of plastic bricks can look real enough to fool even an expert.

Every home can use a few extra shelves, whether they are rough-and-ready storage shelves in the basement or decorative, adjustable shelves on a living room wall. Why not put shelves up along an entire wall with spaces for books, records, and a stereo unit?

Create a "fun" wall. Make your own family "rogues' gallery" by covering a hall or den wall with framed or mounted photographs. Fill in large, blank areas with colorful posters. Hang mirrors like a professional. All you need is know-how and a willing assistant.

Try any of these "wall ideas" to renew unexciting walls and to brighten the decor of your home.

Wallpapering

Wallpapers, or more properly, wall coverings, are produced in a variety of materials, textures, and finishes. They are made of paper, often coated with plastic, metallic foils, solid plastics, woven cloths, and grasses and other natural fibers.

Wallpaper may be printed by hand or by machine. Naturally, hand-printed papers are more expensive. Colors used in modern wallpapers are usually waterproof, and most papers are washable. However, don't take anything for granted—ask your dealer. Be sure to use washable paper in areas that will be given heavy use.

Flocked papers, which give a dimensional velvetlike effect, come in both modern and traditional patterns. Some look like old tapestries.

In order to simplify matters, all wall coverings will be referred to as *wallpapers*.

Wallpapers are available in single, double, and triple rolls. A single roll always contains 36 square feet. Double and triple rolls contain two and three times as much. These measurements are standard throughout the wallpaper industry.

Wallpapers are manufactured with a *selvage,* or waste edge, which must be cut away; this is usually done at the factory. If you buy a paper which still has the selvage attached, ask your dealer to trim it for you; he has a special machine for this purpose.

How to Measure a Room for Wallpaper

Measure the length of each wall. Multiply the total wall length by the height of the wall (*all measurements in feet*), and divide by 30; this gives you the number of single rolls required, with an allowance for waste. Or you can arrive at the same figure by consulting the table in Figure 1.

Deduct one single roll for every *two* wall openings such as doors, windows, and fireplaces, and then add one single roll to your total. This gives you the number of single rolls needed to paper a room with a nonmatching wallpaper or one with a repeat pattern no more than 4 inches high. You will need more if you are planning to use a paper with a larger repeat pattern. To be safe, get more paper than you think you will need. Although you can return unused paper if you have a complete unopened roll left over, it is a good idea to save some paper for repairing damaged areas (page 82). And you can always think of decorative ways to use extra paper, so don't worry about its going to waste.

When in doubt, take your measurements to your dealer, who is experienced in calculating the amount of paper needed.

The easiest wallpaper to put up is one that does not require matching of adjoining strips. Grass cloths and cloth-textured papers can be successfully hung by beginners.

If you live in an old house, check each door and window frame and each wall for vertical exactness before you try to hang a paper with a pronounced vertical or horizontal stripe (see page 172). If walls or frames are even slightly slanted, stay away from striped papers.

It is very difficult to hang wallpaper on a ceiling; the weight of the pasted paper makes it tend to pull away from the surface and the angle at which you must work makes it hard to align the strips correctly. If you must paper a ceiling, don't do it alone—get an experienced person to help.

Preparing a Wall for Papering

Wallpaper can be applied over any smooth, dry surface. You can paper over old wallpaper if it is firm, with no loose areas. If there are just a few loose spots, tear the paper away from the wall and "feather" the edges with sandpaper, so that they blend into the wall.

Don't apply wallpaper over vinyl wall coverings, metallic foil papers, flocked papers, or any wall covering that has been waterproofed; these must be removed before new wallpaper is applied.

SIZE OF ROOM IN FEET	HEIGHT OF CEILING						SIZE OF ROOM IN FEET	HEIGHT OF CEILING					
	8'	8½'	9'	10'	11'	12'		8'	8½'	9'	10'	11'	12'
9 x 9	10	11	11	12	14	15	11 x 20	17	18	19	21	23	25
9 x 10	11	11	12	13	14	16	11 x 21	18	19	20	22	24	26
9 x 11	11	12	12	14	15	16	11 x 22	18	19	20	22	25	27
9 x 12	12	12	13	14	16	17	12 x 12	13	14	15	16	18	20
9 x 13	12	13	14	15	17	18	12 x 13	14	15	15	17	19	20
9 x 14	13	14	14	16	17	19	12 x 14	14	15	16	18	20	21
9 x 15	13	14	15	16	18	20	12 x 15	15	16	17	18	20	22
9 x 16	14	15	15	17	19	20	12 x 16	15	16	17	19	21	23
9 x 17	14	15	16	18	20	21	12 x 17	16	17	18	20	22	24
9 x 18	15	16	17	18	20	22	12 x 18	16	17	18	20	22	24
10 x 10	11	12	12	14	15	16	12 x 19	17	18	19	21	23	25
10 x 11	12	12	13	14	16	17	12 x 20	18	19	20	22	24	26
10 x 12	12	13	14	15	17	18	12 x 21	18	19	20	22	25	27
10 x 13	13	14	14	16	17	19	12 x 22	19	20	21	23	25	28
10 x 14	13	14	15	16	18	20	12 x 23	19	20	21	24	26	28
10 x 15	14	15	15	17	19	20	12 x 24	20	21	22	24	27	29
10 x 16	14	15	16	18	20	21	13 x 13	14	15	16	18	20	21
10 x 17	15	16	17	18	20	22	13 x 14	15	16	17	18	20	22
10 x 18	15	16	17	19	21	23	13 x 15	15	16	17	19	21	23
10 x 19	16	17	18	20	22	24	13 x 16	16	17	18	20	22	24
10 x 20	16	17	18	20	22	24	13 x 17	16	17	18	20	22	24
11 x 11	12	13	14	15	17	18	13 x 18	17	18	19	21	23	25
11 x 12	13	14	14	16	17	19	14 x 14	15	16	17	19	21	23
11 x 13	13	14	15	16	18	20	14 x 15	16	17	18	20	22	24
11 x 14	14	15	15	17	19	20	14 x 16	16	17	18	20	22	24
11 x 15	14	15	16	18	20	21	14 x 17	17	18	19	21	23	25
11 x 16	15	16	17	18	20	22	14 x 18	18	19	20	22	24	26
11 x 17	15	16	17	19	21	23	14 x 19	18	19	20	22	25	27
11 x 18	16	17	18	20	22	24	14 x 20	19	20	21	23	25	28
11 x 19	16	17	18	20	22	24	14 x 22	20	21	22	24	27	29

Figure 1. Number of single wallpaper rolls needed for various-sized rooms

Papered wall

Remove old wallpaper by either *soaking* or *steaming*. To soak off wallpaper, prepare a bucket of warm water, get a large brush or sponge and a wide-bladed painter's knife.

Apply the water to the wallpaper until it can absorb no more. At this point it should be easy to strip it off with the painter's knife. Try not to gouge holes in the wall with the knife. Paint stores sell products which can be added to the water, making it easier to remove wallpaper.

Metallic papers, or multiple layers that are stubborn and do not respond to simple soaking, may require the use of a *steamer* (Figure 2),

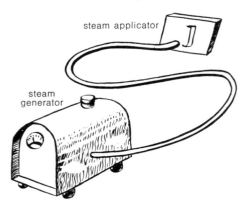

steam applicator

steam generator

Figure 2. Wallpaper steamer

which contains a water tank and some means of heating the water to generate steam. Some steamers use kerosene; others are heated electrically. Steam is applied to the wall, where it saturates the paper and loosens old paste. When the paper is limp, scrape it off with the painter's knife. You can rent a steamer from your wallpaper dealer or a do-it-yourself tool rental firm.

After the paper has been removed, wash the wall with warm water and a sponge to remove any bits of paper which may still be adhering to it.

Painted wall or wall covered with adhesive-backed material

If the wall is painted rather than papered, the glossy surface will have to be dulled. Wash the wall with warm water and ammonia—about 1 cup of ammonia to each quart of water.

Decorative sheet plastics with adhesive backings are often used as wall coverings. If you are lucky, you can simply peel them off. If they are firmly stuck in place, you have a problem; the adhesive backing will have to be softened with lacquer thinner.

Wear plastic or rubber gloves. Test your gloves before you start the job by wetting a small area with lacquer thinner. If the gloves soften up when exposed to the thinner, get another pair that will not.

Cover the floor next to the wall with several thicknesses of newspaper so that thinner can't drip onto the floor.

Start at the top of the wall. Loosen as much of the plastic sheet as you can, using an old brush to soak the back of the plastic and soften the adhesive. After the wall covering has been removed, wash the wall with lacquer thinner applied with a cloth.

Cautions

Close the doors to the room in which you are working. Open all the windows. If possible, set up an electric fan to bring in fresh air and exhaust the fumes given off by the thinner.

Do not smoke. Lacquer thinner is highly flammable.

Keep children and pets out of the room while you are working, and until the smell of the thinner has disappeared.

After the wallpaper has been removed and the wall has been washed, repair any cracks, dents, or other wall blemishes. Unless you do, they will show up after your new wallpaper has dried (see page 141).

Sizing

It's a good idea to *size* all walls that are to be papered. Size is a glue preparation which is usually sold in granular or powdered form. It is mixed according to directions on the container, then sponged or brushed onto the wall. Sizing usually dries in about an hour. It provides a smooth, adhesive surface to which the wallpaper will stick. It also seals porous walls so that they do not absorb water from the wallpaper paste, thus causing it to dry too fast and lose its strength.

Hint

If you are planning to paint the ceiling or woodwork, do so *before* you hang the paper when it doesn't matter if you splatter the walls.

Paperhanging Table

If necessary, you can cut and match wallpaper strips on the floor, but it's almost impossible to apply paste to paper unless you work on some sort of table.

Professional paperhangers use a special table that can be taken apart and folded up for easy transport from job to job. You might consider buying one if you expect to do a great deal of paperhanging.

In a pinch, you can use an ordinary kitchen table as a work surface, but you'll be cramped. A kitchen table isn't long enough to permit you to roll out, cut, and paste wallpaper strips.

You can improvise a paperhanging table that can last indefinitely and will make your work easier. Buy a 4 feet x 8 feet plywood panel, ½ inch thick. Have the lumberyard dealer cut it lengthwise, to give you two pieces, 2 feet x 8 feet.

If you are a homeowner, you can find storage space for them in a basement or attic. If you live in an apartment, have the pieces cut to a length of 7½ feet. This will enable you to store them in the back of a clothing closet.

Make a work surface by simply laying the panels on a table, side by side. Protect the surface of the table by covering it with an old blanket or layers of newspapers. Or lay the two panels across a pair of saw horses.

HOW TO HANG WALLPAPER

You will need:

> Worktable
> Stepladder
> Two 5-gallon pails
> Large sponge
> Paste brush
> Smoothing brush
> Seam roller
> Metal triangle, about 12 inches long
> Single-edged razor blade in holder
> Large scissors
> Steel rule or yardstick
> Wallpaper paste
> Plumb line or thin cord with weight attached
> Colored chalk
> Thumbtack
> Newspapers
> Eggbeater (optional)

Mixing the paste

1. Mix the paste according to directions. Pour the required amount of water into a pail and slowly add the paste, stirring with a stick at the same time. Or you can whip the paste mixture to a smooth, even consistency with an egg beater.

2. Tie a cord across the top of the pail, making a rest for the paste brush (Figure 3).

Figure 3. Paste brush set across top of pail

Cutting the paper

1. Hold the wallpaper roll, pattern-side up, near the right-hand end of the table. Unroll about two feet and pull it firmly over the table edge to remove the curl (Figure 4). This end represents the *top* of the pattern, which will be pasted next to the ceiling.

Figure 4. Unrolling end of wallpaper by pulling paper down over edge of table

2. Measure the height of the wall, from baseboard to ceiling. Unroll the paper and cut off a strip about 8 inches longer than the wall height.

3. Unroll another length of wallpaper, and lay it alongside the strip you have just cut. Match the pattern on the *left* edge of the second strip with the *right* edge of the first strip. Be sure to match the entire length of the strip. Trim the top and bottom of the second strip so that it is the same length as the first one.

4. Place the second strip on top of the first one, pattern-side up. Match and cut succeeding strips in the same way. Place each newly cut strip on top of the preceding one.

5. Cut enough strips to go around the room (excluding doors, windows, and fireplaces). Example: Suppose your wallpaper is 28 inches wide. Measure and count the number of 28-inch widths needed to go around the four walls. Each width represents one wallpaper strip.

6. Turn the pile of matched strips over so that they are face down. You are now ready to apply paste to the strips.

Applying paste

1. Cover the table with several layers of newspaper. Move the pile of wallpaper strips to the edge of the table farthest from you. Remove the top strip (the first one you cut), and align it with its left end and near edge even with the left edge and front edge of the table.

2. Apply paste to the strip, covering the area that rests on the table; this will be about two-thirds of the strip. Use plenty of paste. Do not brush it out, but flow it on evenly without bearing down on the brush.

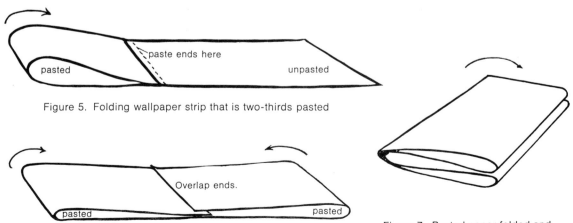

Figure 5. Folding wallpaper strip that is two-thirds pasted

Figure 6. Folding wallpaper strip with only one inch left unpasted

Figure 7. Pasted paper folded and ready for hanging

3. Fold the strip, pasted side to pasted side, bringing the left end to within two inches of where the paste ends (Figure 5). Do not crease the folded end or it will leave a mark on the paper. The edges of the folded part must be exactly even. Align them by placing the palms of your hands on the paper and sliding it. The paper should move easily; if it doesn't, you haven't used enough paste.

4. Shift the wallpaper strip so that the unpasted portion is resting on the table. Apply paste to the rest of the strip, stopping about one inch from the end. Fold this end over to the left so that the unpasted end overlaps the opposite, pasted-down end (Figure 6).

5. Now fold the whole piece in half, as in Figure 7.

6. Paste up enough strips to cover one wall. Fold them as you did the first one, and stack them one on top of another. Then turn the entire pile upside down so that the first one you pasted is on top and the last one is on the bottom. Hang them in that order.

Hanging the paper

1. Start at a corner or at the edge of a door or window frame. Make a pencil mark on the wall to the right of your starting point, one inch less than the width of your paper.

2. Use a thumbtack to attach one end of a plumb line to the wall near the ceiling; the other end should hang near the floor. The line must lie directly over the pencil mark. You can easily improvise a plumb line by using any thin, strong cord and attaching a small weight to the bottom. Almost anything will do—a nut, bolt, spoon, fork, or even a pair of scissors.

3. Coat the plumb line with colored chalk. Hold the bottom of the line so that the string is taut, then pluck it with your fingers; this will snap a vertical chalk line onto the wall. Or, after the plumb line has come to rest, use it as a guide to draw a line on the wall with pencil and yardstick.

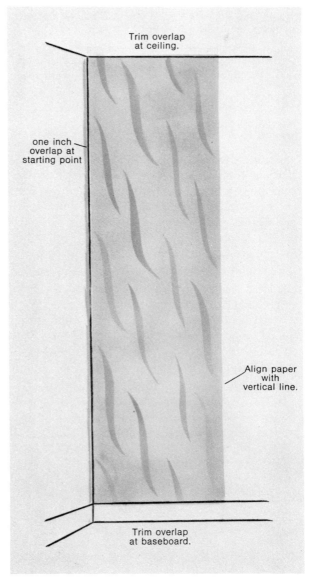

Figure 8. Hanging first wallpaper strip

4. Set the ladder near the wall so that you will be able to reach the ceiling. Place the smoothing brush on top of the ladder. A *smoothing brush* is a wide brush with stiff bristles used to sweep pasted paper against the wall. Hang the first wallpaper strip by unfolding the top of the strip and handling it by the top (the unpasted end). Allow the bottom of the strip to remain folded.

5. Place the paper against the wall; it should overlap the ceiling by about three inches. The right-hand edge of the paper should be perfectly aligned with the vertical line on the wall; the left edge should overlap the starting point (door, window, or corner) by one inch. Slide the paper into exact position with the palms of your hands.

6. Unfold the bottom portion of the paper and align the right edge with the vertical chalk line (Figure 8). Sweep the paper with the broad smoothing brush. Make a long stroke down the center, then work out to each side. Using the end of the bristles, tap the paper firmly into each corner.

7. Press the edge of the metal triangle into the corner between the wall and the ceiling. Using at as a guide, trim the paper with a single-edged razor blade at the exact spot where it meets the ceiling (Figure 9). Next trim the paper at the baseboard. (Use this method to hang any strip of wallpaper: overlap at top and bottom, then trim off excess.)

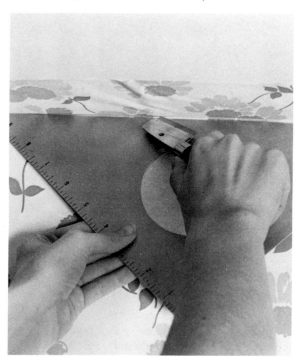

Figure 9. Trimming paper with razor blade

8. In the same way, trim away the paper that overlaps your starting point. If the starting point is a door or window frame, trim the overlap about ¼ inch. Use a sharp single-edged razor blade and cut freehand.

9. You can also use a pair of scissors to trim wallpaper. First use the smoothing brush to tap the paper into the corner. Then, with the point of the scissors, score a line where the paper is to be trimmed. Peel the paper partly away from the wall; the scored line will be visible and can easily be cut with the scissors. Sweep the paper back into place with the smoothing brush.

10. Keep clean water in your second pail. Use it to sponge off the excess paste from each strip of paper that has been hung. Be sure to wash paste from ceiling and woodwork as well.

11. Paste the second strip to the wall, butting its *left* edge against the *right* edge of the first strip. Match the pattern by sliding the paper as previously described. Sweep the paper firmly against the wall with the smoothing brush, then trim the ends at the ceiling and baseboard.

12. After about fifteen minutes, when the paste has partially dried, run over each wallpaper seam with the seam roller. Wash off any paste that may be squeezed out in the process.

Most walls are not vertical and the corners are therefore imperfect. If you try to paper around such a corner, the paper would buckle. To avoid this, *split* the paper.

To make a split

1. Cut the wallpaper strip vertically so that it is just wide enough to overlap the corner by one inch (Figure 10). Match and paste the strip to the wall; smooth and pat it into place with the smoothing brush. One inch now extends around the corner, onto the adjoining wall.

2. Measure the width of the balance of the split paper strip. Mark the same distance from

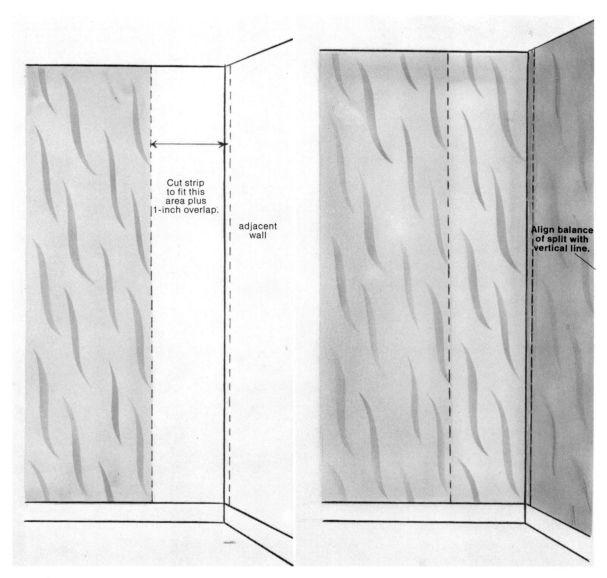

Cut strip
to fit this
area plus
1-inch overlap.

adjacent
wall

**Align balance
of split with
vertical line.**

Figure 10. Making a split

Figure 11. Fitting balance of split into corner

the corner and strike a vertical line on the wall with your plumb line. Hang the paper with its right edge aligned with the vertical line. The left edge should fit snugly into the corner of the wall, overlapping the paper which was pasted around the corner (Figure 11). If necessary, use scissors to score and trim the paper so that it fits the corner perfectly, *but*

on no account change the position of the right edge; this must be vertical.

3. Split the paper whenever you come to a door or window frame. Cut it one inch wider than the distance between the last pasted-up strip and the door or window frame. Hang the split. Snip the paper at the top of the frame so that it can lie flat on the wall.

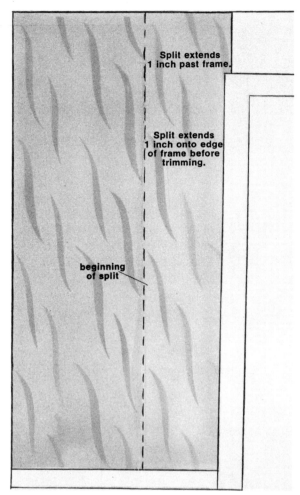

Split extends
1 inch past frame.

Split extends
1 inch onto edge
of frame before
trimming.

beginning
of split

Figure 12. Bringing split up to a door frame

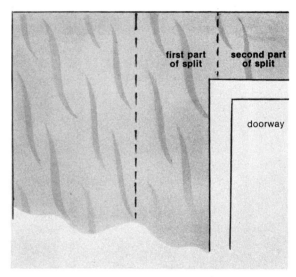

first part
of split

second part
of split

doorway

Figure 13. Matching paper over doorway

Figure 14. Cutting paper away from wall outlet

One inch of the split will extend onto the side of the door or window frame. Tap it firmly into place, then trim it (Figure 12).

4. Cut a matching piece from a wallpaper strip to fit across the top of a door or the top and bottom of a window frame (Figure 13). The remainder of the strip can be used to match other small areas.

To paper around electrical outlets and switches

First, turn off the current (see page 5), then remove the wall plate (see page 9). Paper over the outlet, then use scissors or a razor blade to cut away the paper, exposing the electrical box and its contents (Figure 14).

Use the smoothing brush to sweep the paper back against the wall around the outlet, then replace the cover plate and turn on the current.

Hints

If you have no wallpapering tools, you can buy a kit which contains everything you will need.

Be sure you get the proper adhesives for the paper you are hanging. Wallpaper adhesives are highly specialized, formulated especially for different types of coverings.

Mix wallpaper paste with warm water, but allow the paste to cool before you use it. Ready-to-use paste should have the consistency of creamed soup.

Any paint brush at least 3 inches wide makes a satisfactory paste brush.

Allow paste to soak into the strips for at least fifteen minutes before you hang them. This softens the fibers of the strips, so they will make strong contact with the wall.

Check the edges of the pasted, folded wallpaper strips before you start to hang them. If they have dried out, repaste them.

Check with your dealer to determine whether your paper is colorfast. If it is, you can use water liberally to sponge off excess paste. If not, wipe it off with a dry, or slightly damp, sponge or cloth.

Use clean water for sponging wallpaper; change the water frequently. Both the sponge and the water in your pail become contaminated with paste, so if you are not careful, you may be sponging on a layer of diluted paste instead of cleaning the wallpaper.

You may occasionally find air bubbles under the wall covering as you are hanging it. These show up as soft, bumpy areas. Brush them away to one side of the paper with the smoothing brush. If you can't eliminate them by brushing, perforate them with a pin or razor blade, then tap them smooth with the brush.

For trimming, use a single-edged razor blade in a holder. It is not only safer, but makes it easier to reach into corners.

Razor blades dull quickly when used for trimming wallpaper. Keep at least a half dozen on hand, and switch to a new one whenever the one you are using shows signs of dragging.

If you are hanging a large-patterned paper over a fireplace, first center a strip directly over the fireplace, aligning one edge with a plumb line. Then hang paper in both directions from each side of the central strip.

HANGING PREPASTED PAPERS

Some wall papers are *prepasted*; their backs have already been coated with adhesive. They are hung and trimmed on the wall exactly like other wall coverings. However, instead of brushing paste on the back of the paper, you wet the adhesive that is already there by immersing each strip of paper in a container of water.

Prepasted papers are not available in as great a variety of patterns and materials as regular wallpapers. Consequently, they are not as widely used. They are very handy, however, for someone who wants to do only one wall or for someone who is not prepared to cope with all the tools and preparations needed to do regular wallpapering.

What to do:

1. Unroll and cut the paper into matching strips (page 75). Strike a plumb line on the wall as a guide for hanging the first strip (page 77).

2. You will need a pasteboard container or water tank, which you can obtain from your wallpaper dealer. Place it on the floor directly under the area to be covered with the first wallpaper strip. Pour in water until it is about three-quarters full.

3. Roll up the strip of wallpaper you are going to hang first. Immerse it in the water. Take hold of the top edge of the wet paper and unroll it from the container. Reach up to the ceiling, align the paper's edge with the vertical plumb line, and sweep the paper against the wall with your smoothing brush. Trim with a razor blade.

4. Slide the container along the floor, moving it into position for hanging the next strip; continue in this way around the room until the job is done.

Hints

Don't soak all the strips at once; doing so may remove all the adhesive, and as a consequence, they won't stick to the wall.

It's not a good idea to soak wallpaper strips in the bathtub—unless you are papering the bathroom. A water tank is inexpensive and you can have it where you need it. By dashing from room to room carrying wet paper, you run the risk of dripping a glue mixture all over your floors.

Cleaning wallpaper

Small marks on wallpaper can often be removed with a gum eraser. Don't rub too hard or you will leave a light spot that won't match the rest of the paper.

You can clean washable paper with mild soap and water or mild detergent solution applied with a soft sponge. Don't confuse the word "washable" with "scrubbable." If you scrub wallpaper, or use a strong household detergent, you are likely to remove both the color and the finish.

Repairing damaged spots

If for any reason you must replace paper over a small area, tear (don't cut) a piece large enough to cover the damaged spot. The trick here is to end up with a piece of paper that matches the pattern on the wall. While cut edges of paper would show up readily, torn paper is practically invisible when it is pasted down. Use wallpaper paste.

Repasting the edges

Wallpaper edges that have lifted away from a wall can easily be repasted. Best for this purpose is wallpaper paste. If you have none, mix a little flour with *hot* water. Mix it well so that there are no lumps and allow it to cool before using. Sponge the edge with clean water after pasting it.

Don't use white glue, library paste, or any kind of cement.

Other Wall Coverings

Resilient Floor Tiles

All types of resilient floor tiles can be used as wall coverings—you can use asphalt, vinyl-asbestos, or vinyl tiles. The installation procedure is the same as that used for laying tiles on a floor (see page 131).

Important: Be sure to buy the proper adhesive for the tile you are using. Read directions and follow them carefully. With some adhesives *you must wait* before setting tiles into place. If you don't, they may sag out of position.

Apply tiles only to an uncovered wall. Do not tile over wallpaper, no matter how sound it may seem to be.

Plastic Wall Tiles

Plastic tiles are available for installation on walls. Some have self-adhesive backs. Others must be cemented in place, in the same way as ceramic tile (see page 133).

Ceramic Tiles

You can use these to cover a whole wall or a small area, such as a sink splashback. They come in a beautiful array of colors and designs and are as practical as they are attractive. (See page 133 for directions on installing ceramic tiles.)

Cork Squares

Some cork squares have self-adhesive backs and are simply pressed into place. Others, less expensive, can be cemented to a wall, using floor-tile adhesive. Cork is not only decorative, but also provides good insulation.

Synthetic Brick

Some synthetic bricks are made of plastic about ¼ inch thick, cleverly fabricated to look like used bricks. They can be applied over any clean, dry surface—but *not* over wallpaper.

APPLYING SYNTHETIC BRICKS

You will need:

> Synthetic plastic bricks
> Special adhesive cement
> Painting knife or trowel

What to do:

1. Use the painting knife or trowel to apply a layer of adhesive about ¼ inch thick to the wall area to be covered.

2. Butter the back of each brick with a dab of adhesive in three places, as in Figure 15.

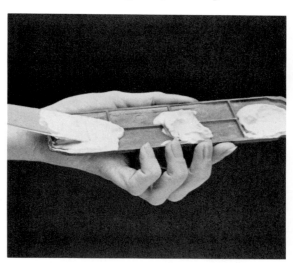

Figure 15. Buttering plastic brick with adhesive

3. Set each brick into the adhesive with firm pressure, twisting it slightly as you press it into place. Leave spaces of ¼ inch to ½ inch between bricks to simulate mortar joints.

4. Some adhesive will be squeezed up between the bricks. Don't disturb it, as this helps create the illusion of real brick.

5. Begin at either the top or the bottom of the area you wish to cover. Be sure to line up the bricks in even rows, with equal spaces between them. It's not necessary to measure the spaces exactly; minor variations aren't important. However, rows should be horizontal; check their alignment with a level, as in Figure 16.

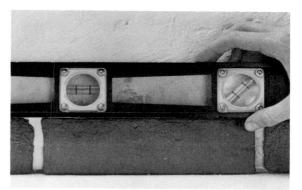

Figure 16. Checking alignment of plastic bricks with a level

Figure 17 shows a plastic-brick installation on a small kitchen wall under a cabinet.

Figure 17. Plastic bricks on kitchen wall under cabinet

Hints

Check the adhesive you are using. Some are slow-drying types, which enable you to cover a large area before applying the bricks. Others dry rapidly and can only be applied to one small area at a time. Some synthetic wall materials are available with self-adhesive backing.

One type of synthetic brick or stone is made in thin, hollow plastic sheets, each of which is

Figure 18. Sheet-plastic stones

several square feet in size (Figure 18). Installation is simple and rapid. Depending on the particular type, apply adhesive either to the wall, the back of the sheet, or both, then press the sheet against the wall.

Although they are decorative, hollow sheets are structurally weak and therefore not as desirable as separate plastic bricks. Separate bricks, cemented to a wall, will actually strengthen it. Plastic bricks should be applied with the adhesives recommended by the manufacturer.

Metallic Wall Tiles

These are thin, metal tiles, 4½ inches square. Most have self-adhesive backs. Grouting is not necessary as there are no spaces between the tiles.

INSTALLING METALLIC TILES ON A SINK SPLASHBACK

You will need:

> Metallic wall tiles, self-adhesive type
> Ruler
> Pencil
> Scissors or tin snips

What to do:

1. If tiles are to be laid under a window, make a pencil mark in the center of the windowsill to use as a guide.

2. Peel the protective paper from the adhesive tabs on the back of a tile. Press the tile against the splashback with its bottom edge pressed against the sink counter and one side lined up with the center mark on the windowsill. Press tiles into place to complete the bottom row of the splashback. There should be no spaces between tiles.

3. Install the second row of tiles. Each tile must fit exactly over one in the bottom row. If necessary, use scissors or tin snips to cut tiles to fit as was done in the completed splashback in Figure 19.

Figure 19. Completed splashback with tiles cut to fit

WOOD PANELING

Wood panels make very attractive indoor wall coverings. They can be applied over any smooth, dry surface, including painted or unpainted walls and firm wallpaper.

Panels are usually 4 x 8 feet and ⅛-, ³⁄₁₆-, or ¼-inch thick. Most are made of plywood, which is composed of thin sheets of wood glued together with their grains running at different angles. You can also find panels made of lumber-cored veneers; in these a thin sheet of good wood is glued over a core of common wood.

Almost every kind of wood can be obtained as a wall panel. There are softwoods, hardwoods, domestic woods, and exotic imported woods. They are usually prefinished—either stained or antiqued, then treated with a protective sealer, lacquer, plastic, or polyurethane finish. All you have to do is attach them to the wall.

Other panels are made of compressed, ¼-inch thick sheets of wood fiber covered with vinyl that has been imprinted to look like wood. Some are realistic enough to fool an expert even at close range.

Or you can use inexpensive, vinyl-covered gypsum board panels, which also look very much like wood.

You will need:

> **Wall panels**
> **Matching nails**
> **Pry bar**
> **Wood blocks**
> **Hammer**
> **Panel adhesive**
> **Caulking gun**
> **Screwdriver**
> **Stepladder**
> **Steel tape or yardstick**
> **Level**
> **Plane**
> **Plastic corner moldings, inside and**
>   **outside, to match panels**
> **Plastic edge molding (optional)**
> **Electric saber saw**

If you do not have an electric saber saw, you will need the following:

> **Hand or electric drill**
> **½-inch drill bit, with shank turned down**
>   **to fit your drill**
> **Keyhole saw**
> **Crosscut saw**

What to do:

1. Measure the width of the walls in feet, all around the room; include doors and windows.

Divide this figure by 4 in order to obtain the number of panels needed to go around the room. Subtract one panel for each door and a half panel for each window. If your total is a fraction, buy the next larger number of panels. For example, you may have three windows in your room and need a total of twelve and a half panels; buy thirteen panels.

2. Use the pry bar to remove the ceiling molding by inserting it carefully between the molding and the wall. Place a small wood block between the bar and the wall to give you leverage, and exert pressure on the pry bar (Figure 20). Don't try to remove the molding all at once. Instead, work it loose gently, prying all along its length at intervals of about two feet. Be careful not to break the molding, as it will have to be nailed back into place later.

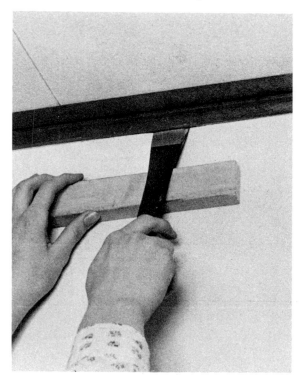

Figure 20. Use pry bar to remove ceiling molding.

3. Using the same procedure, remove the baseboard cap molding. In some homes you can't do this, for there is no separate cap molding; the baseboard and cap are milled in

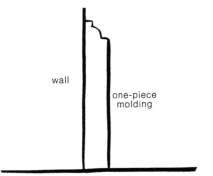

Figure 21. One-piece baseboard and cap molding

one piece (Figure 21), so don't try to remove it.

4. Use a screwdriver to remove wall plates from switches and outlets.

5. Measure the distance between the ceiling and the top of the baseboard. Use your crosscut or saber saw to trim all panels to this height, minus ¼ inch.

6. Work from left to right, using a corner of the room as a starting point. Slip a piece of inside corner molding over the left edge of a panel (Figure 22). Check to see how the panel fits by pressing it into the corner of the wall and resting its lower edge on the baseboard. Hold a level up against the right-hand edge of the panel to see whether it is perfectly vertical, or plumb. If it isn't, move the panel to make it plumb. You should be able to do this without disengaging the panel from the corner molding; the panel can be moved inside the molding if adjustment is needed.

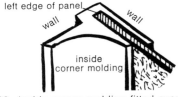

Figure 22. Inside corner molding fitted over left edge of panel

7. When you have adjusted the panel, set it aside, and install a cartridge of wall-panel adhesive into your caulking gun (see page 150), after having snipped off the end of the tube and pierced the inner seal according to directions on the label.

8. Apply adhesive to the back of the panel by squeezing it out in long strips all around the panel, about 2 or 3 inches from each edge. Then make a large X with the adhesive to cover the entire back of the panel.

9. Press the panel against the wall, exactly where it is to be installed. Then pull it away and stand it somewhere until the adhesive is partially dry; this will take about ten minutes. Now press the panel back against the wall in the same place as before. The partially dry adhesive will "grab" the panel and hold it in place.

10. Use the level again to check the vertical line of the right side of the panel. Since the adhesive is not yet hard, you can adjust the position of the panel, if necessary, by pressing your palms against it and pushing it into its proper place.

11. Fasten the panel at the top and bottom with two or three nails. Use nails that match the color of the panel (these may be obtained from dealers who sell paneling). Or use ordinary finishing nails and set them slightly below the surface of the wood with a nail set. You can then hide the nail heads with matching color sticks (see page 60).

12. Using a hammer, tap a piece of scrap wood firmly against the panel (Figure 23); go along its entire surface. This will spread the adhesive and bond the panel to the wall.

Figure 23. Tapping panel with hammer to secure it

13. Cement—that is, attach with the adhesive —the next panel to the wall with its left edge pressed up against the right edge of the previously installed panel. Continue in this way, working from left to right, all around the room.

14. When you come to an inside corner, trim the right-hand edge of the panel so that it fits into the corner molding. Do this before you apply panel adhesive (Figure 24).

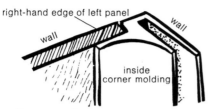

Figure 24. Right-hand edge of left panel fitted into inside corner molding

15. Continue onto the adjacent right-hand wall; the left-hand edge of the next panel will fit into the corner molding. Check it with a plumb line to see that it is perfectly vertical before you cement it in place, just as you did when you installed the first panel.

To make cutouts for wall outlets or switches

Wherever panels cover wall outlets or switches, they must be cut out to expose the metal wall box. This must be done before the panel is cemented to the wall.

1. Put the *uncemented* panel in place against the wall. Measure off the exact position of the wall box (including its flanges and a small fraction of an inch for play). Mark this rectangle on the back of the panel with a pencil—it must be large enough to insert the switch, but small enough to be covered by the wall plate.

2. If you have a saber saw, cut out the rectangle you have marked (see page 185). If not, drill ½-inch holes in each corner of the rectangle, being careful not to drill outside the rectangle. Insert a keyhole saw and connect the four holes by sawing along the lines which form the rectangle (Figure 25). Then use the saw to square up the corners where the holes have been drilled.

3. Place the panel back against the wall; the opening should coincide perfectly with the switch-box opening. If not, make it fit by using a coarse file or wood rasp.

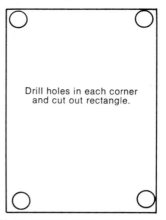

Drill holes in each corner and cut out rectangle.

Figure 25. Holes provide places to insert keyhole saw.

Splits for doors or windows

When you reach a door or window, unless the panel fits exactly against the edge of the frame, you will have to make a "split."

1. Suppose that the last panel you installed is 12 inches from a window frame. Cut a strip 12⅛ inches wide from another panel.

2. Plane down the edge to remove all saw marks and fit the piece perfectly against the window frame. Cement and nail it in place (Figure 26).

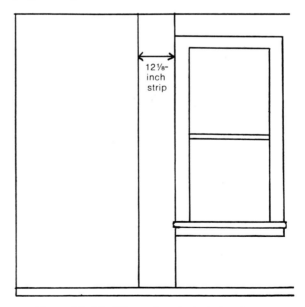

12⅛-inch strip

Figure 26. "Split" panel against window frame

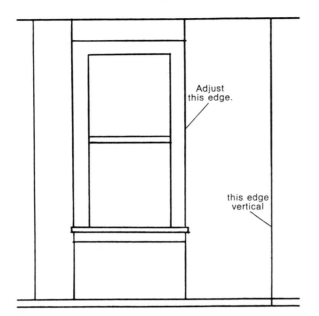

Figure 27. Remainder of "split" panel against right edge of window frame

3. Now take the panel from which you cut the 12⅛-inch piece, and smooth its edge with the plane.

4. Install this at the right-hand edge of the window frame; cement and nail it in place after you check the plumb of its right edge. If it isn't plumb, adjust it by planing the *left* edge which rests against the frame (Figure 27).

Install all the full-length panels, then use leftover pieces to fill spaces over doors, and under and over windows.

Outside corners

If necessary, add outside corner molding.

1. Be sure to cut your panels so that they are flush with the outside corner.

2. Press a length of outside molding against the corner; the left side of the molding will cover the edge of the panel you have just installed, while the other, wider side extends around the corner (Figure 28).

3. Secure the molding by driving nails through the wide side into the wall from top to bottom at intervals of about one foot. Any

common (flat-headed) nail about 1½ inches long will do.

4. Move around to the right side of the corner and press a panel against the wall, sliding it into the molding as in Figure 28. Check the right edge of the panel for verticality, then cement and nail it into place. The corner is now finished.

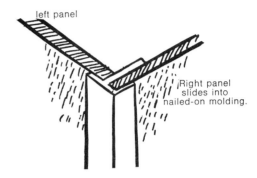

Figure 28. Outside corner molding

Finishing touches

1. Replace ceiling and baseboard moldings by simply nailing them back into place, using the nails which originally held the molding.

2. Before you replace switch and outlet wall plates, loosen the two screws which hold each switch or outlet to the wall box by giving each screw three turns to the left (Figure 29). When

Figure 29. Loosening screws in switch

you put on the wall plate, the short wall-plate screws will now be able to reach the loosened switch or outlet. When the wall plate screws are tightened, they draw the switch (or outlet) and the wall plate tightly together.

Hints

If you simply replace ceiling and baseboard cap moldings without treating them in any way, they are bound to look somewhat battered after having been pried loose and then rehammered. Repaint or stain them before you nail them back.

If you can remove both ceiling and baseboard cap moldings, it makes no difference whether the cut end of the panel is at the top or at the bottom. However, if your baseboard and cap molding are in one piece, install all panels with their cut ends at the top, next to the ceiling. Any imperfections will then be covered by the ceiling molding; the bottom, uncut ends will fit snugly against the baseboard.

If the ceiling molding is too battered to reuse, cover the top, cut ends of the panels with plastic edge molding instead. Press the molding against the ceiling *before* you install any panels, and nail it to the wall. Then slide each panel under the overlapping lip of the molding as in Figure 30.

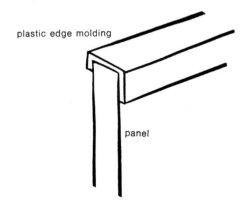

plastic edge molding

panel

Figure 30. Plastic edge molding with panel slid under lip

Get someone to help you handle the panels. Even though thin panels don't weigh much, they are awkward to handle.

To Fasten Things to Walls

Exterior Walls

To fasten screws to solid brick, concrete, and cinder-block walls, you must first drill a hole with a masonry drill (see page 169). Make the hole just large enough to accommodate a plastic, lead, or fiber plug. You can improvise a plug by filling the hole with thin pieces of soft scrap wood driven into place.

Tap the plug into the wall; it should fit snugly. Screws driven into the plugs will hold; as the screw is turned, it forces the plug walls apart, anchoring it in the hole (Figure 31).

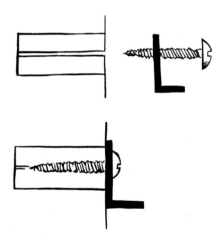

Figure 31. Installing screws in plugs

Interior Walls

Interior walls are hollow. Lightweight objects can be held by drilling a pilot hole (see page 201), then driving in a *sheet-metal screw*. The screw's wide threads hold very well in plaster or wallboard.

If you can locate a stud (see page 92), drill a pilot hole, lubricate screws with soap, then drive them through the wall into the stud.

If you must support a heavy weight and cannot reach a stud, use either a *toggle bolt*, or an *expansion fastener*.

Toggle bolt

Drill a hole large enough to admit a toggle bolt with its wings folded, and detach the screw from the wing portion. Pass the screw through the object to be hung, then rethread it into the wings. Insert the folded wings through the hole in the wall where they will spring open. Then turn the screw clockwise; this will simultaneously draw up the wings so that they are pressed firmly against the back of the wall and secure the object you are hanging to the front of the wall (Figure 32).

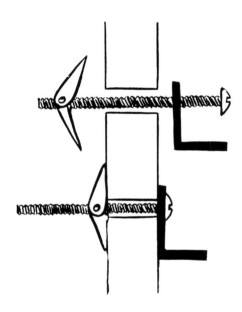

Figure 32. Toggle bolt

Expansion fastener

Drill a hole just large enough to admit the body of the fastener. Tap it into the hole with a hammer; the expanding portion of the unit is now behind the wall. Turn the screw clockwise; as shown in Figure 33, this draws the expanding part up against the back of the wall. Withdraw the screw, pass it through the object to be hung, then screw it back into the fitting.

Another type of expanding fastener has a sharp point that makes its own hole. Instead of drilling a hole through which to pass it, hammer it into the wall.

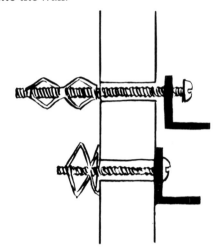

Figure 33. Expansion fastener

HANGING PERFORATED HARDBOARD

Perforated hardboard, or pegboard, makes excellent racks for tools, kitchen utensils, or almost anything else you might want to hang on a wall. Lumberyards and hardware stores usually carry it in a variety of sizes. If you can't buy the exact size you need, get the next larger size and trim it with a crosscut saw (see page 182).

A perforated hardboard panel that is to be used as a rack must be installed with a space between the panel and the wall to allow hanger fittings, or hooks, to be pushed through from the front. The simplest way to do this is to fasten furring strips (wood strips) to the edges of the back of the panel. This not only provides space for the pegboard hooks, but also prevents warping.

If you don't want the hooks on which the board is hung to show, prepare furring strips and hang the board by one of the methods described on pages 91–92.

MAKING A TOOL RACK

You will need:

> Perforated hardboard (pegboard) panel,
>   cut to size
> White glue
> 1 x 2 inch wood strips (furring strips)
>   to fit around the edges of the panel
> Hammer
> Crosscut saw
> ¾-inch wire nails
> Stud finder
> 2 C-clamps or 6 spring-type clothespins
> 2 screw hooks
> 2 screw eyes
> Tool hangers

What to do:

1. If necessary, cut the panel to the size needed.

2. Cut furring strips to fit around the edges of the panel as in Figure 34.

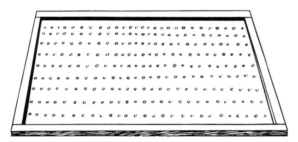

Figure 34. Perforated hardboard with furring strips attached to back edges

3. Apply glue to the 2-inch face of a wood strip. Line it up with the back edge of the panel, and clamp both together. Use two C-clamps or a row of spring clothespins (Figure 35).

4. Nail the pegboard panel to the wood strip by driving the nails through the hardboard into the wood. Remove the clamps. Glue and nail the three other strips of wood to the back edges of the panel, and the rack is finished. Hang it on a wall or on the inside of a closet door. Do this in one of several ways, depending on where it is to be hung.

Figure 35. Clothespin clamps

Hanging it on a solid wood door or wall

Drive two screw eyes into the wood strip at the top edge of the rack (see page 203). Then drive two screw hooks into the wall or door, matching the positions of the two screw eyes. Hang the rack by slipping the screw eyes over the screw hooks (Figure 36).

Figure 36. Hanging a pegboard rack with screw eyes and screw hooks

Hanging it on a hollow door

Fasten a strip of wood across the door, securing it with nails or screws at both ends. At these points you will be going directly into the structural frame of the door, which is solid. Check the strip before you fasten it in place; it should be as wide as possible, yet should not interfere with the closing of the door.

Hang the rack from screw hooks driven into the wood strip (Figure 37). Use the same procedure when hanging a tool rack on a paneled door.

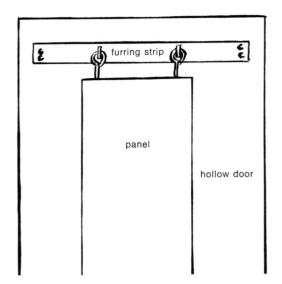

Figure 37. Panel hanging on wood strip screwed to door

Hanging it on a hollow wall

Suspend the rack from screw hooks which have been driven into wall *studs*. Studs are vertical lengths of 2 x 4 inch lumber which form the core of every house wall. They are usually spaced with their centers 16 inches apart, though in many old houses, studs may be 24 inches apart or even set at random.

How to locate wall studs:

By tapping the wall: Use a hammer to tap horizontally across a section of a wall. When you tap over a hollow portion of the wall, you will hear a low-pitched thud. Over a stud, the sound will change, becoming higher in pitch with less of an echo. Mark the position of the stud with a pencil. You can usually expect to find another stud 16 inches from that spot.

Using a stud finder: A stud finder is a device which uses a freely rotating magnet to locate nails. Since baseboards are nailed to studs, you can find a stud by locating a nail in the baseboard.

Hold the stud finder horizontally and pass it slowly along the baseboard. Where there is nothing to attract the magnet, it will lie to one side as in Figure 38. When the finder passes over a nail, the magnet points directly at the nail (Figure 39).

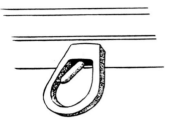

Figure 38. Stud finder with magnet on one side

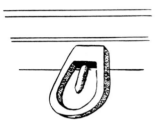

Figure 39. Stud finder with magnet pointing to nail

If your tool rack is wider than the space between two studs, hang it from screw hooks which have been driven into the studs (Figure 40).

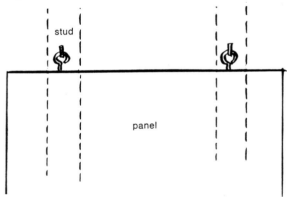

Figure 40. Screw hooks driven into studs

If the rack is narrower than the distance between two studs, hang it from a strip of wood which has been nailed across two studs as in Figure 41.

Hints

You can also hang a rack by first drilling holes through the perforated hardboard and wood strip frame, then securing it to the wall with 2-to 2½-inch screws driven into studs.

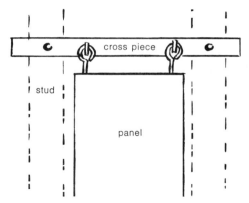

Figure 41. Panel hanging from crosspiece driven into studs

Paint the tool rack. When the paint has dried, outline each tool as it hangs in place. Fill in the outlines of the various tools with different color paints. This will enable you to locate instantly the places to which tools should be returned after use (Figure 42).

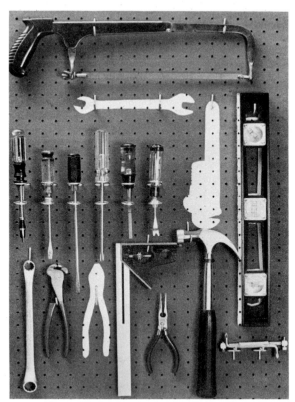

Figure 42. Tool rack, showing tool outlines

Specially shaped fittings of heavy steel wire are made for perforated hardboard racks, thus making it possible for you to hang articles of various shapes and sizes (see Figure 42).

HANGING MIRRORS

Some mirrors are sold in 12-inch squares. They have self-adhesive backs and can be installed on any smooth wall by simply pressing them into place. Others must be cemented into place. Your dealer can recommend the proper type of cement and tell you how to apply it.

You can form a large mirror by butting these mirror squares together. Make up a mirror that is bright and modern, tinted, or antiqued. If the wall is not absolutely flat, put up a ¼- or ⅜-inch plywood backing, using one of the methods described on pages 91–92. Be sure the backing measures exactly the same size as the combined mirrors. Make certain, too, that no nail or screw head protrudes above the surface of the wood. Then apply the mirror squares to the backing.

Hanging a Mirror on a Door

Door mirrors are long and narrow—some are framed, but most are sold unframed.

You will need:

> **4 or 6 mirror clips**
> **Screwdriver**
> **Push drill**

What to do:

1. Decide where the bottom of the mirror is to go and draw a line on the door at that level, making it the same width as the mirror. About two inches in from each end of the line, make pilot holes with the push drill for two mirror clips. Fasten a clip at each pilot hole, using the screws that are supplied with the clips (Figure 43).

When installing the two bottom mirror clips, leave them slightly loose.

2. Place the mirror against the door with its bottom edge resting on the two clips. Have

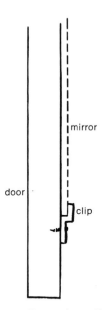

Figure 43. Door-mirror clip

someone hold the mirror in place while you install two clips at the top edge. To make certain the mirror won't move in any direction, you can, if you like, also install two extra clips along each side.

3. After the mirror has been placed against the door, tighten the clips by turning the screws a few times. Don't apply so much pressure that you crack the glass; just allow the clips to make contact with the mirror. Do the same with the two top clips.

Use sheet-metal screws when installing clips on a hollow door; they'll hold better than ordinary wood screws.

Hanging a Large, Unframed Mirror

A large mirror can be very heavy, so don't try to handle it by yourself; it's a job for two people.

You will need:

>**Chrome shoe, the same length as the width of your mirror**
>**Common nails, 1½ inches long**
>**Hammer**
>**Steel rule**
>**2 or 4 mirror clips with screws supplied**

Push drill
Hand or electric drill
Center punch
Level

A *chrome shoe* is a chrome-plated, U-shaped metal channel used by professional glass craftsmen to hang large mirrors (Figure 44). Your local glass and mirror shop can sell you a piece *exactly* as long as the width of your mirror.

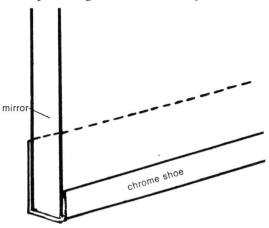

Figure 44. Chrome shoe

What to do:

1. Measure the mirror you are going to hang, then decide where it is to go on the wall. Use a pencil to mark the distance from the floor and the width of the mirror on the wall. Locate a stud (see page 92) and mark its location with a small, lightly penciled X.

2. Place the chrome shoe against the wall *exactly* where it is to be fastened. Level it (see page 172). Make a pencil mark under the shoe so that you can later replace it in exactly the same place.

3. Mark the back of the shoe to show the stud position. If the shoe is long enough, it may cover more than one stud. Since studs are usually 16 inches apart, mark off 16 inches to each side of your first stud marker.

4. Use a center punch to make a dent at each mark; then drill a ⅛-inch hole at each spot (see page 168).

5. Place the chrome shoe on the wall, lining it up with the pencil line you made. Drive a nail through each hole in the back of the shoe to fasten it securely to the wall. The shoe should be nailed to at least one stud.

6. With the help of your assistant (or assistants, if the mirror is too heavy for two people to handle), pick up the mirror, place it against the wall, and lower it into the chrome shoe.

7. While someone holds the mirror against the wall, position a clip against one of the side edges, near the top. Use the push drill and go through the hole in the clip, making a *thin* pilot hole in the wall (see page 167). This will probably dull the drill, but it's worth it. Drive a screw through the clip to hold the mirror. Fasten another clip to the opposite edge.

8. If you like, you can also install a clip on each side of the mirror near the bottom edge. They aren't needed to hold the mirror, but they make the installation symmetrical.

HANGING PICTURES

Any room can be enhanced by hanging framed paintings, prints, or photographs on the walls. Before hanging your pictures, work out an interesting grouping that will complement the area around it and show the artwork to best advantage. Be sure that pictures are hung at a comfortable viewing level; no one should have to crane his neck or stoop in order to see them.

Hanging a Small Framed Picture

You will need:

> Picture hanger
> Push drill
> Picture wire
> Pliers
> Screw eyes
> Cutting pliers
> Steel tape
> 1-inch wire brads
> Level
> Hammer

What to do:

1. Place the face of the framed picture on a flat surface, top edge up. Drill a pilot hole in each side of the frame, about two inches above the center. Install a screw eye in each hole. Thread the end of a length of picture wire through one of the screw eyes. Bend it back over the screw eye and twist it around the wire five or six times to keep it from slipping loose. Pass the other end of the wire through the opposite screw eye. Pull the wire through, leaving it slack between the screw eyes.

2. Draw the center of the wire up toward the top of the frame; stop when it is about two inches from the top (Figure 45). Cut the wire. Still maintaining the slack in the wire, bend the end back and twist it behind the screw eye as before.

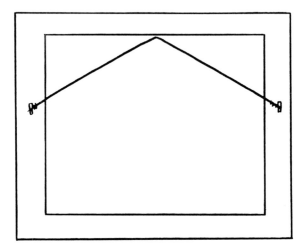

Figure 45. Center of picture wire drawn up toward top of frame

3. Now hook your finger under the center of the wire, and with the picture facing outward, place it against the wall at the proper height. Your finger indicates where the picture hanger is to go. Mark this spot with a pencil. Cover it with a 1- to 2-inch piece of cellophane tape, which will keep any cracked plaster from falling out when the nail that holds the hanger is hammered into the wall.

Hangers are made in several sizes to accommodate pictures of different weights, so use the one most suitable for the picture you are going to hang. You will note, too, the hangers are so constructed that the nail holding each one is driven into the wall at an angle (Figure 46); this ensures that the weight of the picture, when it is hung, will not pull the nail out.

Figure 46. Picture hanger; note the angle at which the nail is inserted.

4. Hold the picture hanger flat against the wall over the tape, hammer the nail in, and hang the picture. Place a level on top of the frame and adjust it so that it is perfectly horizontal. Then drive a brad into the wall at each side of the bottom of the frame. This will prevent the picture from shifting out of position.

Hanging a Large Framed Picture

1. Install screw eyes and picture wire just as though you were hanging a smaller picture. However, allow for more slack in the wire between the screw eyes so that you can draw it toward the top with two fingers to look like Figure 47 and still have about two inches between the wire and the top of the frame.

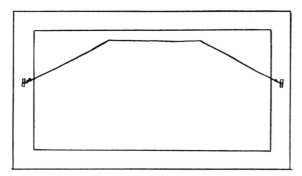

Figure 47. Push picture wire toward top of frame.

2. Your fingers indicate the positions of *two* hangers, each about one-third of the way in from the side edges of the frame. Measure the distance between these two points and divide the figure in half (measurement A).

3. Hold the picture up against the wall at the proper height and make a tiny pencil dot on the wall above the center of the top frame edge. Put the picture aside. Below the dot on the wall, mark off 2 inches. Then to each side of this second dot, mark off measurement A. The final two dots drawn indicate where the hangers are to be nailed. Cover each spot with cellophane tape to prevent any cracked plaster from falling out when you hammer in the nails. Now nail the two hangers into the wall.

4. Hang the picture, level the top of the frame, and drive brads into the wall at each side of the bottom of the frame.

Hang heavy, framed mirrors the same way: use two heavy-duty picture hangers.

Mounting and Hanging an Unframed Photograph

You will need:

> **Composition wallboard, soft type,
>   cut to size**
> **Contact cement**
> **Finishing nails, 1½-inch**
> **Cutting pliers**
> **Hammer**

What to do:

1. Remove the white border from the photograph and trim the edges cleanly.

2. Cut a piece of composition board exactly the same size as the photograph. If you can't cut it accurately, perhaps your hardware or lumber dealer will do it for you.

3. Coat the composition board and the back of the photo with contact cement. When both coats of cement have almost dried but are still tacky, place the photo on top of the wallboard and press it down. Smooth it all over (Figure 48).

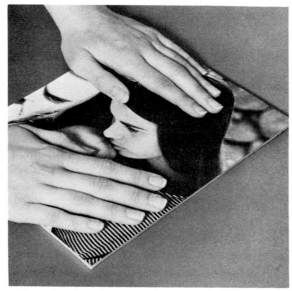

Figure 48. Pressing photo against composition board

Important: Once the two coated surfaces make contact, you can't slide or move them, so be extremely careful when you put them together.

4. Paint the edge of the wallboard in any color you choose. (Red contrasts nicely with the grays in a black-and-white photograph.)

5. Place the photo against the wall, exactly where it is to hang. With tiny pencil dots, mark the corners of the picture. Set the picture aside. Drive two nails into the wall on a line with the center of the picture area. Use the cutting pliers to snip off the nailheads at a slant, leaving sharp points (Figure 49); if necessary, tap them into the wall so that they project no more than ½ inch.

6. Align the mounted photo with the pencil dots on the wall. Then press it against the wall to impale it on the two headless nails.

Hints

Use the same system for mounting and hanging posters. However, you will need an assistant when it comes to placing the coated poster on the backing. Remember, you can't move it once it makes contact with the coated wallboard.

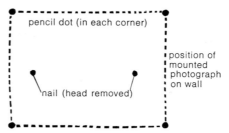

Figure 49. Nails driven along center line of picture area

PUTTING UP SHELVES

The simplest way to put up a shelf is by using brackets which are made to hold shelves of all different widths (Figure 50). Use plain, inexpensive brackets for basement shelves. You can get fancy wrought-iron and brass brackets for use upstairs as well as for use with pre-finished hardwood shelving. Fasten brackets to walls using any one of the methods described on pages 91–92.

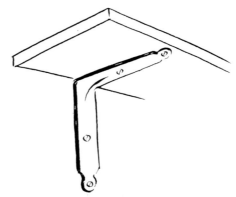

Figure 50. Bracket holding shelf

What to do:

1. Put up one bracket and fasten it to the wall.

2. Hold a second bracket against the wall and bridge them both with either a long level or a straightedge with a level on top (see page 172).

3. Adjust the second bracket so that both are on the same level, then fasten it to the wall.

4. Screw the bracket to the underside of the shelf.

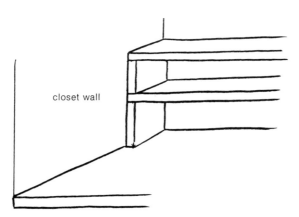

Figure 51. Divided shelf installation

DIVIDING A SHELF FOR EXTRA STORAGE SPACE

You can install one or more narrow shelves at the back of a wider shelf (Figure 51). For example, above one wide shelf in your linen closet, make a couple of narrow shelves on which to stack soap and other small articles.

You will need:

>   Lumber (an old shelf or a piece of
>   common, 1-inch thick lumber)
>   Try square
>   Crosscut saw
>   White glue

What to do:

1. Cut a piece of lumber the same length as the original shelf over which you are going to install the new one. The new shelf can be any width you choose.

2. Decide how high it is going to be and cut two more pieces of the same wood to this length; these two small pieces will serve as supports for the new shelf. Use the try square to mark the wood accurately before you cut it (see page 205).

3. Dab a little glue on one side of one of the small pieces and insert it into the corner of the original shelf with the glued side against the wall; do the same thing in the opposite corner

with the other small piece.

4. Place the new shelf on top of both and the job is done.

Add as many supports and shelves as you like by simply stacking them on top of each other. If you don't want to put them in permanently, don't use glue. The weight of the shelves on top will hold the bottom ones in place.

INSTALLING ADJUSTABLE SHELVES

Adjustable shelves rest on metal brackets, which fit into slotted metal standards. Standards are sold in sizes from 1 to 4 feet long. Brackets are made to accommodate shelves from 6 to 15 inches wide. Here is a practical method for installing adjustable shelves. It can be expanded to take in as much wall space as you like or be restricted to a small area.

You will need:

>   **Metal standards**
>   **Brackets**
>   **Flat-headed screws, 1½-inch, No. 10**
>   **Screwdriver**
>   **Electric drill**
>   **Level**
>   **Straightedge**
>   **Shelving to fit brackets**
>   **Stud finder**

What to do:

1. Position the first standard on the wall directly over a wall stud (see page 92). Place a level against the standard and adjust it so that it is absolutely vertical.

Note: Each standard has a top and a bottom. Put two of them side by side and you'll see the difference. Be sure to install all standards the same way.

2. Use a pencil to mark the wall through the top and bottom screw holes. Drill pilot holes at each mark (see page 201). Lubricate the screws with soap and drive them through the standard into the wall. These screws are long enough to reach the studs. Now drill pilot holes through the remaining screw holes and drive screws through them into the wall.

3. Fit bracket into a slot in the first standard. Fit a second bracket into another standard at exactly the same place as the first one. For example, if the bracket in the first standard is inserted in the third slot from the top, insert the bracket in the other standard in the third slot from the top also.

4. Hold the second standard against the wall, directly over a stud. If you have a level more than 16 inches long, place it across both brackets. If not, lay a straightedge across the brackets and place the level on the straightedge (Figure 52). A straightedge can be any length of unwarped wood or metal that is perfectly straight. Adjust the height of the second standard so that the level is perfectly horizontal.

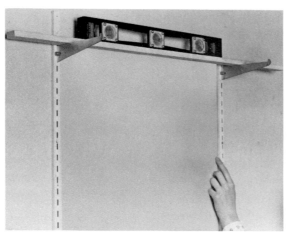

Figure 52. Using level to align standards

5. Mark through one of the screw holes in the second standard. Drill a pilot hole in the wall, and drive a screw through the standard, holding it against the wall. Check to see that the standard is vertical. If necessary, make adjustments.

6. Drill the remaining pilot holes and install screws.

7. Repeat the procedure, installing as many standards as needed. Check each one against

the preceding one, making sure all brackets are level with each other.

Install more brackets as needed, again making sure that they, too, are level with each other, and add the shelves; they should lie flat.

Hints

Shelves installed in standards 16 inches apart and screwed into studs are capable of supporting solid rows of books. For most purposes, you can install standards in every other stud, 32 inches apart.

If the positions of your standards do not permit you to screw them to studs, use one of the fastening methods described on page 90.

INSTALLING SHELVES AND MOUNTING POLES IN A CLOTHES CLOSET

Most clothes closets are poorly designed with lots of wasted space. You can easily double the capacity of your closet by installing two poles instead of one and adding extra storage shelves.

You will need:

    Pry bar
    Hammer
    8d (eightpenny) nails
    1 wooden clothes rod
    1 set of wooden clothes-rod brackets
    2 pieces of 1 x 4 inch wood, the same
        length as the depth of the closet
    Level
    2 flat-headed screws, 1¼ x 8 inches

What to do:

1. Lift out the shelf already in the closet and put it aside for future use. Then lift out the wooden clothes rod to give you easy access to the shelf area. Use the pry bar and a piece of scrap wood (for leverage) to remove the strips of wood which supported the shelf (there may be two strips—one on each side of closet; or

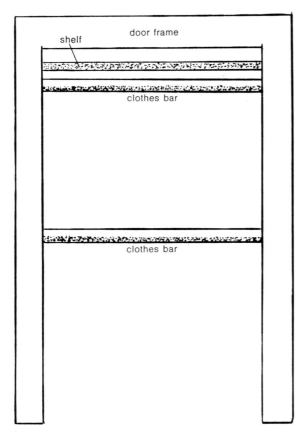

Figure 53. Redesigned closet

three—one on back of closet as well as on sides). Leave the rod brackets in place.

2. Renail the two or three pieces of wood to the same walls, 88 inches above the floor. Check them with the level before you nail them permanently in place; they should all be on the same level line.

3. Reinstall the clothes rod and replace the shelf on the wooden strips. If the shelf originally consisted of two separate boards, use only one and push it against the back wall. If you use both boards, you'll never be able to get at the shelf to store or retrieve anything; it will be too deep and the front of the shelf will be too close to the top of the door frame. If it is a wide one-piece shelf, saw it down the middle or use another piece of board about half the width of the old shelf.

4. Nail a piece of 1 x 4 inch wood to one side of the closet, 44 inches high. Level it before you nail it permanently. Nail the other piece of 1 x 4 inch wood to the other side of the closet; level this one, too. Screw rod brackets to the center of each wood piece.

5. Cut the new clothes rod to the exact size needed to fit between the two brackets.

Figure 53 shows the completed installation. Instead of one clothes rod, there are now two. Use the shelf for storing items you are not likely to use often.

Hints

Spackle all holes, and paint the inside of the closet before you hang clothing in it (see page 141).

You can install clothes rods to meet specific needs. For example, you may prefer only one high rod with a chest of drawers underneath. This is a good spot for a piece of unpainted furniture; or you can use two small pieces, side by side.

INSTALLING FIXTURES ON BATHROOM WALLS

Plaster or Wallboard Walls

You will need:

    Push drill
    Hand drill or electric drill
    Screwdriver
    Sheet-metal screws
    Sharp pencil

What to do:

1. Hold the fixture in place on the wall. Use a sharp pencil to mark the wall through the screw holes. Drill a pilot hole at each mark; it should be considerably smaller in diameter than the screw you are going to use (see page 167).

2. Lubricate the screws with soap and attach the fixture to the wall.

Hints

Sheet-metal screws are perfectly adequate for installing towel racks and hooks on which to hang shower caps and bathrobes. However, should they work themselves loose in time and you find you can no longer tighten them, reinstall fixtures by using toggle bolts or expansion fasteners (see page 90).

Tile Walls

You will need:

Masonry drill
Electric drill
Screwdriver
Sheet-metal screws
¼-inch fiber or plastic plugs

What to do:

1. With a felt-tip pen, mark the tiles where holes are to be drilled. Use the masonry drill to bore holes in the tile at each mark you have made.

2. Hold the drill steady to prevent it from skittering across the tile. If you are using a variable-speed drill, start it at low speed with little pressure. Increase both speed and pressure as you go on.

3. Press a fiber or plastic plug into each hole. Lubricate screws with soap. Pass them through the fixture to be hung and then drive the screws into the plugs.

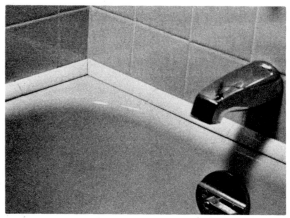

Figure 54. Bathtub sealing tiles in place

CAULKING BETWEEN BATHROOM WALL AND TUB

A frequent source of trouble is the crack that develops between the bathtub and the wall. Water seeps in, causing tiles to loosen; wall studs can consequently rot, resulting in extensive damage.

The simplest way to stop water seepage is by caulking the crack. You can add to the effectiveness of your caulking by installing ceramic tile units around the edge of the tub, where it meets the wall (Figure 54). Seen in cross-section, these tiles look like quarter-cylinders; their edges fit perfectly against the tub and the wall (Figure 55).

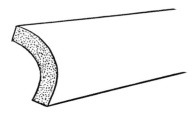

Figure 55. Bathtub sealing tile

You will need:

Bathtub sealing kit, consisting of
    tile and cement
Tube of latex caulking compound
Hacksaw

What to do:

1. First caulk the crack between the tub and the wall with latex caulking compound. It is a good idea first to knead the tube slightly to make the compound flow more easily. Also be sure the tube is at room temperature. Press the nozzle of the tube against the crack and squeeze, spreading the compound around the perimeter of the tub.

2. When applying the ceramic pieces, both tile and wall surfaces must be clean or the cement will not stick. Wash off soap residue and wipe the surfaces clean. Begin at a corner, squeezing a bead of cement (supplied with the kit) along the back and bottom edges of a mitered piece. Press it into the corner. Squeeze cement along the edges of a matching corner piece and press it into the same corner, making a mitered joint. Be sure to apply ceramic tile cement liberally and *press* the units into place —don't just lay them down. With a damp cloth, wipe off any cement that oozes out. Then polish the tiles with a dry cloth.

3. Apply mitered units to the other corner.

4. Starting from each corner, install pieces toward the center.

5. You may have to cut the last piece to fit it in place. Hold it in a vise and score the back heavily with a hacksaw. It can then be broken off at the crack.

6. Now apply tiles from the corners to the open ends of the tub. Special corner units give the ends a professional-looking finish.

5

WINDOWS
Get-Ready Jobs for Curtains, Drapes, and Shades

A window does more than admit light and air. It also provides a decorative area that breaks the monotony of a large wall. Curtains and draperies provide interesting contrasts of color, texture, and pattern, and they can make a wall seem higher or wider, depending on whether the window treatment accents its height or width. It is easy to install curtains and draperies yourself.

Like everything else, however, windows need care and maintenance. Every type of window can develop problems. *Double-hung* windows, with upper and lower sashes which can be raised or lowered, are the most common type of window. Paint that has gotten into the side spaces tends to make the sashes stick. *Casement* windows swing outward. Some are adjusted by hand; others are manipulated with a crank—either type can stick or cause other problems. *Awning* windows are hinged at the top. When cranked out, the bottom of the window extends farther away from the house than the top. Cranking mechanisms sometimes bind. *Sliding* windows move horizontally in a track which requires periodic lubrication to prevent the windows from sticking.

Householders frequently run into these and other small problems, such as patching a hole in window screening, replacing a broken sash cord, or stopping a window from rattling. You should be able to replace the screening in either wood or aluminum frames as well as install a set of invisible catches or a friction spring.

You can also put up window shades—and even design and make your own, using leftover wallpaper. It is also helpful to learn how to install curtain rods, traverse rods, and venetian blinds. Your window treatments can be much more imaginative, and your window parts will work much more efficiently, once you learn how to take care of all these problems yourself.

Buying Curtain Rods

Measure the width of the area to be covered by the curtain or drape. Buy a drapery rod that does not have to be extended more than half its original length to meet your required length, for a rod that is extended to its full length is likely to sag. When buying a traverse rod (page 105), be sure that when it is closed, it is at least three-quarters as long as the distance to be spanned.

INSTALLING SIMPLE CURTAIN RODS

There are several types of simple curtain rods; all are hung on brackets which are fastened to the window casing (the front of the window frame). Nails or screws are included with each pair of brackets.

You will need:

Push drill
Hammer or screwdriver

What to do:

1. Hold a bracket on the left side of the casing from 1½ to 2 inches below the top as in Figure 1. Use a sharp pencil to mark the frame through the nail or screw openings.

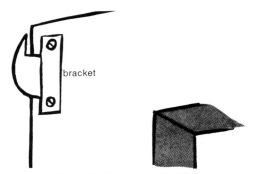

Figure 1. Curtain-rod bracket

2. Select a push drill slightly smaller in diameter than the nails or screws you are using. Drill pilot holes (see page 201) at each mark.

3. Using the nails or screws supplied, fasten the bracket in place. Lubricate the screws with soft soap before you insert them.

4. In the same way, install a bracket on the casing at the other side of the window frame. The ends of the curtain rods fit over the brackets as shown in Figure 2.

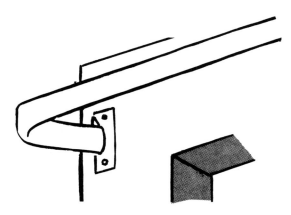

Figure 2. Curtain rod fitted over bracket

Hints

Double brackets are available which enable you to hang one curtain rod inside another.

A loose rod bracket is a common household problem which can be fixed in one of two ways. If the loose screws are driven into wood (such as a stud), replace them with longer ones. If the loose screws are driven into the wall (not a stud), replace the screws with expansion fasteners (page 90).

Sagging drapery rods can be fixed by installing a bracket that supports the center of the rod.

To make a window look wider, attach a swinging crane, or a swinging rod, to the wall on each side of the casing to hold a narrow drapery.

Extension plates, screwed horizontally to the top of a window casing, extend the distance between the rod brackets, giving the effect of a wider window (Figure 3). To add height, screw the extension plates vertically to the top of the window casing. The draperies will then hang from above the window frame. Brackets are fastened to each end of the extension plate with small machine screws and nuts which come with the bracket.

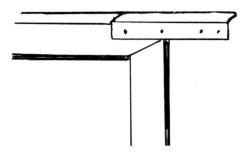

Figure 3. Extension plate screwed to window casing

INSTALLING CAFE-CURTAIN RODS

Café curtains are sewed or clipped to rings which are hung loosely from long rods. The rods are held about 3 inches away from the window by brackets which are screwed to the casing. You need two brackets (one for each side of the window) for a single rod. Sometimes café curtains are hung in layers—one pair over the top half of the window and another pair over the bottom half. In such cases, two rods as well as four brackets are required. The following directions are for a single rod to accommodate one pair of café curtains over the lower half of the window.

You will need:

> **Push drill**
> **Screwdriver**

What to do:

1. Hold a bracket against the front of the left-hand window casing, even with the top of the lower sash. Make pencil marks on the casing through the screw holes in the bracket.

2. Select a push drill slightly smaller in diameter than the screws you are going to use.

Figure 4. Café-rod bracket

Drill pilot holes at each pencil mark (see page 201); this will prevent the screws from splitting the wood. Lubricate the screws with soft soap and fasten the bracket to the wall (Figure 4).

3. Hold the other bracket against the front of the right-hand window casing. Rest the curtain rod on both brackets, adjusting the position of the bracket so that the rod is level and parallel to the top of the lower window sash. Mark through the screw holes, drill pilot holes, and install the bracket. The curtain rod rests on the brackets as in Figure 5.

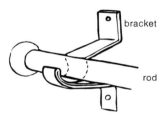

Figure 5. Café-rod resting on bracket

Hints

Rods are made in several diameters and many styles, ranging from simple, thin brass rods to elaborate fluted poles.

For repairing loose brackets and sagging rods, see page 104.

INSTALLING TRAVERSE RODS

A traverse rod is more than just a rod. It consists of a sheet-metal track in which a set of plastic slides moves freely; the curtains or draperies are fastened to these slides. The track is equipped with a pulley arrangement through which a double cord runs (Figure 6). Pulling one cord opens both drapes at the same time and pulling the other cord closes them.

Traverse rods usually come equipped with the hardware needed to install them on walls, windows, or ceilings. If they are more than four feet long, they require a central supporting bracket.

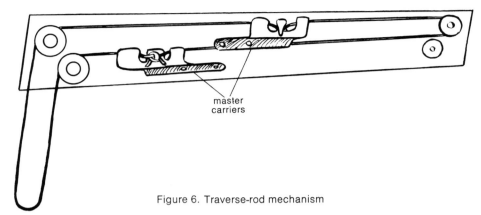

Figure 6. Traverse-rod mechanism

Window Installation

You will need:

> **Push drill**
> **Screwdriver**
> **Traverse-rod mounting brackets**
>   **and screws**
> **Soap**

What to do:

1. Position a mounting bracket at the upper left-hand corner of the window casing. Mark through only two screw holes with a sharp pencil.

2. After selecting a push-drill bit smaller in diameter than the screws you are going to use, drill pilot holes at each of the pencil marks (see page 201).

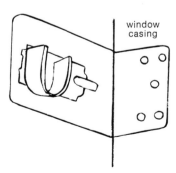

Figure 7. Traverse-rod bracket

3. Lubricate the screws with soap and screw the bracket to the window casing (Figure 7).

4. Then install a bracket on the other side of the casing and fit the traverse rod into the two brackets.

Wall Installation

You can use the same brackets for both wall and window installations.

You will need:

> **Traverse-rod brackets**
> **Sheet-metal screws**
> **Push drill**
> **Screwdriver**
> **Soap**

What to do:

1. Decide how wide the traverse rod is to be, then mark the wall with a pencil to show where the brackets are to be fastened.

2. Hold the brackets in place on the wall and mark through the screw holes with a sharp pencil.

3. Use a push drill to make one pilot hole in the wall for each bracket. The drill bit must be smaller in diameter than the screws you use. *Note:* Don't use the screws that come with the traverse rod. They will hold in wood, but they are too small for use in a wall. Use the largest sheet-metal screws that can pass through the screw holes in the brackets.

4. Lubricate a screw with soap and screw a bracket to the wall. If it holds, make another pilot hole and drive in a second screw.

5. Secure the other bracket to the wall.

When installing a very long traverse rod, if it is possible, locate the wall studs and screw the brackets into the studs.

If the sheet-metal screws do not hold, but continue to turn after they should have become tight, you will have to secure the brackets with either toggle bolts (page 90), screw plugs (page 200), or expansion fasteners (page 90).

Ceiling Installation

Most traverse rods can be mounted on either walls or ceilings. To install a rod on a ceiling, pass fasteners through holes in the tops of the end brackets. It is also advisable to use mounting clips, which hold the rod and are fastened to the ceiling.

Special traverse rods are available for ceiling mounting. They do not require the use of end-mounting brackets, but have holes in their tracks, through which you·can insert toggle bolts, or expansion fasteners. Do not use screws for ceiling mounting.

Hints

The long, metal slides on a traverse rod are the *master carriers.* If your draperies do not open or close when you pull the cord, one of the cords has probably become disengaged from the master carrier. See that the cord is looped *under* the down-pointing hook on the slide (see Figure 6).

You can add plastic slides to, or subtract them from a traverse rod through the opening, or gate, in the end of each rod.

For repairing loose brackets and sagging rods, see page 104.

WINDOW SHADES

Window-shade brackets come in pairs; one has a slotted opening (Figure 8) and the other has a hole (Figure 9). Mounting screws or nails are included with each pair.

Figure 8. Left-hand (slotted) window-shade bracket, inside type

Figure 9. Right-hand window-shade bracket, inside type

Inside shade brackets are used when installing window shades inside a window frame. *Outside* brackets are fastened to the casing (the front of the window frame) to take shades that are wider than the window sash.

You will need:

> **Window shade**
> **Window-shade brackets**
> **Push drill**
> **Hammer or screwdriver**

Installing Inside Window-Shade Brackets

What to do:

1. Hold the slotted bracket, with the open end of the slot on top, against the top of the left-hand stop molding. (The stop molding, Figure 21, is nailed to the inside of the window casing in front of the lower sash to prevent the sash from falling out of the window frame.) Mark the two screw or nail openings with a sharp pencil.

2. Select a push drill slightly smaller in diameter than the nail or screw you are going to use and drill pilot holes at each pencil mark (see page 167). This will keep the screws from splitting the molding.

3. Lubricate screws with a little soft soap and nail or screw the bracket to the molding.

4. Use the same procedure to fasten the other bracket to the right-hand stop molding.

Installing Outside Window-Shade Brackets

1. Drill pilot holes, then fasten the left-hand (slotted) bracket (Figure 10) to the front of the window casing.

2. Fasten the right-hand bracket (Figure 11) to the front casing of the other side of the window.

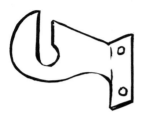 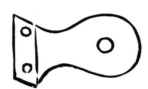

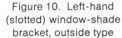

Figure 10. Left-hand (slotted) window-shade bracket, outside type

Figure 11. Right-hand window-shade bracket, outside type

Hints

After hanging a window shade in a set of brackets, pull it all the way down and test to see that it returns all the way up.

If the shade won't go back up, pull it all the way down and remove it from the brackets. Rolling it up by hand will tighten the spring in the roller mechanism. Replace it in the brackets.

If the shade won't stay down, roll it all the way up, remove it from the brackets and partially unroll it to loosen the spring in the roller mechanism.

When ordering new inside shades, give your dealer the distance between stop moldings. If you already have outside brackets in place, measure the exact distance between brackets; your new shade roller should be ¾ inch smaller than this distance. If you are replacing a worn shade, take it to your dealer, so he can duplicate the size exactly.

REPLACING WINDOW SHADE MATERIAL

You can add an exciting decorator touch to any room by devising your own custom-made window shades. Make a shade to match the surrounding wallpaper, slipcover fabric, or bedspread material. Or use a bright accent color to carry out a decorating scheme. This is an inexpensive way to add interest and color to a room, and decorated shades are ideal low-cost substitutes for draperies. Although ordinary fabric doesn't have enough body to make a good window shade, you can buy iron-on shade backing material. Iron it to the back of any wallpaper or fabric to get exactly the right degree of stiffness.

You will need:

> **Vinyl wall covering or other shade material (decorative fabric or wallpaper)**
> **Scissors**
> **Staple gun, or hammer and No. 2 tacks**
> **New window-shade roller, or old window shade**
> **Iron-on shade backing material (optional)**

What to do:

1. If you are using an old shade, separate the the shade material from the roller by removing all tacks or staples. Remove the wooden strip from the bottom of the shade as well.

2. Using the old shade as a pattern, cut a new shade from a strip of vinyl wall covering or a decorative fabric. Vinyl wall covering can be used to make a shade without doing anything further to it.

3. Tack or staple the top end of the shade to the roller.

4. Fold back the bottom end, and turn the edge under. Then sew it to make a 1½-inch hem into which you can slide the wooden strip.

5. Roll up the shade and hang it.

6. If you wish, install a shade pull and decorative trim at the bottom. Sew the trim to the shade, just above the hem.

Making a New Shade

1. If necessary, install shade brackets in the window (see pages 107–108). Measure the exact distance between the brackets and buy a roller to fit. Or, if you have an old roller that is too long, cut it down to fit (see below).

2. Cut the shade material. It should be ½ inch narrower than the width of the roller and 8 inches longer than the length of the window.

3. Fold back the bottom end of the material and sew it, making a hem into which a wooden strip can slide.

4. Tack or staple the top end of the shade to the roller.

How to Cut Down An Old Shade Roller

Each roller has a spring end (with a screwdriverlike tip) and a pin end (with a round, nail-like tip) made of either metal or plastic. Use a knife or screwdriver to pry the pin end from the roller. Don't touch the spring end.

Measuring from the spring end, mark the point at which the roller is to be cut—don't forget to include the pin end in your measurement. With a saw, cut off the excess and then hammer the pin end back onto the roller.

The spring end of a roller is *always at the left;* the pin end is *always at the right.*

Hint:

If a window shade keeps falling out of the brackets, use a screwdriver to pry out the pin end just a bit.

VENETIAN BLINDS

Venetian-blind brackets come in pairs. You can't interchange the left and right side brackets.

You will need:

> 2 venetian-blind brackets
> Push drill
> Screwdriver
> Soap

What to do:

1. Press a left-hand bracket into the upper left-hand corner of the window casing. Using a sharp pencil, mark the casing through two screw holes in the bracket.

2. Select a push drill smaller in diameter than the screws you are going to use. Drill pilot holes at each pencil mark.

3. Lubricate the screws with soap. Hold the bracket in place and screw it to the casing (Figure 12).

Figure 12. Venetian-blind bracket

4. Following the same procedure, install the right-hand bracket.

5. Open the front section of each bracket and slide in the venetian blind, then close the hinged fronts.

SCREENING

Whether your screens are framed with wood or aluminum, they are always vulnerable to damage—the screening itself can tear or develop holes, or the molding can loosen. To avoid costly repair bills and save both time and annoyance, remedy these problems yourself.

Repairing Holes in Screening

To repair small holes and tears in screening, simply coat the damaged areas with transparent cement, such as clear epoxy or any model-airplane cement.

Larger areas (up to 2 square inches) can be repaired with ready-to-use screen patches. To use a patch, just press it into place; double-curved prongs on the patch hold it securely and prevent it from falling off.

Replacing the Screening

Screening is made of aluminum, fiberglass,

or bronze (all rustproof). The longest lasting is fiberglass, which is tough and resilient and withstands practically everything. Aluminum screening is good, too, but is not recommended for seaside areas because it is likely to corrode in time. Since screening comes in standard widths, in increments of one inch, all you have to do is measure the width of your old screening and buy an exact replacement. Lumberyards and large hardware stores sell both screening and screen molding.

RESTORING A WOOD-FRAME WINDOW SCREEN

You will need:

New screening, (fiberglass or aluminum, 3 or 4 inches longer than old screening)
New screen molding (if needed)
Putty knife or flat chisel
Claw hammer
1-inch wire brads
Two 4-inch C-clamps
Tin snips or heavy-duty scissors
Tack hammer and No. 3 tacks, or staple gun with bronze or monel staples
Screwdriver or tack remover
Crosscut or backsaw (only if replacing moldings)
Single-edged razor blade in holder
2 pieces 2 x 4 inch wood, at least as long as the length of frame
2 pieces wood, about 1-inch thick, any width, at least as long as the width of frame

What to do:

1. Use a chisel or putty knife to pry off the screen molding. Try not to damage it, for you are going to use it again.

2. With a tack remover or screwdriver, remove tacks or staples which hold the old screening in place. Discard the old screening.

3. Place the two pieces of 2 x 4 inch wood on your work surface; this may be a workbench, table, or two sawhorses.

4. Lay the screen frame on the two lengths of wood, with the sides of the frame even with the wood. The side of the frame on which the screening is to be tacked should face up.

5. Slip the shorter lengths of 1-inch thick wood under each end of the frame; these can be lengths of furring strip or any other wood about 1 inch thick.

6. Clamp both sides of the center of the frame to the 2 x 4 inch pieces. This bends the frame, making it lower in the center. Figure 13 shows how a clamp is applied.

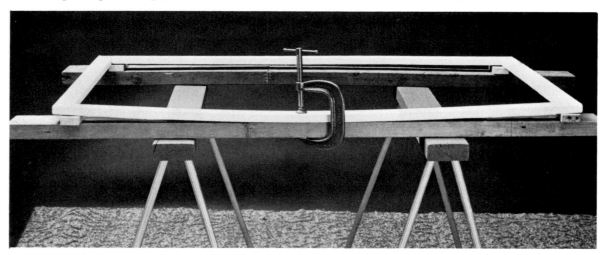

Figure 13. Clamping center of screen frame to wood pieces

7. Unroll the new screening material and center it on the frame. Use tin snips or scissors to cut it 3 or 4 inches longer than the old screening.

8. Secure the screening along one end of the frame with a row of staples or tacks about one inch apart. Pull the screening to the other end, stretching it so that it lies flat, without ripples. Again, tack or staple it down (Figure 14).

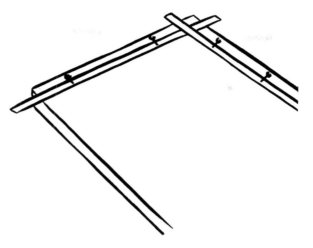

Figure 15. Screen moldings with temporary nails

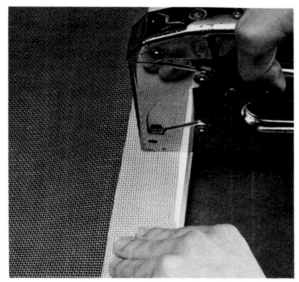

Figure 14. Stapling down ends of new screening

9. Release the clamps. The frame will spring back to its normal position, stretching the screening taut.

10. Remove the 1-inch-thick wood strips from under the ends of the frame. Tack or staple the screening along the sides of the frame.

11. Retack or staple the original molding, using 1-inch wire brads. If necessary, nail down new molding: nail it temporarily along the top and bottom exactly where the old moldings were, covering the edges of the screening. Place two nails in each molding, but do not drive them in all the way. Then nail side moldings in the same way, placing nails near the center of each strip. These moldings must be long enough to cross over the top and bottom moldings with a couple of inches to

spare at each end (Figure 15).

12. Using a backsaw or crosscut saw, cut a freehand miter in each corner by holding the saw vertically and cutting through *both* moldings at a 45-degree angle (Figure 16).

Cut through both moldings at this angle.

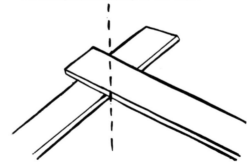

Figure 16. Mitering molding at corner

Stop when you have sawed almost through the bottom molding. Then complete the cut with a utility knife. When the waste scraps of molding are removed, the corners will fit perfectly.

13. Remove the temporary nails which presently hold the moldings. Then renail them, this time permanently, shifting them slightly so that the spaces left by the saw cut in each corner are closed.

14. If your screen has a center brace, cut a piece of molding to fit across it and nail it down.

15. Use a single-edged razor blade to trim off any excess screening. Cut close to the molding (Figure 17).

Figure 17. Cutting away excess screening with razor blade

RESTORING AN ALUMINUM-FRAME WINDOW SCREEN

No tacks or staples are used to hold screening to an aluminum frame. Instead, the screening is forced into a channel or slot, then wedged in place with plastic cord.

You will need:

    New screening
    Single-edged razor blade in holder
    Screwdriver
    Plastic cord (optional)
    Screen roller

What to do:

1. Lay the screen on a table, floor, plywood sheet, or other flat work surface.

2. Using a screwdriver, pry up one end of the plastic cord (Figure 18). Pull the cord out of the slot. This frees the screening so that you can lift it out and discard it. Save the cord, however.

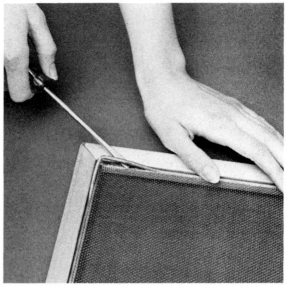

Figure 18. Prying up old plastic cord

3. Place a new piece of screening over the opening in the frame. It should be about two inches longer than the distance between the slots. The wires in the screen should lie parallel to the edges of the frame. Using the round-edged wheel on the screen roller, roll the screening into the slots around the frame. Don't push it all the way into the slot—only enough to keep it in place (Figure 19).

Figure 19. Rolling screening into slot

4. Place an end of plastic cord into the slot on top of the screening. Using the concave end of the screen roller, roll the plastic cord into the slots while simultaneously pushing the screen down (Figure 20). Do not exert too much pressure. Work your way all around the frame, lightly at first, then with enough force to seat the screening at the bottom of the slot. At this point the screen should be taut.

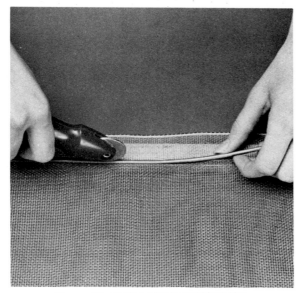

Figure 20. Rolling plastic cord into slot

5. Use the single-edged razor blade to trim excess screening from the slots.

FREEING STICKING WINDOWS

Most windows stick because they have been painted into place; the dried paint actually glues the window sash to the frame.

Double-Hung Sash Windows

You will need:

> Large paint scraper
> Sharp penknife
> Hammer
> Scrap wood
> Silicone lubricant (either spray or jelly)
>   or dry lubricant

What to do:

1. First break the paint seal that holds the sash to the frame by running the tip of a sharp knife all around the sash wherever it makes contact with the frame or sill. Do this with both upper and lower sashes.

2. Insert the blade of a paint scraper between the sash and the frame; if necessary, use a hammer to force the edge of the scraper through the paint barrier. Free the sash at all points of contact.

3. Unfasten the sash lock. Place the heels of your hands under the top rail of the bottom sash and push upward. If you are lucky, the sash will move. If it doesn't, continue to work with the flat scraper blade, inserting it between sash and frame and moving it back and forth until the sash has been freed.

4. Pull on the scraper handle to force the sash and frame apart just a bit. As soon as any space shows, spray it with silicone lubricant.

5. Continue to alternately pry the sash loose with the scraper and attempt to work it loose by hand. Sometimes you can break the paint seal by placing a small block of scrap wood at each end of the top of the lower sash, and striking it lightly with a hammer. As soon as you can move the sash, lubricate all points of contact with silicone; then move it up and down until it is entirely free.

Casement Windows

Casement windows often stick and fail to close properly because they have been given too many coats of paint.

What to do:

1. Remove accumulated paint with paint remover or by scraping it off. Give the window a coat of metal primer, followed by enamel.

2. Lubricate the window after it has been painted. Use light machine oil on the cranking mechanism and window hinges.

Awning Windows

Like casement windows, awning windows

are cranked out. Treatment for sticking awning windows is the same as that used for casement windows.

What to do:

1. Look for accumulated layers of paint on the bottom edge of the window and scrape them off.

2. Lubricate crank mechanisms with light machine oil.

Sliding Windows

Sliding windows are moved by hand, so there aren't any crank mechanisms to go out of order. However, the tracks in which the windows run should be brushed clean and vacuumed from time to time, and lubricated with silicone spray. Don't use oil.

Hints

You can easily avoid painting windows together. After a window is painted, do not close either the top or bottom sash all the way. Instead, leave each one open an inch or two, until the paint is thoroughly dry. Then push the upper sash *up* to break the new paint bond; push the lower sash *down*. Lubricate all window channels with silicone.

If the handle of a window crank mechanism breaks, you may be able to get an exact replacement. Bring the broken handle to a hardware store so that it can be matched.

INSTALLING A FRICTION SPRING

Many older houses have windows which were originally equipped with sash cords and weights. In time, sash cords become brittle and break, weights fall, and the sash becomes unbalanced and unmanageable.

The obvious remedy is to replace the broken sash cord. This can be a messy job in an older house, particularly if the woodwork has been painted a number of times. You will have to scrape away accumulated layers of dried paint, and pry off moldings that have been painted in place for years.

One solution is to install a friction spring, a simple gadget that can be installed in a matter of minutes and works like a charm.

What to do:

1. If the lower sash has a broken cord, raise the sash as high as possible.

2. Slide the spring between the sash and the frame, with the prongs facing the frame (Figure 21).

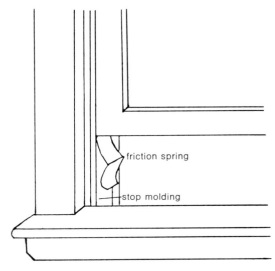

Figure 21. Installing friction spring

3. Close the window; the prongs will become imbedded in the frame, and provide enough friction for the sash to work very well. The spring will not only provide enough friction to hold the sash securely, but it will also help to eliminate window rattling.

4. To install a spring in an upper sash, drop the sash as low as you can, insert the spring with its prongs facing the frame, and raise the sash.

INSTALLING INVISIBLE WINDOW CATCHES

Most window catches don't do what they are supposed to: safeguard the house by preventing anyone from entering through the window. A professional burglar can either neutralize or force any visible lock or catch. But what about an invisible catch that can't be forced and can only be released by someone inside the house? Installation is simple and it costs practically nothing.

You will need:

> Hand or electric drill
> Two 8d (eightpenny) finishing nails
>   for each window
> 7/64-inch twist drill

What to do:

1. Close the window and tighten the window latch.

2. Tighten a 7/64-inch twist drill in a hand or electric drill. Measure the length of the drill that protrudes from the chuck; between 2¼ and 2½ inches should be exposed. In the top

Figure 22. Drilling hole for nail in window sash

rail of the bottom sash, about one inch from the right-hand window frame, drill a hole the full length of the exposed drill (Figure 22). This hole must go through the top rail of the bottom sash and into the bottom rail of the top sash (Figure 23).

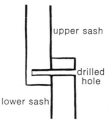

upper sash

drilled hole

lower sash

Figure 23. Hole drilled through lower sash into upper sash

3. Insert an 8d nail into the hole. That's all there is to it. The nail will effectively hold everything in place, and prevent any up-and-down movement of the two window sashes.

4. To open the window, just grasp the nailhead and pull it out, so that the top and bottom sashes are free to move.

Hints

For a truly invisible installation, file the head off the nail, and drill the hole deep enough to accept its full length. The nail must slide smoothly in and out without binding, so use a ⅛-inch drill to make the hole. Since the nail has no head and is completely hidden in the wood, you must use a magnet to withdraw it. Most hardware stores sell small, powerful magnets that do the job nicely.

WEATHERSTRIPPING

Weatherstripping serves several important functions by closing up spaces in door and window frames. This eliminates drafts, keeps out dust and dirt, and prevents doors and windows from rattling. Furthermore, weatherstripping can cut down your heating bill, for it keeps heat from leaking out.

Although metal weatherstripping is the best, it must be installed by a professional because it involves removing window sashes, cutting special grooves, and carefully refitting a sash when it is replaced. It is definitely *not* a job for a beginning do-it-yourselfer.

However, there are other types of weatherstripping you can install yourself without difficulty. Kits are available at your local hardware store which contain enough weatherstripping to do one door or one window. Or buy rolls of weatherstripping material by the foot. Among materials used are felt, vinyl tubing, plastic foam, wood and vinyl strips, and aluminum and vinyl strips.

Weatherstripping a Window

What to do:

1. Weatherstrip a window from the inside. First do the upper sash by fastening the weatherstrip material to the *parting strip* (the strip of wood that separates the tracks for the upper and lower sashes). Then press it against both sides of the upper sash. It should not impede the movement of the upper sash, but should eliminate any looseness or window rattling.

2. Fasten it in place with tacks or staples.

3. Next weatherstrip the lower sash. Place weatherstripping material flat against the stop molding at each side with its edge pressed against the sash.

4. Fasten it in place with tacks or staples.

Figure 24. Installing self-adhesive weatherstripping

Hint

Self-adhesive weatherstripping, which is often preferred by beginning do-it-yourselfers, is available in a wide variety of materials, all of which are efficient.

6

DOORS

Entrance and closet doors can present home-owners with an array of fix-it problems, most of which can be solved very easily.

Because houses are constantly settling, door frames often warp out of shape, causing doors to sag or bind so that they won't close properly. Varying weather conditions can cause swelling with the same result—a door that won't close.

When sliding closet doors jump the track and doors rattle every time the wind blows, you have yet another set of problems to remedy.

In some instances, you may have to take down a door. Although this isn't too difficult, you shouldn't try to do it by yourself. Get help. Find a neighbor with whom you can exchange fix-it-yourself time. It's important to have an extra pair of helping hands for this kind of job.

Even when your doors close properly, you may have problems with the hardware. If the latch doesn't work, a simple adjustment of the strike plate (opposite the latch on the door frame) is the answer. Perhaps you'd like to refinish your old doorknobs or replace them with new decorative types. These simple jobs take only a few minutes.

Locks and other security mechanisms are very important for the protection of your home and family. Although you may not be able to install a new lock, you can attach a chain to your door or install a peephole. Sometimes, in cold areas, moisture freezes in the opening of a lock, making it impossible to insert the key. Thawing the lock is not at all difficult.

You are bound to encounter one or more of these door problems eventually. When the time comes, fix-it-yourself!

FREEING A STICKING DOOR

Doors often rub or stick because they sag in their frames. In addition, they are affected by seasonal changes, swelling during hot, humid weather, and shrinking when the heat is turned on. As a result, some doors can only be closed during the winter.

Before you do anything more complicated, try tightening all the hinge screws. This may pull the door snugly against the frame, and solve your problem immediately. If this doesn't work, try the following.

You will need:

> **Large screwdriver**
> **Hammer**
> **Smooth block or rasp plane**
> **Woodworking chisel**
> **Stepladder**
> **Cardboard**
> **Matchsticks or toothpicks**
> **White glue**
> **Old magazines or newspapers**

What to do:

1. If you find a loose screw that doesn't grip when you turn it, remove it. Open the door part way, and wedge it in place with magazines or newspapers to keep it from moving. Remove the rest of the screws from the hinge leaf, and swing the hinge back, exposing the wood underneath.

2. Break the heads from a couple of wooden matches. Dip the ends of the matches into white glue, and hammer them into the screw hole that's too large. (If you don't have matches, use toothpicks). Wait until the glue sets (about a half hour), then shave off the excess matchstick-wood with a woodworking chisel.

3. Replace the screws in the hinge. Start the screw in the packed hole by tapping it with a hammer.

If the door still sticks, find out where it rubs against the casing by looking for worn paint. You can often adjust an out-of-line door by in-

stalling a cardboard shim behind a hinge; this will move that portion of the door farther away from the casing.

1. To do this, open the door part way, and wedge it in place with magazines. Remove the hinge screws from the casing, and swing out the hinge leaf.

2. To make a shim, cut a piece of cardboard that just fits the cutout where the hinge leaf goes.

3. Reset the hinge leaf on top of the cardboard shim. Use a nail to poke holes in the shim, then install the screws.

If a door rubs *near the top* of the latch side, place a shim behind the *lower* hinge (Figure 1).

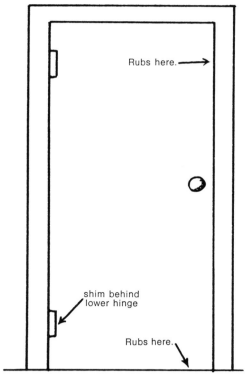

Figure 1. When door rubs near top part of frame or at bottom edge, shim lower hinge.

Do the same if the *bottom edge* on the latch side rubs against the saddle on the floor.

If the *top edge* or the *lower part* of the latch side rubs, install a shim behind the *upper* hinge. (Figure 2).

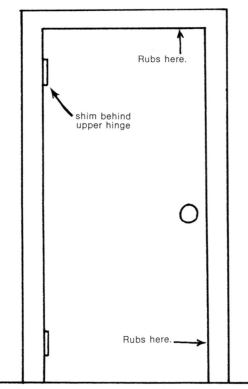

Figure 2. When door rubs at top edge or lower part of latch side, shim upper hinge.

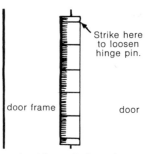

Figure 3. Removing hinge pin from door

Shimming may not cure the condition completely, so if a door still rubs, shave it down with a plane until it clears the casing. You can easily plane the top or edge of a door while it is in place, but you will have to remove the door in order to plane the bottom edge.

REMOVING A DOOR

You will need:

Hammer
Old screwdriver
Old magazines

What to do:

1. Open the door part way and wedge old magazines in the space between the door and the floor to keep it ajar.

2. Place the tip of a screwdriver under the knob of the hinge pin. Strike the handle of the screwdriver with a hammer, forcing the hinge pin up and out (Figure 3).

3. Remove both hinge pins, and then have someone help you take the door out of the frame.

Replacing a Door

1. Stand the door in the frame.

2. Block it up with magazines so that the hinge halves on the door match those on the frame.

3. Replace the pins in the hinges.

Hints

It may be difficult to remove hinge pins that have been painted into place. Scrape off excess paint with the tip of a screwdriver.

Lubricate hinge pins with a drop of oil to facilitate their removal.

HOW TO STOP A DOOR FROM RATTLING

If a door rattles, it is not firmly seated against the stop molding when it is latched. The stop molding is the molding against which the door closes.

What to do:

1. Pry off the molding at the latch side of the door casing (see page 179); do it carefully in order not to split it. Scrape off accumulated paint from both molding and casing.

2. Close the door so that the latch catches. Replace the molding, moving it closer to the door to prevent the door from rattling.

ADJUSTING SLIDING DOORS

A sliding door may need adjustment from time to time. It may jump its track, stick at the bottom, or require lubrication. In all cases, the cure is simple.

Each door has two fittings attached to the top near each edge. The fittings contain wheels which run in a track fastened to the underside of the top door casing (Figure 4). The bottom of the door may run between plastic angles, or it may be fitted with two narrow fins which slide in a grooved sill on the floor. All adjustments to a sliding door are made in the fittings at the top. All you need is a screwdriver.

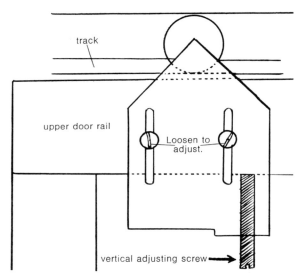

Figure 4. Inside view of sliding-door fitting

If a door has jumped out of its groove in the sill, it is probably too high, and must be lowered. To do this, loosen the small screws which hold the fitting to the door. *Don't* remove them; just give each screw a full turn to the left.

Turn the vertical adjusting screw (shown by an arrow in Figure 4) counterclockwise. The weight of the door will cause it to drop. The more you turn the screw, the lower the door will be. When the fins at the bottom of the door engage the slot in the sill without the bottom of the door scraping against the sill, tighten the screws you have loosened.

If a door sticks at the bottom, turn the vertical screw clockwise in order to raise the door.

To silence a squeaky sliding door, lubricate the wheels and the tracks in which they run. You can either apply ordinary petroleum jelly or spray the wheels and track with silicone lubricant.

TRIMMING A DOOR TO FIT NEWLY LAID CARPETING

The carpet installer usually removes the door before he lays a carpet. Try just rehanging it; it may not need any alterations. But if it binds at the bottom, you will have to take the door down and trim it. This prevents the door from rubbing against the carpeting and wearing it out.

Depending on the type of carpeting laid, you may have to remove as much as 1 inch from the bottom of a door that opens into a newly carpeted room.

You will need:

> Ripsaw or saber saw
> Plane
> Medium-grade sandpaper

What to do:

1. In order to determine how much to trim off, measure the distance between the lower edge of the half hinge on the door frame and the carpeting minus ¼ inch (Figure 5). Or, if

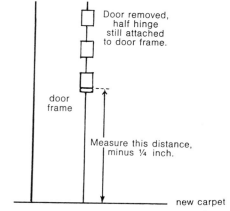

Figure 5. Measuring from bottom of hinge to carpeting

a new sill has been installed in the doorway, measure the distance between this sill and the hinge, and subtract ¼ inch.

2. With a pencil, mark off this distance on the door, measuring from the lower edge of the half hinge to the door bottom. Also make a pencil mark at this point on the other side of the door. A line joining both marks will serve as a cutting guide.

3. If you must take off only ¼ inch (or less), plane it. Get someone to help you remove the door and hold it while you plane the bottom edge *from each side toward the center.* You will find that planing from one side will give you a smoother cut than planing from the other side; this is because you are planing with the wood grain. Therefore continue to plane only from that side.

4. If more than ¼ inch must be removed, saw it off. Lay the door on a table, with the bottom edge protruding over the tabletop. Use a ripsaw to cut a strip from the bottom (Figure 6). Hold the door firmly and keep your fingers

Figure 7. Cutting bottom of door with saber saw

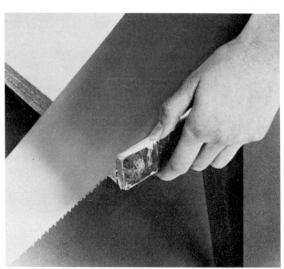

Figure 6. Cutting bottom of door with ripsaw

away from the path of the saw blade. Or use a saber saw (Figure 7).

5. After you have sawed the piece off, plane a few thin shavings from the bottom. Smooth with sandpaper, then rehang the door.

MAKING A DOOR LATCH WORK

A door usually fails to latch properly because the *latch bolt* does not engage the opening in the strike plate (also known as the *strike*). This often happens when the door frame sags, throwing the latch and strike plate out of alignment.

Examine the latch bolt while you open and shut the door. As the door is shut, the bolt is compressed against the strike plate; spring action then clicks it into the rectangular opening in the plate. If this does not happen, you will have to alter the strike-plate opening.

If the Latch Bolt is Too Low

You will need:

    Screwdriver
    File, not more than ¾ inch wide
    Wood chisel, ¾ inch wide
    Hammer
    Vise

What to do:

1. Check the latch-bolt action on the door to determine where the fault lies. In Figure 8 the latch bolt is too low to engage the opening in the strike plate.

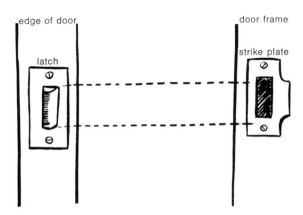

Figure 8. Latch bolt too low for strike opening

2. Remove the screws which hold the strike plate. Place the strike plate in a vise and file the bottom of the opening (Figure 9). Remove enough metal to permit the latch bolt to fall into place.

Figure 9. Filing bottom of the opening in strike plate

3. Replace the plate, then try the door. If necessary, remove the strike plate and chisel out a bit of wood from the bottom of the opening in the door frame.

Hint

It is often possible to enlarge a strike-plate hole without removing the plate from the door frame. Simply file it in place.

If the Latch Bolt is Too Short to Reach the Strike Plate

You will need:

> Screwdriver
> Utility knife
> Hard cardboard, about ⅛ inch thick
> Sharp pencil

What to do:

1. If necessary, file the opening in the strike plate so that it is aligned with the latch bolt.

2. Remove the strike plate and carefully trace around it on a piece of cardboard to make a shim. Place the cardboard on a piece of scrap wood or an old magazine, and with a utility knife, cut out the piece you have traced.

3. Replace the strike plate, with the cardboard shim behind it. Check the action of the latch bolt; if it still doesn't catch in the strike-plate opening, install a second shim, or even a third, if necessary.

Hint

After installing shims, you may find that the screws which hold the strike plate will be too short. Replace them with longer screws of the same diameter.

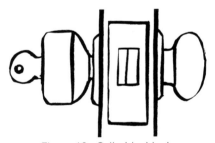

Figure 10. Cylindrical lock

DOOR LOCKS

The lock on your front door is a security device. Unfortunately, most door locks provide little or no security.

The most commonly used type is a *cylindrical lock* (Figure 10); the key fits directly into the knob. This is considered the least secure of all available lock types.

If your home is equipped with a key-in-the-knob lock and you are concerned about security, have a locksmith install a second lock. The best type in this case, and one of the strongest you can buy, is a lock that has a *vertical bolt* (Figure 11).

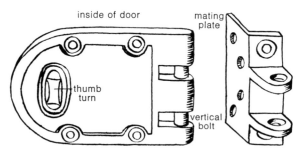

Figure 11. Vertical-bolt lock

Vertical-bolt locks are opened and closed from the outside with a key that fits into a *cylinder*. A thumb turn makes it possible to turn the lock from the inside.

If the lock is to be installed on a door with glass panes or thin wood panels, get one with a *double cylinder* (Figure 12). The second cylin-

Figure 12. Double-cylinder lock

der takes the place of the thumb turn on the inside of the lock. Should an intruder smash a door panel or somehow get an arm inside, he would probably be able to unlock the door by turning the thumb turn; but he would *not* be able to open a double-cylinder lock without the key for the inside cylinder.

Hang the key out of reach of the door, but within reach of every member of the family. Be sure everyone knows where the key is, and how to unlock the door in case you should have to get out of the house quickly during an emergency.

Hints

If your house *key fits loosely* in the lock and can be wiggled from side to side, the cylinder is worn; have it replaced by a locksmith. The cylinder should also be replaced if you can open the lock with the key only partly inserted.

If a *key breaks off* in a lock, try to grasp the broken end with needle-nose pliers or eyebrow tweezers; then pull it out. If you can't reach the broken part, call a locksmith.

A *key may stick* in a worn lock so that you can't pull it out. If you can't budge it by wiggling it gently and pulling at the same time, don't try to remove it with brute force; you may damage the cylinder. Call a locksmith, who can dismantle the lock and remove the key. If necessary, he will install a new cylinder.

To lubricate a lock, never use oil, for it will eventually deteriorate and become gummy. Also, oil can freeze solid during very cold weather. Lubricate stiff-working locks with powdered graphite, which comes in a squeeze tube. Hold the nozzle of the graphite container against the opening in the lock cylinder and squeeze it so that powder is blown into the lock. One good squeeze is enough; too much graphite can prevent a key from working properly.

Have you ever tried to use a key, and found that the lock was *frozen*? It's an easy problem to solve, provided you first heat the key with a match or cigarette lighter. (Since it's cold, you'll probably be wearing gloves, so the hot key won't burn your hand.) Gently insert the hot key into the lock. As soon as you can get part of the key in, apply more heat. Work the key in gradually. Reheat it so that it can melt the ice surrounding it, and you will be able to turn it in the cylinder.

INSTALLING A DOOR CHAIN

One of the simplest security devices is a door chain (Figure 13). It enables you to open the door wide enough to see and speak to someone outside, but it keeps the door chained until it is unbolted from the inside. Some types can be opened with a key from the outside. A door chain is screwed to the casing and to the door.

Figure 13. Door chain

What to do:

1 Drill pilot holes before driving in the screws. Use sheet-metal screws on metal casings and doors (see page 202).

2. Fasten the small unit (the one to which the chain is attached) to the casing. Slide the end of the chain into the slotted unit and pull it in the slot as far as it will go.

3. Position the slotted unit on the door, at the same height as the part already attached to the casing. With the door open about four inches, move the piece until the chain is taut. Fasten the slotted unit to the door at exactly that spot.

INSTALLING A PEEPHOLE

You can install a *peephole* in your front door to enable you to see someone outside without having to open the door (Figure 14). Buy one at a hardware store. Installation is simple.

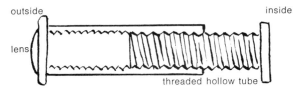

Figure 14. Peephole

What to do:

1. Between 4½ and 5 feet from the floor, drill a hole through the center of the door. (Manufacturer's directions will tell you what size drill to use.) The peephole unit consists of two sections.

2. Push the section with the lens through the drilled hole from the outside. Push the threaded tube into the hole from the inside.

3. Turn the tube clockwise until it is tight.

REPLACING A DOORKNOB

Replacement knobs come in all styles. They may be plain or fancy, and made of metal, glass, ceramic, or plastic. They are usually sold with matching spindles.

One commonly used type of door latch uses knobs which are attached to a threaded spindle and held in place by setscrews (Figure 15).

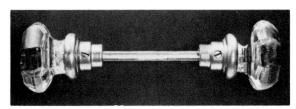

Figure 15. New doorknobs showing setscrews

You will need:

Doorknobs
Screwdriver

What to do:

1. Loosen the setscrew on one doorknob, and remove the knob by turning it counterclockwise. If it does not turn freely, remove the setscrew entirely.

2. Pull the knob-and-spindle assembly out of the door latch.

3. Thread one new doorknob onto the spindle, and tighten the setscrew. If both the new and the old spindles are the same size, it doesn't matter which one you use.

4. Push the spindle through the door latch, and thread on the other new knob. Tighten the setscrew.

Hints

Don't turn the new knobs up so far that they press against the door plate; this will prevent them from turning freely. If the knobs are too tight, loosen one setscrew, give the knob a quarter turn to the left, and retighten the setscrew.

REFINISHING BRASS DOORKNOBS

Brass doorknobs are attractive when they are new, but unfortunately they soon lose their neat, smart appearance. Normal usage wears off the lacquer coating that protects the metal finish underneath; or they may become spattered and smeared if they are not removed before doors are painted.

You can easily restore brass knobs to their original condition.

You will need:

Paint remover, any type
Paint thinner (mineral spirits)
Rubber or plastic gloves
Screwdriver
Old paintbrush, about 1 inch wide
Clear metal lacquer
Steel wool, any grade

What to do:

1. Remove the knobs from the door latch (see page 124). Unscrew and remove the flanges, the circular plates which fit between the knob and the door.

2. Some knobs and flanges can't be separated. Removing the screws from one of the flanges will free both knobs and spindle, enabling you to withdraw them from the door. (Figure 16.)

3. Put on rubber or plastic gloves. Coat the

Figure 16. Removing knob and flange unit

knobs, flanges, and screw heads with a thick layer of paint remover. Wait about ten minutes, then rub all the surfaces with steel wool. If the old paint or lacquer does not come off, apply another layer of paint remover, wait a few minutes, and rub again.

4. After all old paint has been removed, wash the pieces with paint thinner to remove all traces of paint remover.

5. Wipe each piece with a dry cloth, then polish it with clean steel wool. Rub hard to eliminate scratches; this will give the metal a soft, satiny finish. Brush or wipe each piece to get rid of any small bits of steel wool.

6. Fasten a wire to one of the pieces. Dip the piece into a container of clear metal lacquer. Hold it over the container to allow excess lacquer to drip off. Do the same with the other pieces, making sure you coat each knob, flange, and screw.

7. Place the partially dry pieces on a paper towel or newspaper, or better still, hang them up to dry. Don't touch freshly lacquered surfaces while they are drying or you'll leave fingermarks.

8. When everything has dried thoroughly (overnight), reassemble the knobs and flanges on the doors.

Hints

Lacquer protects the metal and prevents it from tarnishing. So long as the lacquer coating is unbroken, the knobs will stay new-looking.

If you remove knobs and flanges before painting a door, you can keep them in perfect condition.

ADJUSTING AN AUTOMATIC DOOR CLOSER

Automatic door-closing units are used on storm doors and screens. The unit consists of a cylinder and a piston (Figure 17). Regulating

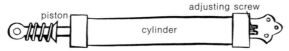

Figure 17. Automatic door-closing mechanism

the flow of air at one end of the cylinder controls the movement of the piston so that it can move rapidly or slowly.

Since the piston is connected to the door, its movement controls the door movement. If the piston moves rapidly, the door will close rapidly. If the piston moves slowly, the door will close slowly.

You will need:
>Screwdriver
>Light machine oil

What to do:

1. Find an air-relief hole near the end of the piston. Apply one or two drops of light machine oil to the hole, but *do not overoil!* Move the door back and forth a few times, distributing the oil throughout the cylinder.

2. Check the door movement; if it closes too rapidly and smashes against the door frame, cut down the amount of air passing through the cylinder by turning the adjusting screw clockwise. If the door now closes too slowly and does not latch properly, open the adjusting screw by turning it counterclockwise.

3. Find the correct position of the adjusting screw by experimenting; turn it either in or out, and try the door. When it closes slowly but firmly and clicks into place, that's the proper setting.

Hint

Lubricate storm and screen doors as you would any others. Apply one or two drops of oil to each hinge, and open and shut the door a few times to distribute the oil.

Repairing a Screen Door (see page 109).

WEATHERSTRIPPING A DOOR

Doors are weatherstripped on the outside. Some types, such as wood and vinyl weatherstripping, must be nailed in place.

What to do:

1. First close the door. Be sure it latches.

2. Cut lengths of weatherstripping to fit the sides and top of the door. Hold one piece on one side flat against the stop molding (the molding against which the door closes), and press it firmly against the door.

3. Using 1½-inch finishing nails, nail it to the stop molding.

4. Following the directions in Step 2, nail lengths of weatherstripping to the stop molding at the top and other side of the door frame.

5. Test the installation by opening and closing the door. It should latch firmly. You may have to use a little pressure in order to close it, but that makes for a good, tight, draft-free job.

Other types of weatherstripping have adhesive backs and don't require nailing. Simply unroll, cut to fit the required space, peel off the protective backing, and press into place. Be sure the surface against which you press the weatherstripping is clean; the adhesive will not stick to a dirty surface.

Some weatherstripping materials must be stapled or tacked into place. Use either brass or monel staples or copper tacks.

Hints

Self-adhesive weatherstripping materials are best for beginning do-it-yourselfers. They are available in a wide variety of materials, all of which are efficient.

You can buy heavy-duty vinyl weatherstripping for garage doors. If you have a heated, attached-to-a-house garage, and the door is not weatherstripped, nail or staple weatherstripping to the sides and bottom of the door to conserve heat.

7

FLOORS
The Beautiful Cover-ups

A floor can be the focal point of any room, depending on the floor treatment you choose. The many different materials available today for use as coverings make it possible for you to have a floor that is literally made-to-order. You can buy and lay tiles made of asphalt, vinyl, vinyl asbestos, cork, carpeting, or ceramics. Some tiles have self-adhesive backs and are merely pressed into place. Others must be laid on adhesive which is applied to the floor. Both types are easy to install.

Many modern, resilient tiles are patterned after old, traditional designs. Reproduced in vinyl, they are almost indistinguishable from the originals. Carpet tiles, some of which are self-adhesive, are available in many forms from flat indoor-outdoor types to high-pile shag carpets.

To make a waterproof, stainproof, easy-to-clean floor, consider laying down ceramic tiles. Many potteries are producing tiles that are exact reproductions of those found in historic châteaux and palaces. You can buy tiles singly or in sheets, depending on their size.

Unfortunately, everyone eventually has a problem with their flooring. It may simply be a loose floorboard that squeaks when you walk over it, a loose tile on the kitchen floor, or a rip or cigarette burn in a carpet. With a little experience, you will be able to solve these as well as other problems.

HOW TO FIX A SQUEAKY FLOOR

Squeaks are often the result of loose floorboards rubbing against each other. If you simply nail them down, the movement of the boards will soon loosen the nails, and they will work their way out of the wood. Floorboards must be *toenailed*: this means driving two nails into each loose board at opposite angles.

You will need:

Hammer
8d (eightpenny) finishing nails
Nail set
Hand or electric drill
3/32-inch twist drill
Putty stick to match the color of the floor
Shellac
Shellac thinner (alcohol)
Cotton swab or small, pointed brush
Chalk
Single-edged razor blade in holder

What to do:

1. If your squeaky floor is carpeted, you will have to pull up the carpeting first. Then make a chalk mark on the floor wherever a board squeaks. Drill two pilot holes at the chalk mark at a 45-degree angle, about two inches apart (see page 201). The holes should go through the floor and partly into the subfloor (Figure 1).

2. Drive an 8d finishing nail into each hole. Leave about ¼ inch of the head protruding above the floor. Use a nail set to sink the nailheads about ⅛ inch below the surface of the floor.

3. Fill each nail hole by rubbing a putty stick across it. Scrape off excess putty with a razor blade.

4. Use a cotton swab or small brush to coat each putty spot with shellac.

5. Clean the brush by rinsing it thoroughly in two clean changes of shellac thinner (alcohol).

Hints

As a temporary expedient, try dropping talcum powder between squeaky floorboards. Or spray between boards with silicone lubricant.

Various methods have been used to remedy squeaky stairs; but most of them don't work. There isn't anything you can do unless you have access to the understructure of the stairway, and usually this understructure is covered and inaccessible from everywhere but the cellar.

REFINISHING WOODEN FLOORS

The only way to salvage a badly scratched or discolored wooden floor is to remove the old finish. This is done by *scraping* it. Scraping in this case means sandpapering, done with a special floor-scraping machine.

Unless you are willing to risk ruining your floor completely, give the scraping job to a professional who will also coat the newly sanded floor with a special sealer. Then if you really want to have a hand in the floor-finishing process, give the floor a coat of polyurethane or epoxy-type finish.

Polyurethanes are used directly from the can. Epoxy finishes come in two cans whose contents must be mixed together just before use. The mixture has a short life, so it must be used soon after it is prepared or it will harden in the can.

Both types of finishes are extremely durable and will resist scuffing and scratching.

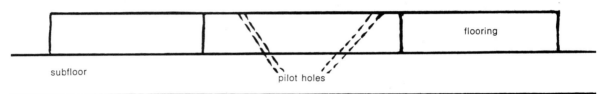

Figure 1. Pilot holes drilled through floor and partly into subfloor

PORCH AND PATIO FLOORS

Porch and patio floors that are exposed to the weather should be refinished with special porch-and-deck finishes. These are usually enamels that dry to a hard, lustrous finish. (See page 148 for preparation and painting.)

RESILIENT FLOOR TILES

Resilient floor tiles are squares of nonrigid floor-covering material which are available in a wide range of colors, textures, and designs. Today's tiles are designed for do-it-yourself installation and easy maintenance. And they make the floor as decorative and colorful as the rest of the room. The three most common types of tiles are made of asphalt, vinyl, and vinyl asbestos.

Asphalt tile is the oldest and least expensive type on the market. It requires a special, water-based adhesive, and can be polished only with water-soluble wax. These tiles are usually 9 x 9 inches in size, and are available only in marbleized grays and browns.

Vinyl-asbestos tile has largely supplanted asphalt tile, for it is more flexible and is available in many more colors, patterns, and embossed designs. These come in 9 x 9 and 12 x 12 inch sizes. Although it costs more than asphalt tile, vinyl-asbestos tile lasts longer because it is both abrasion- and burn-resistant.

Vinyl tile is the best of these three types of tile, but it is also the most expensive. In addition to being more durable than the other two, it is available in more varied patterns, colors, and textures. Some look exactly like elegant antique ceramic tiles. They are made in three sizes: 12 x 12 inches, 18 x 18 inches, and 36 x 36 inches.

There are, of course, many other types of floor tile. One of the most recent innovations is a no-wax vinyl with a specially coated surface that requires only minimum maintenance. Ask your dealer about what is presently available.

One of the most attractive characteristics of floor tiles in general is the ease with which they

can be installed. Although some tiles must be cemented to the floor with special adhesives, others are self-sticking. To install the latter, just peel off the protective backing and lay them on the floor. When buying tiles, it is a good idea to ask your dealer if there are any restrictions on the type of floor the tile will cover.

When laying tiles, it is often necessary to cut them to fit the room or to fit around a pipe, appliance, or irregular corner. All three common types of tile can be cut by scoring them with a sharp knife, then bending them so that they break at the scored line. Or cut them with a pair of scissors, tin snips, or a sharp utility knife. But don't try to cut tile if the temperature is below 65°F. The warmer the tile, the easier it is to cut and lay. Asphalt tiles are brittle at low temperatures and can easily crack. To prevent this, place them in a warm oven (set oven at lowest setting) for about one hour before they are to be used. Don't allow them to get so hot that they can't be handled.

The amount of maintenance required to keep tiles bright and clean is, of course, an important criterion when buying tiles. Many manufacturers supply information about the care of their tiles and recommend specially formulated cleaning products. Be sure to ask your dealer if such care booklets or special products are available.

How to Prepare a Floor for Tiling

You can usually lay tiles on any clean, smooth, unyielding surface (unless the particular tile is restricted to a specific use). Cover concrete, hardwood, plywood, or even old tiles and linoleum that are in good condition. Just be sure the surface is free of dirt and wax.

A smooth wooden floor with no loose boards can be prepared simply by covering it with a layer of *lining felt*. Tiles are then laid on top. Lining felt is made especially for this purpose and is sold in floor-covering stores. It is cemented down with a special adhesive.

Don't try to lay tiles directly over a bumpy wooden floor. Even if you should succeed in getting them to lie flat, they will wear rapidly at the floor's high spots, eventually showing the shape of every bump underneath. Floors of this type should first be covered with ½-inch plywood or hard, synthetic board called *underlayment*, which must be nailed down firmly. Tiles may then be cemented to the underlayment.

How to Measure and Determine the Number of Tiles You Will Need

Measure the length and width of the floor in feet. If you are using 12-inch square tiles, you need the same number of tiles as there are square feet in the floor. For example, to cover a 9 x 12 foot floor, you need 108 tiles. To this, add two or three tiles to allow for waste, giving you a total of 111 tiles.

Consult Figure 2 to determine how many tiles you will need in order to cover a given area. Always get at least six extra tiles (in addition to the two or three extra ones for immediate use), and keep them in reserve. You never know when you may have to replace a damaged tile.

HOW TO LAY A TILE FLOOR

You will need:

Resilient floor tiles
String, a few inches longer than the length of the floor
Chalk
Notched trowel
Carpenter's square (optional)
Hammer

SIZE OF AREA IN FEET	NO. OF 9'' x 9'' TILES	NO. OF 12'' x 12'' TILES	SIZE OF AREA IN FEET	NO. OF 9'' x 9'' TILES	NO. OF 12'' x 12'' TILES	SIZE OF AREA IN FEET	NO. OF 9'' x 9'' TILES	NO. OF 12'' x 12' TILES	SIZE OF AREA IN FEET	NO. OF 9'' x 9'' TILES	NO. OF 12'' x 12'' TILES
4 x 4	29	16	7 x 9	112	63	9 x 14	224	126	11 x 20	392	220
4 x 5	36	20	7 x 10	125	70	9 x 15	240	135	12 x 12	256	144
4 x 6	43	24	7 x 11	137	77	9 x 16	256	144	12 x 14	299	168
5 x 5	45	25	7 x 12	150	84	9 x 17	272	153	12 x 16	342	192
5 x 6	54	30	8 x 8	114	64	9 x 18	288	162	12 x 18	384	216
5 x 7	63	35	8 x 9	128	72	10 x 10	178	100	12 x 20	427	240
5 x 8	72	40	8 x 10	143	80	10 x 12	214	120	12 x 22	470	264
5 x 9	80	45	8 x 11	157	88	10 x 14	249	140	12 x 24	512	288
5 x 10	89	50	8 x 12	171	96	10 x 16	285	160	13 x 13	301	169
6 x 6	84	36	8 x 13	185	104	10 x 18	320	180	13 x 15	347	195
6 x 7	75	42	8 x 14	200	112	10 x 20	356	200	13 x 17	393	221
6 x 8	86	48	9 x 9	144	81	11 x 11	216	121	14 x 14	349	196
6 x 9	96	54	9 x 10	160	90	11 x 12	235	132	14 x 16	399	224
6 x 10	107	60	9 x 11	176	99	11 x 14	274	154	14 x 18	448	252
7 x 7	88	49	9 x 12	192	108	11 x 16	313	176	14 x 20	498	280
7 x 8	100	56	9 x 13	208	117	11 x 18	352	198	14 x 22	548	308

Figure 2. Number of tiles needed

6d (sixpenny) nail
Scissors
Pencil

What to do:

1. Find the center of one of the end walls. Drive a 6d nail halfway into the floor at this point, next to the wall. Tie one end of the string to the nail. Find the center of the opposite wall and mark this spot on the floor.

2. Rub chalk on the whole string, and then hold the free end directly over the mark on the floor. Stretch the string taut and snap it to make a chalk line that divides the room exactly in half.

3. Mark the center of the chalk line. Lay the carpenter's square on the line at this point, and make a pencil line on the floor that is perpendicular (at right angles) to the chalk line. If you do not have a carpenter's square, use a couple of new tiles as guides for marking the perpendicular.

4. Now take one end of the chalked string and go to one of the side walls. Have someone stand at the opposite wall, holding the other end of the string. Move the string into position directly over the perpendicular line and snap a second chalk line onto the floor, from side wall to side wall; the floor is now divided into four equal parts.

5. Lay a row of tiles along the perpendicular line; this will help to adjust the guideline. Begin at a side wall, and lay tiles up to the first chalk line you made (Figure 3). There will

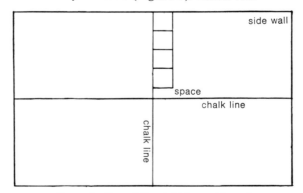

Figure 3. Row of tiles laid from side wall

probably be a space between the last tile and the chalk line that will be narrower than the width of one tile. If there is such a space, you will have to relocate the chalk line, so that it coincides with the edge of the last tile (Figure 4). Have your assistant hold one end of the chalked string while you stretch the other end, and snap a new line onto the floor.

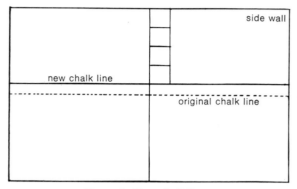

Figure 4. New chalk line

6. Next lay a row of tiles from an end wall up to the perpendicular chalk line (Figure 5). If necessary, relocate this line also so that it falls exactly at the edge of the tile.

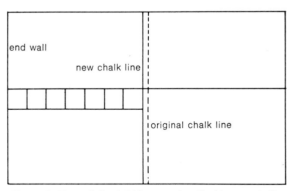

Figure 5. Row of tiles laid from end wall with new chalk line

You have now made whatever adjustments are necessary to assure that the tiles on the finished floor will be properly centered. Pick up the loose tiles that you used for this purpose and put them aside with the others for the time being.

7. Using a notched trowel, apply adhesive to one half of the floor. Don't use a trowel with a smooth edge; this will lay down an uneven layer of adhesive, whereas a notched trowel controls the amount of adhesive deposited. Avoid applying too much adhesive; it will only be squeezed up between tiles and stain them. Consult the directions on the container to determine how long you must wait, after applying the adhesive, before you can lay down the tiles.

8. Now place a tile *exactly* at the point where the two chalk lines cross, and press it against the floor. Continue to lay tiles on the prepared floor, working from the center toward the walls. Fill in one quarter of the floor at a time. Butt the edges of the tiles firmly together *before* you press them down. Don't slide them sideways after they have been laid or you'll force adhesive up between them.

9. Now apply adhesive to the other half of the floor, and wait the required time before you lay the tiles.

10. Cut pieces to fill narrow spaces between the full tiles and the walls. Place the tile to be cut *directly* on top of the one in the last row laid. Use another tile as a guide by placing it on top of the tile to be cut, with its edge pressed against the wall. Run a pencil line along its opposite edge, marking the tile beneath (Figure 6). Cut the marked tile with

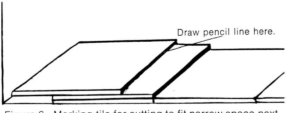

Figure 6. Marking tile for cutting to fit narrow space next to wall

scissors, and it will now fit snugly into the space between the full tile next to it and the wall.

Hint

If you are using tiles that must be cemented

down, be sure to get the proper adhesive. Follow the manufacturer's directions; some adhesives must be allowed to dry until they are no longer tacky, while others must be used as soon as they are applied.

REPLACING LOOSE OR BROKEN FLOOR TILES

A tile may become badly stained, cracked, gouged, or otherwise in need of replacement. If it is loose, simply lift it up with a putty knife. If it is firmly cemented down, heat it with a hot iron with a cloth under it, an electric paint remover, or a heat lamp. This will soften both tile and cement, making it easy for you to scoop up the tile with a putty knife or scraper.

You will need:

> Putty knife or paint scraper
> Contact cement or floor-tile adhesive
> Stiff cardboard, about 3 x 5 inches

What to do:

1. Remove the loose or broken tile. Use the putty knife or paint scraper to remove all dried adhesive from both the floor and the bottom of the tile.

2. You may have some leftover adhesive from a recent job. If so, use the cardboard to apply a coating not more than ⅛ inch thick to the floor. Be careful not to spread any on the edges of adjoining tiles. Wait until the adhesive is ready; the exact time is given on the container. Never lay a tile on fresh adhesive unless manufacturer's directions tell you to.

(When using contact cement, apply a thin coating to both the underside of the tile and the floor. Wait until it feels slightly tacky.)

3. Drop the tile into place; step on it to press it down evenly.

Hint

Don't use anything but the approved adhesive when replacing asphalt tile. The wrong type may soften the tile.

CERAMIC TILES

Ceramic tiles are made of fired clay in many different sizes, colors, and textures. They may be glazed or unglazed, with mat, semi-mat, crystalline, or glossy surfaces.

The smallest tiles are about ⅜ inch square and are usually glued to an open mesh backing; they are sold in one-foot square sheets. Larger tiles may be similarly backed, or sold singly in sizes from 4 to 12 square inches.

Tiling surfaces

Tiles can be laid on any smooth, dry, unyielding surface. This includes painted or bare wallboard, resilient tiles in good condition, plywood, plastic bonded to plywood, plaster, concrete, and firm wooden floorboards. You can even lay new ceramic tiles over old ceramic ones.

How tiles are applied

Tiles are cemented in place with a mastic adhesive. This is spread with a notched trowel which deposits an even coating on the surface to be tiled. Tiles are then pressed into place against the tacky cement. It is not necessary to remove the mesh backing from sheet tiles before cementing them in place.

Grout, a plasterlike mixture, is packed into the spaces between the tiles (see page 63). After excess grout is wiped off, polish the tiles with a clean cloth.

HOW TO CUT CERAMIC TILE

Small tiles can be easily cut with a *tile nipper*, which looks like a pair of end-cutting pliers.

You will need:

Tile nippers
Pencil

What to do:

1. Mark a pencil line on the tile, showing where it is to be cut. Place the open jaws of the nippers on the line and squeeze the handle If the line is too far in from the edge, it may be necessary to nibble away at the tile (Figure 7).

Figure 7. Tile nippers cutting up to line

2. Cut curves by nibbling away small bits at a time (Figure 8).

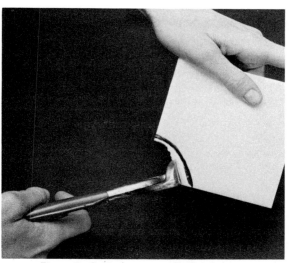
Figure 8. Cutting a curve with tile nippers

Hints

If you have a large number of tiles to be cut, it might be worth your while to rent a commercial *tile cutter* from your dealer. This tool, designed to make straight cuts on tiles, is practically foolproof.

You can use ceramic tile to cover a tabletop (see page 62) or to resurface a fireplace hearth or entrance foyer. Installation methods are identical to those used when applying tile to any other surface.

RECEMENTING A LOOSE CERAMIC TILE

You will need:

Paint scraper or putty knife
Contact cement
Tongue depressor, ice-cream stick,
   or wood scrap
Grout
Paper cup
Clean cloths

What to do:

1. Use the tongue depressor to pry the loose tile away from the floor. Don't work too hard trying to remove it; if real force is needed, it isn't loose at all—it needs regrouting.

2. Use a pencil to mark the back of the tile so that you can replace it in the same position.

3. Scrape all the old adhesive from the back of the tile. Using contact cement, coat the back of the tile and the floor area into which it fits. Wait three to five minutes, then press the tile into place in its original position.

4. Mix a small amount of grout in the paper cup and regrout the spaces around the tile (see page 63).

Hints

You can use ceramic-tile adhesive instead of contact cement.

Follow the same procedure when replacing a missing tile. First find one to match the others on your floor and try it in place to be sure it fits. Then apply cement, press into place, and grout.

REGROUTING TILES

Old grout sometimes crumbles, particularly after having been subjected to moisture over a long period of time. This leaves spaces that can lead to serious troubles. Moisture can seep in between tiles, weakening the structure and sometimes providing a haven for termites. Such a surface should be regrouted.

You will need:

Grout
Paper cup
Tongue depressors, ice-cream sticks,
   or wood scraps
Grouter
Soft cloths
Beer-can opener

What to do:

1. Using the pointed end of the can opener, probe vigorously between tiles to remove all loose grout.

2. Mix grout in the paper cup (see page 63). With a tongue depressor, ice-cream stick, or wood scrap, transfer some grout from the cup to the floor. Use the grouter to force the grout into all spaces between tiles.

3. Dampen a cloth and wipe off excess grout.

4. Polish the tiles with a clean, soft cloth.

CARPET TILES

Carpet tiles are 12-inch–square pieces of carpet, available in many different colors, patterns, and textures. Some are designed for either indoor or outdoor use, while others must be used indoors exclusively. Some tiles have self-sticking backs; others must be cemented in place. Another type has no adhesive on its back, but seems to grip the floor when it is laid. You can lift it easily, but you can't slide it on the floor without a great deal of difficulty. Most carpet tiles have padded backs.

Lay self-sticking carpet tiles exactly as you would resilient floor tiles (see page 130).

Hints

Since carpet tiles are 12 inches square, the number of square feet in your floor is equal to the number of tiles you will need to cover it (see page 130).

Use a sharp, single-edged razor blade in a holder or a utility knife to cut carpet tiles. Since the carpeting will not unravel, you can cut in any direction.

Though you can cut through the face of the carpet tiles, the simplest way to cut them is from the back. Tiles with deep piles, however, call for special handling: first part the individual fibers; then cut through the backing of the tile—not through the pile fibers on the face.

REPAIRING A HOLE IN A CARPET

Use either of the two following methods to repair holes, burns, or tears from which the threads have *unraveled*.

Working from the Front of the Carpet

Work from the front of the carpet if you want to do a quick repair job or if the damage has occurred near the center of the rug.

You will need:

> Liquid latex
> Single-edged razor blade in holder
> Scissors
> Stick for applying latex
> Piece of matching carpet

What to do:

1. With the razor blade, remove the damaged area by cutting a square or rectangular area out of the carpet. Cut from the front. If you have a shag or high-pile carpet, separate the pile so that you can cut through the carpet backing without severing the fibers of the pile. Lift out the section you have cut.

2. Lay a piece of matching carpet on the one you are repairing. Turn it so that the piles of both carpets face in the same direction. If they don't, one will appear darker than the other.

3. Cut a plug from the matching piece to fit the hole in the carpet. Use the cut-out piece as a pattern, tracing around it so the new piece will be exactly the same size as the hole.

4. Drop a little latex cement into the hole opening and spread it so that the padding under the carpet and the edges of the cut-out section are coated.

Figure 9. Spreading latex on back of carpet plug

5. Next coat the back of the carpet plug with latex (Figure 9) and place it carefully into the cut-out hole, taking care not to get latex on the carpet fibers. Press it into place. If you have followed directions, the repair will not be noticeable.

Working from the Back of the Carpet

You can make a stronger repair if you turn the carpet over and work from the back. This is easy to do if the damaged area is near the edge of the carpet—simply fold the edge over to expose the back. If the edge is tacked down, pry up the tacks with a screwdriver or putty knife. To remove the edge of a carpet from a "tackless" installation, pry it up with a screwdriver.

When the damaged area is in the center of the rug, you'll have to remove all the furniture to get at it. (To avoid this, you may prefer cutting and installing a carpet plug from the front, as previously described.)

Gather together the materials listed above.

You will also need:
> Seaming tape
> Stiff cardboard, about 3 x 5 inches
> Scissors

What to do:

1. Cut out the damaged area (see step 1, above), and turn the carpet over, exposing the back of the cut-out hole.

2. Cut a strip of seaming tape long enough to overlap the cut-out section by about 3 inches on each side.

3. Apply a liberal coat of latex to the back of the carpet around the hole. Press the tape over the hole.

4. Turn carpet over, face up, and proceed as on page 135, cutting a matching carpet plug, applying latex to the opening and the plug, and inserting the plug (Figure 10).

Figure 10. Inserting carpet plug

Hints

You can buy liquid latex at most carpet stores in either pour-spout cans and plastic containers or pressurized spray cans.

A coat of latex applied to the back of a throw rug will prevent it from sliding underfoot. Allow the latex to dry before turning the rug face up.

REPAIRING A TORN CARPET

Use the following technique to repair clean tears, from which no threads are missing.

You will need:

    Seaming tape
    Scissors
    Liquid latex
    Stiff cardboard, about 3 x 5 inches

What to do:

1. Turn the carpet over, exposing the back of the torn area.

2. Cut a piece of seaming tape about 4 inches longer than the tear.

3. Use the cardboard to spread a coat of latex over the side of the tape that has threads sewn to it (Figure 11).

Figure 11. Spreading latex on thread side of seaming tape

4. Apply a coat of latex to the area of the carpet back that will be covered by the seaming tape.

5. Press the latex-coated side of the tape against the carpet back, covering the tear.

6. Turn the carpet right side up. Push the torn edges together, and at the same time, press the repaired area against the seaming tape underneath. Maintain the pressure for about five minutes, to give the latex a chance to set.

Hint

If it is not possible to turn the carpet over in order to work on the back, try this: carefully separate the torn edges; then coat each edge of the carpet backing with latex, taking care not to get any on the carpet pile. Squeeze the edges of the tear together while simultaneously pressing down on them. Continue to exert this pressure for about five minutes, or long enough for the latex to set and cement everything together.

CARPET AND FLOOR-TILE EDGING

Metal strips, or edgings, are used to protect the edges of floor coverings when they are exposed in doorways. They are usually sold in strips 3 feet long, and come with matching nails or screws. Indentations or holes indicate where the nails or screws are to be inserted.

How to Install Carpet or Floor-Tile Edging

You will need:

> Metal edging
> Screws or nails to match the edging
> Screwdriver or hammer
> Push drill or hand drill
> Tin snips or hacksaw
> Steel tape

What to do:

1. Measure the door opening and with tin snips or a hacksaw, cut the edging to fit (Figure 12).

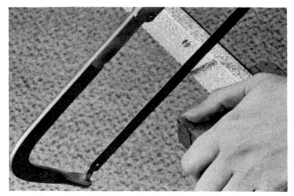

Figure 12. Cutting metal edging with hacksaw

2. Lay the edging in the doorway so that it covers the edge of the floor covering. Figure 13 shows edging that covers carpeting in one room and tile in the adjoining room.

Figure 13. Metal edging strip covering edges of carpet and tiles

3. Use a hand drill or push drill to make pilot holes slightly smaller in diameter than the nails or screws that are to hold the edging down (see page 167).

4. Starting at one end of the strip, insert the nails or the screws in the places indicated.

COVERING STAIRS

Carpet Runners

One way to cover old, worn stairs is to install a carpet runner. Runners make stairs softer, quieter, and safer.

You will need:

> Carpet runner long enough to cover stairway
> Magnetic hammer and No. 6 carpet tacks or staple gun and staples
> Single-edged razor blade in holder

What to do:

1. Measure the depth of the stair tread and the height of the riser to determine how much carpet you need. Give the dealer these measurements, and tell him the number of steps you wish to cover; he'll sell you the proper length of carpeting.

2. Runners are often installed with just one row of tacks or staples on each step at the point where the tread and the riser meet (Figure 14). Begin at the top step. Fasten the runner to the top of the riser with a row of tacks or staples.

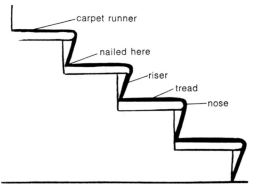

Figure 14. Installing a carpet stair runner

3. Pull it down firmly and fasten it where the tread and riser meet. Stretch the runner over the tread, pull it down firmly and evenly, tacking or stapling it to the same meeting place of tread and riser on the step underneath.

4. Work your way down the stairs, attaching the carpet at each step. When you reach the bottom, fasten the carpet to the bottom of the riser, then cut it off even with the floor.

Preformed Treads and Risers

Made of rubber, vinyl, rubber-backed fabric, or vinyl and fabric, preformed treads and risers really simplify stair-covering. They are available either as separate treads and risers or as a combination of the two, and are usually used in playrooms, basements, and on back stairs. Fastening methods vary, so consult your dealer for specific information.

Bullnose Moldings

Another way to cover stair treads is by the combined use of bullnose moldings (Figure 15) and resilient floor tiles. The moldings are available in extruded aluminum or plastic.

You will need:

> Molding for each step
> Hacksaw
> Electric or hand drill
> Pilot drill
> Screwdriver
> Floor tiles of vinyl asbestos or vinyl
> Floor-tile adhesive
> Notched trowel

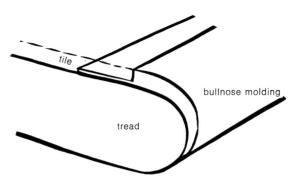

Figure 15. Bullnose molding

What to do:

1. Measure the stair width and use the hacksaw to cut molding to fit the width of each stair.

2. Press the molding into place against the nose of the stair tread.

3. Drill a pilot hole at each of the prepared screw holes. Use soap to lubricate the screws, which are usually furnished with moldings, and drive them through the holes. Install a molding at each step.

4. Cut tiles to fit the stair treads. The front edge of the tile should fit snugly against the molding; the rear should fit against the riser.

5. Using a notched trowel, apply floor-tile adhesive to each stair tread. Allow the adhesive to dry for the recommended time, then lay the tiles in place.

Figure 16. Bullnose molding installed on stairs

Another type of bullnose molding is inserted *over* the tiles (Figure 16). With this type, the tiles are laid first and then the molding is pushed over the edge of the stair tread and screwed into place as above.

Hints

Carpet runners are all 27 inches wide; this is standard throughout the carpeting industry.

In addition to carpet runners, preformed pieces, and moldings, you can use stair pads. These are carpet rectangles bound with a decorative brass strip. Attach them to stair treads with brass nails.

You can cover the stair risers with tiles, too. Or use self-sticking carpet squares.

8

HOUSE PAINTING
Indoor and Outdoor Magic

A fresh coat of paint serves two important functions: first, it can brighten a drab house and change the character of a room completely. In addition to this cosmetic effect, paint also serves as a wood preserver. Outdoors, unpainted wood can dry out, shrink, split, warp, or even rot. Paint fills wood pores, forming a waterproof, dirtproof seal that withstands heat and cold. Indoors, periodic painting provides a sanitary, washable surface.

Thanks to modern paints and equipment, it is simple to do your own painting. Most paints are odorless, and they dry quickly without streaks. You can paint a room a day, or even just one ceiling, leaving walls and woodwork for another time. Outdoors, you can work your way around the house by painting one side or one window each day.

Plan your work carefully. Gather all the materials you will need to prepare the surface to be painted, and buy the proper paint and painting equipment. Paint is available in stores in every conceivable tint and shade. Or you can make your selection from a dealer's color chart and he will probably be able to mix it for you right then and there. He will also clamp the can of paint into a vibrating machine and shake it up so that you won't have to do any stirring. (*Note:* some paints should only be stirred— never shaken.) You'll need both a brush and a roller. Use the brush to paint woodwork and the roller for large flat areas such as ceilings and walls.

Painting Interiors

Using a Ladder Safely

In order to paint ceilings and the upper parts of walls and windows, you will need a ladder. Don't stand on a stepstool, wooden crate, or anything else—use a stepladder that opens like a large letter A and has a platform on which you can place your paint container.

Never stand on the top of a ladder. If your ladder is so short that you must stand on top in order to reach the ceiling, borrow or buy another one. A six-foot ladder is perfect for indoor work.

Don't use a ladder unless it is in good condition. It should stand solidly when it is open, and support your weight without swaying. If you are planning to buy a ladder, get an aluminum one; it's lighter and stronger than those made of wood.

Be sure the two halves of the ladder are fully extended before you use it. A partially open ladder is unstable and dangerous.

Always remove the paint container from the ladder before you move the ladder to another location.

Never reach so far from a ladder that you lose your balance. Be safe: move the ladder instead of reaching.

Types of Interior Paint

Oil-base paints

Oil paints form a tough finish that can last for years. They usually contain linseed oil, and must be thinned with either paint thinner (mineral spirits) or turpentine.

However, there are some things you must know if you plan to use oil paints. You can't paint over a surface unless it is absolutely dry; even the slightest trace of moisture can cause the paint to blister. Never paint outdoors on a damp day. If the weather forecast predicts rain, hold off. If it starts to rain while you are painting, stop! Moisture and oil paints just don't go together. Wait until the sun shines, and the surface is absolutely dry.

Cleaning up oil paints can be a messy job. Brushes must be rinsed in two changes of paint thinner, then cleaned with soap and water (see page 46). Clean your hands with a cloth dipped in paint thinner, then with soap and water. *Dispose of all rags at once if they have either thinner or paint on them.* Place them in a covered, metal trash container. Otherwise, they are a fire hazard.

Water-base paints

Modern water-base paints are highly recommended for both indoor and outdoor work. You can do a professional job even if you have never painted anything before. With a few exceptions, tough, acrylic-latex paints can be used for practically all purposes. Unlike oil paints, you can apply them over damp surfaces. Spills and spots can be wiped up with a wet cloth, but don't wait too long to do it, as the paint dries in about a half hour. Best of all is the easy cleanup. You can clean yourself and your tools with warm, soapy water.

How Much Paint to Buy

Measure the width and height of each wall to be painted and multiply the two figures to get the total number of square feet in the room. Paint cans are marked to show the number of square feet that the contents of the can will cover. Count the number of windows and doors, and consult your paint dealer to determine the amount of paint needed for trim.

Whether painting indoors or outdoors, always be sure to read the instructions on the can.

Preparing a Room for Painting

Remove draperies, curtains, window shades, paintings, mirrors, and removable shelves. Cover large, in-place mirrors with an old sheet or taped-on newspaper. Remove picture hooks unless mirrors or pictures are to be rehung in the same place. In short, leave the walls bare.

Remove all doorknobs and flanges (see pages 124-125).

Remove as much furniture as possible by stacking pieces in another room. Heavy, non-removable furniture can be moved to the center of the room. Cover both the furniture and the floor with cloth, paper, or plastic drop-cloths.

PREPARING A PAINTED SURFACE

This consists of repairing all cracks in the ceiling and walls, and removing any loose or heavily built-up layers of paint.

You will need:

> **Paint knife**
> **Beer-can opener**
> **Ready-to-use spackle**
> **Paint scraper**
> **Sandpaper, medium grade**
> **Electric paint remover or liquid paint remover**
> **Paintbrush, any size**
> **Rubber gloves or heavy canvas gloves**

What to do:

1. Use the pointed tip of the can opener to scrape all loose materials from a crack. Dip a brush into water and wet the crack thoroughly. With a paint knife, force spackle into the crack. Smooth it, making it even with the surface of the ceiling or wall.

2. After the spackle has dried, sandpaper the area so that it blends with the surrounding surface. Also use spackle to fill spaces in door and window casing joints.

3. Remove old paint. You may encounter areas on woodwork that are thickly encrusted with dried, hard paint. This not only looks unsightly, but it may also prevent doors and windows from closing properly. It's not a good idea to apply more paint to an already messy area.

The easiest way to remove old paint is by using an electric paint remover. This is nothing more than an enclosed heating element with a handle.

Hold the tool, element side up, and plug it into the nearest outlet. If you use an extension cord to reach the outlet, it must be heavy enough to conduct the current needed to heat the tool. For distances up to 50 feet, you need a cord with No. 14 wire. From 50 to 100 feet, use a cord with No. 12 wire.

Put on a pair of heavy gloves, such as you might use for gardening, to protect your hands from radiated heat and any hot, spattering paint.

When the element is red-hot, turn it face down with the element next to the area to be scraped (Figure 1). Hold it there for a moment, then move it slowly. Follow about an inch behind the paint remover with a paint scraper. The paint will come off easily.

Figure 1. Electric paint remover

If the paint starts to burn, you are probably moving the tool too slowly. On the other hand, if the paint is hard to scrape off, you are moving the tool too rapidly. (NOTE: Keep a container of water handy when using an electric paint remover. You never know when a bit of burning paint may fall on a flammable surface.)

If you don't have an electric paint remover, use liquid paint remover; be sure to wear rubber gloves (see page 44).

Preparing a Wallpapered Surface

It is not advisable to try to paint over wallpaper. The seams will inevitably show, particularly if they had been overlapped when the paper was hung. Any loose areas of paper will swell and come away from the wall when paint is applied. Frequently, too, the red pigments in wallpaper will "bleed" through paint.

Remove all old wallpaper (see page 74), and sandpaper the wall to remove paper scraps. Then size the wall and allow it to dry before painting.

APPLYING PAINT

Use acrylic-latex paint. Flat paints are generally used on ceilings and walls. The only difference between ceiling and wall paints is that wall paints are made to be scrubbed, while ceiling paints are not. On woodwork, use either flat wall paint, or semi-gloss enamel.

You will need:

Acrylic-latex ceiling paint
Acrylic-latex wall paint
Acrylic-latex semi-gloss enamel
    for woodwork (optional)
9-inch paint roller and tray
2- or 3-inch nylon paintbrush for
    woodwork
Small corner roller or pad (optional)
Roller extension handle
Masking tape

What to do:

1. *Paint the ceiling first.* Set up the ladder near a wall, making it possible for you to reach the edge of the ceiling without stretching.

2. Pour about 1 inch of paint into the deep portion of the paint tray. Paint a strip about 3 inches wide all around the edge of the ceiling. Use either a brush, a small offset roller to reach into corners, or a paint pad made for painting the edges of ceilings and walls.

3. You can paint the rest of the ceiling without using the ladder. Screw the extension into the handle of the roller. This will enable you to reach the ceiling while standing on the floor.

4. Fill the deep portion of the paint tray. Dip the roller into the paint, then roll it on the upper part of the tray to distribute the paint evenly (Figure 2).

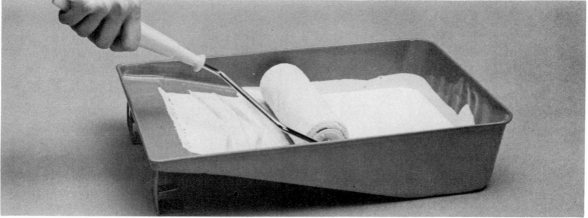

Figure 2. Distributing paint evenly on roller in paint tray

5. Press the roller *lightly* against the ceiling, and roll it in all directions, at random, so that paint will be deposited in an even layer (Figure 3). Roll slowly! The faster you go, the more the paint will spatter. After a few strokes, the roller will have given up all its paint, so you'll have to dip it into the paint tray once more.

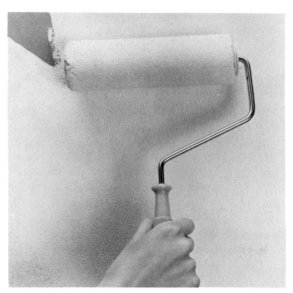

Figure 3. Rolling paint on ceiling

The paint should dry within an hour. If it is streaked or uneven, apply another coat.

6. *Next do the walls.* Paint a band about 3 inches wide, all around the top edges of the walls, in the corners, and next to the baseboard. Use the same equipment as that used for painting the edge of the ceiling.

7. Roll paint on the walls with the same slow strokes that you used on the ceiling.

8. *Do the woodwork last.* Paint in this order: baseboards, doors, door trim, windows. If the woodwork is to be painted in a different color from the walls or with a different kind of paint, *mask the walls.* Wait until the wall paint dries, then apply a band of masking tape to the wall wherever it meets the woodwork. You can then paint the woodwork without smearing the walls. After the woodwork has dried, peel off the tape.

9. When painting windows, follow a definite sequence: upper sash, lower sash, casing. The numbers in Figure 4 indicate the order in which different parts of the window should be painted. For example, paint all edges marked 1 first, then those marked 2, 3, etc. If you follow this system, you are not likely to omit any edges.

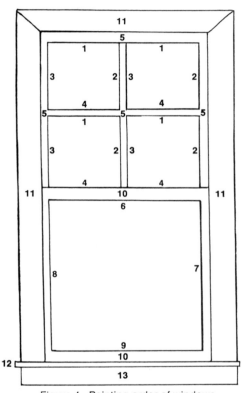

Figure 4. Painting order of windows

If you aren't too steady with a paintbrush, apply masking tape to the glass, right next to the window woodwork (Figure 5). Then paint without a care. After the paint has dried, simply peel off and discard the tape.

Don't shut windows all the way after they have been painted, or else they may get stuck in place. Leave them open about one inch on the top and bottom.

10. Wash rollers, trays, and brushes with warm, soapy water. (There are special liners you can buy to line roller trays and make cleaning up easier.)

Figure 5. Protecting window pane with masking tape

11. Store partially filled paint cans upside down. Before you turn a can over, replace the lid, then stand on it. Your weight will force the lid into place, making a tight seal.

Summary of steps involved in indoor painting:
Remove everything from walls; leave them bare.
Remove doorknobs and flanges.
Remove or cover furniture.
Cover the floor.
Repair cracks.
Remove old paint.
Paint ceiling, walls, and woodwork, in that order.
Clean brushes and rollers.

Hints
For a supersmooth job, apply two coats of spackle to cracks. Sandpaper between coats, and after the second coat.

Two coats of paint are a good investment. Sometimes a single coat will appear to be enough, only to show streaks later on. Always use two coats when covering a dark wall with light paint.

For uneven ceilings, use sand paint. This paint actually contains sand, and it dries with a textured finish that helps hide irregularities.

For interesting color effects, why not antique the doors and woodwork in a room to harmonize with your furniture? (See pages 56-58 for antiquing directions.)

Remove paint from window glass with a single-edged razor blade in a holder. Allow the paint to dry first. Never attempt to wipe or scrape off wet paint; it will smear.

Painting Exteriors

It's easier to maintain a house in good condition if it is painted regularly. This needn't be done every year; you can judge when repainting is needed. If the old paint has cracked, peeled, blistered, or worn down to the bare wood, you have waited too long. The idea is to repaint before the house begins to look shabby. If you paint over a surface in good condition, you can probably do a fine job with one coat of paint. If you put it off too long, you will have to use two coats; this means twice the work, twice the amount of paint, and twice the expense.

Houses exposed to extremes of weather need painting more often than those in sheltered areas. If you live on the seacoast and your home is constantly scoured by abrasive, sand-bearing winds, you may have to freshen up the exterior paint every couple of years.

On the other hand, a well-maintained house in another area might not need repainting for as long as ten years.

Safety—Know How to Use a Ladder Outdoors
Painting outdoors always involves the use of a ladder. Use a small extension ladder for painting siding (exterior walls). Aluminum ladders are light, and can be handled easily, whereas a wooden ladder can be quite heavy. Don't try to raise one against the house or move it by yourself. Get someone to help.

In most cases you can do very nicely with a stepladder or one half of an extension ladder. The only time you will need both halves of an extension ladder is when painting the peak of a house, near the roof. Unless you are accustomed to working on ladders, don't do it yourself; get someone to help you. And if necessary, pay to have it done.

Be very careful when moving a tall ladder. *Under no circumstances must a ladder touch a power line!* Metal ladders (or damp wooden ones) can conduct enough current to kill you, particularly if you are standing on wet ground.

Stand a ladder on a firm, even surface, and lean the top against the siding. Look out for soft spots in grassy areas; one ladder foot can sink, causing the whole thing to shift sideways. If necessary, place a board under one foot to even things up so that the ladder stands vertically. If you feel insecure on a ladder, even though you aren't far off the ground, have someone hold it while you are working.

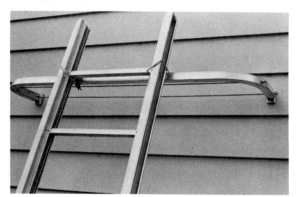

Figure 6. Ladder stabilizer

You can buy a *ladder stabilizer*. This is a 50-inch wide, U-shaped piece that you clamp to the top of the ladder to help keep it steady (Figure 6). The two arms can bridge a window, enabling you to paint it without having to lean far over to one side.

Figure 7. Adjustable ladder step

Another handy accessory is an adjustable *ladder step* that can be attached to any rung (Figure 7). If you know where you are going to stand when painting a particular area, attach the step so that you can work comfortably.

Clothing

Wear expendable clothing when painting. No matter how skillful you may be, you are bound to get some paint on you. Coveralls, slacks, or shorts are acceptable. Use a cap or scarf to keep paint out of your hair, and wear rubber-soled shoes. Avoid shoes with heels, flimsy sandals, or any slick-soled shoes that might slip on a ladder rung.

Types of Exterior Paint

House paints are made for siding, or exterior walls. *Trim paints* are used on doors, windows, shutters, and decorative woodwork. Some companies make house paints that are suitable for both siding and trim; read the label on the can.

Primers are special paints designed to seal surfaces and provide good adhesion for a second, final coat of paint. You must use a primer on bare wood or metal, or on a painted surface that has worn thin.

As a rule, use the same type of paint that has previously been used on your house. If you don't know what kind of paint you are covering, prime it before applying the finishing coat. A properly primed and painted surface can outlast an unprimed one by at least five years.

Self-cleaning paints don't actually clean themselves, but they retain their original brightness for a long time. As the paint ages, its surface becomes chalky. This loose powder is washed away by rain, exposing a fresh paint surface. The paint coat becomes thinner as chalking continues.

Use this type of paint only if the entire house—siding and trim—is painted the same color. Don't use self-cleaning paint on the upper half of a house if the lower part is unpainted brick or shingle. If you do, the lower part will become streaked wherever the old paint washes down the side of the house.

Check the paint you buy; its characteristics are shown on the container.

Suggested Paints for Special Uses

You can't use the same paint for everything. Some paints are specially formulated for different surfaces, as shown in Figure 8.

USE	TYPE OF PAINT RECOMMENDED
Wood siding (exterior walls)	Acrylic-latex house paint. If unpainted or previously oil-painted, use primer first.
Wood shingles	Exterior shingle stain. On previously oil-painted or bare shingles, use acrylic-latex primer and house paint.
Cedar, cypress, or redwood shakes (large, hand-split shingles)	Shakes should not be painted. Use special clear preservative. Allow them to weather to a silvery gray.
Asbestos shingles	Acrylic-latex house paint. If extra coverage is needed, use a primer first.
Redwood siding and furniture	Clear or tinted oil-base or acrylic-latex redwood finish.
Masonry and brick siding	If unpainted, use special masonry paint or acrylic-latex primer and house paint. On oil-painted surfaces, use oil paint or acrylic-latex primer and house paint.
Trim	Acrylic-latex trim paint.
Concrete floors	Epoxy concrete enamel, polyurethane concrete finish, or rubber-base concrete paint.
Wood fences	Any house or trim paint.
Metal fences	Use special primer on bare metal; finish with rust-inhibiting aluminum paint.
Metal play equipment	Rust-inhibiting primer and enamel

Figure 8. Type of paint to use

PREPARING THE EXTERIOR SURFACE

Just as in interior painting, you must prepare the exterior surface before you begin. Remove loose paint, blisters, mildew, and dirt. Caulk all cracks. Scrape out and remove old, brittle caulking and recaulk (see pages 150-151).

Remember to cover foundation plantings and concrete walks when painting outdoors. Use a dropcloth made of paper, plastic, or cloth. It's almost impossible to remove unsightly paint after it has dried.

You will need:

Paint knife or scraper
Sandpaper, medium grit
Old paintbrush, any size
Caulking compound and gun
**Electric paint remover or liquid
    paint remover**
Liquid laundry bleach
Gloves (rubber, plastic, or canvas)

What to do:

1. Prepare one small area at a time, just before you paint it. For example, prepare and paint one window, then move on to the next window.

2. Scrape off loose paint and blisters with a paint knife or a wood scraper, whichever works better. If neither tool does the trick, remove old paint in bad condition with an electric paint remover (see page 141). (Use liquid paint remover if you don't have the electric tool.) Sandpaper the area from which you have removed the old paint, then brush it clean.

3. Caulk cracks. If you allow cracks to remain on the outside of your house, you may be inviting trouble. Not only can moisture seep in, but insects love to get inside where it's nice and warm, and they can build nests and multiply. Furthermore, you will lose heat through cracks in a house. It's impossible to seal off a house completely, but do the best you can.

Look for cracks around doors and windows. Pick out and remove any brittle caulking from old cracks. Use a putty knife, screwdriver, pocketknife, awl, ice pick, hairpin, knitting needle, or anything else that works. Apply a coat of paint to cracks that are to be caulked, whether or not they have been caulked before. Unpainted wood and masonry are porous, and if not sealed, will cause caulking to dry up.

4. Scrub off mildew. Mildew is caused by a fungus, which multiplies wherever moisture is present. Modern paints are mostly mildew-proof, but they should always be applied over an area that has been treated against further infection.

Wearing rubber gloves, scrub mildewed areas with full strength liquid laundry bleach. Allow to dry before you paint.

5. Remove dirt. It's a good idea to wash the house before you paint it, otherwise dirt may cause the paint to streak. A simple way to do it it to first scrub with a brush and detergent (a long-handled auto-cleaning brush is perfect), then flush it down with a garden hose.

Or if you think the house is clean enough to accept a paint job, just dust before you paint. Use an old paintbrush as a duster. Pay particular attention to the corners of windowsills. *Never* paint over dirt.

PAINTING SIDING

Painting siding doesn't require any particular talent, but it's a job which demands muscle and perseverance. You can do it yourself if you live in a one-story house. Painting the siding on a two-story house involves working high up on an extension ladder; this is a job for a professional. Perhaps you may be able to arrange to have someone paint the upper part of the house and leave the lower part for you.

You will need:

   Primer (if necessary)
   House paint
   4-inch nylon brush and paint roller
      or brush pad
   Ladder paint tray
   Ladder

What to do:

1. A ladder paint tray is designed to be suspended from one of the ladder rungs. Pour in some paint, and hang it at a convenient height. Be sure to remove the paint tray every time you move the ladder.

2. Apply primer if necessary. (See page 145.)

3. Start to paint from the top, and work your way down. If you are painting clapboard siding, use a roller and brush combination. Dip the brush about one-third of its length into the paint. Slap the bristles against the inside of the paint container; this removes excess paint, which might otherwise drip off. Don't use the edge of the container to wipe off the paint; this removes too much paint, and you need all that the brush can hold.

4. Paint the lower edge of each clapboard. Do as much as you can comfortably reach from the ladder; don't overreach. Here's a good rule to follow: always hold on to the side of the ladder that is farthest from the area you are painting.

5. Using the roller, paint the face of each clapboard.

6. Shingles and rough stucco can most easily be painted with a *brush*, or *paint*, *pad*; this can get into small crevices more easily than either a brush or a roller (Figure 9).

Figure 9. Brush pad in use

PAINTING TRIM

You will need:

> 2- or 3-inch nylon brush
> Paint roller and tray
> Primer (if necessary)
> Trim paint
> Masking tape (optional)
> Old paintbrush, any size

What to do:

1. Dust the trim with the old paintbrush.

2. Apply primer if necessary. (See page 145.)

3. Apply trim paint. Use the roller on large expanses of trim, such as door and window frames, and doors. When painting windows outdoors, follow the same procedure as painting windows indoors (see page 143).

PAINTING PORCH, PATIO, OR SUNDECK FLOORS

Prepare the floor for painting by scraping off all loose paint with a paint knife, and sandpapering until you have a smooth surface. Then sweep or vacuum it carefully.

Check wooden floors for loose boards. If you find one, nail it down, as on page 128.

You will need:

> Floor paint (see page 146)
> Paintbrush, 2- or 3-inch
> Paint roller with extension handle or
>   brush pad

What to do:

1. First paint a strip about 3 inches wide all around the edge of the floor; use a brush.

2. The simplest way to paint a smooth wooden, concrete, or cement floor is to pour a small amount of paint on the floor, then smooth it with the roller. Rough concrete floors are more easily painted with a brush pad.

Don't paint yourself into a corner. Plan your work so that you can leave the area without stepping on fresh paint.

Summary of steps involved in outdoor painting:

> Scrape off loose paint, scales, and blisters.
> If necessary, burn off loose paint.
> Caulk all cracks.
> Scrub off mildew.
> Remove dirt.
> Where necessary, apply primer.
> Apply finish coat.
> Clean brushes and rollers.

Hints

If you must stop painting for a short while—not more than an hour—wrap the brush or roller in sheet plastic to keep it from drying out. Do the same with your paint tray or paint can.

Should you have to stop for a longer period or overnight, wash the brush, roller, and tray so that no traces of paint remain. Press a layer of sheet plastic over the top of the paint in the can, then put the lid on the can.

9

OUTDOORS
Jobs That Only Look Hard

Home repairs aren't confined to the inside of a house—there are many outdoor problems you may have to solve and many improvements you may wish to make.

It's important to know how to fasten things to exterior walls, whether these walls are made of wood, concrete, cinder block, or cement block. You may have considered hanging up a large, outdoor planter or a piece of decorative wrought iron, but didn't do it because it seemed too difficult. It's as easy as refastening that mailbox that's hanging precariously on the wall.

Loose or damaged bricks in walkways or steps are another common area of concern. You can repair these easily. Perhaps you'd even like to install decorative pavements or garden paths, using bricks, patio blocks, slate, or bluestone.

One of the most frequent sources of trouble might be your home's drainage system. Rain gutters and leaders need constant attention. If your basement is wet after it rains, this may indicate that you should install a splashblock, which will carry the water away from the house. Because cracks develop in the foundation or around door or window frames, you'll also want to know how to caulk.

Maintenance and repair of garden tools is important if they are to remain serviceable. Don't fret if someone accidentally cuts the hose in half while mowing the lawn; it's often possible to mend a hose so that it will be good as new again. You can buy replacement fittings for all hose-repair needs. You should also know how to store a hose to prevent its deterioration. Motorized tools need servicing during the summer and special care before they are stored for the winter.

More serious perhaps than any other problem is the presence of termites. If you make a few simple tests, you may be able to avert a great deal of trouble.

CAULKING

Building materials dry out and shrink during the heating season; in hot, humid weather they absorb moisture and swell. Houses also settle, putting a strain on foundations, walls, and ceilings. As a result, cracks develop between bricks, or around door and window frames and house foundations.

All such cracks can be filled with *caulking*, a soft, puttylike material of the consistency of toothpaste. A good caulking compound should not dry out after application, but should remain elastic indefinitely. Properly applied, it can keep out dirt, dust, insects, heat, cold, and moisture.

Special types of caulking, as indicated in Figure 1, have been developed for specific uses.

How to Apply Caulking

Small quantities of caulking are often sold in soft, squeeze-type plastic tubes, which are easy to use. Simply use scissors to cut off the tip of the tube at an angle, about ½ inch from the end. Press the tip against the crack you wish to fill and squeeze the tube to force caulking out of the tip.

Larger quantities of caulking come in cartridges that fit into a steel, framelike *caulking gun* (Figure 2). Pull the plunger as far back as

SPECIFIC USE	TYPE OF CAULKING
To fill cracks in blacktop driveways and between paving and house foundation	Driveway and foundation sealer
To waterproof storm sash, doors	Window-glazing
To repair leaks in rain gutters	Gutter seal
To repair mortar between bricks	Mortar patch
To fill cracks and small areas of broken concrete	Cement patch
To repair torn shingles, flashing*	Roofing sealant
To seal fine cracks in concrete to prevent absorption of water and further deterioration	Cement crack sealer

*Flashing is an angular strip of metal or roofing paper used as a seal between the chimney and roof.

Figure 1. Uses of different caulking materials

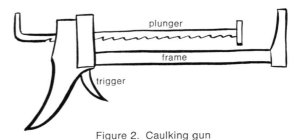

Figure 2. Caulking gun

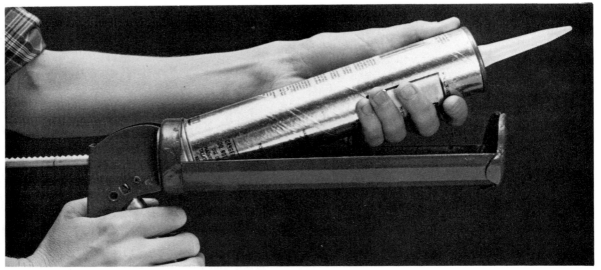

Figure 3. Inserting cartridge in caulking gun

it will go, and place a cartridge of caulking compound into the gun (Figure 3).

Turn the plunger rod so that its notched side faces down; this engages the trigger. In this position, the handle is usually bent up. Squeeze the trigger a few times until you feel a slight resistance; this indicates that the plunger is pressing up against the cartridge.

Cut off the tip of the cartridge at an angle. With a screwdriver, long nail, or ice pick, break the inner seal of the cartridge.

Squeeze the trigger once or twice so that compound oozes out of the cartridge and fills the applicator tip. Holding the gun at an angle, press the opening in the tip firmly against the crack you wish to fill and squeeze the trigger repeatedly. At the same time, move the gun along the crack. Figure 4 shows a gun being used to seal the space between shingles and brick.

To stop the compound from coming out of the tip of the cartridge, turn the handle of the plunger rod so that the notched side of the rod faces up, with the handle bent down. Unless you expect to use the same caulking compound again, remove the cartridge from the gun by pulling the plunger rod all the way back, then lifting the cartridge out.

To prevent the caulking from drying out or becoming hard, plug the applicator tip with a pencil stub, a piece of wood, or anything else that fits in the hole.

Hints

Wait for a warm, dry day to caulk around a house foundation. Most compounds are hard to work with in cold weather.

Caulking compounds are not soluble in water. If you apply compound to a damp surface, it will not stick. Therefore, areas to be caulked *must* be clean and dry. Sweep the crack clean, using either a stiff broom or a wire brush.

REPLACING LOOSE BRICK

Loose bricks in steps should be recemented as soon as possible. If not, water seeping between the bricks will cause others to loosen. In cold areas, this water can freeze and cause further damage. Also, loose bricks located on walkways or steps can be hazardous.

You will need:
Masonry chisel
Hammer
Prepared dry mortar
Mason's trowel or putty knife

Figure 4. Sealing space between shingles and brick

What to do:

1. Use a masonry chisel and hammer to remove all old mortar from both the brick and the area into which it will be recemented (Figure 5).

Figure 5. Removing old mortar with masonry chisel

2. Soak the brick in a pail of water and also soak the steps, particularly the area to which you are going to apply mortar.

3. Mix the prepared mortar in a pail or large can with the amount of water recommended on the container (see the container for complete directions).

4. With a trowel or putty knife, apply a one-inch thick layer of mortar to the spot where the brick is to be set. Then "butter" the brick with a one-inch thick layer of mortar (Figure 6).

Figure 6. Buttering brick with mortar

5. Set the brick in place, tapping it with the handle of your trowel or a piece of scrap wood to align it with the other bricks. Scrape off any mortar that may be squeezed out between bricks. Fill the spaces between the bricks with mortar, using your trowel or a putty knife. Compress the mortar with the handle of the trowel (Figure 7).

Figure 7. Compressing mortar between bricks

6. Cover the repaired area with a wet cloth or a large piece of cardboard to protect it from direct sunlight and to prevent it from drying out. Keep it moist and covered for two or three days before walking on it.

Hints

Here's a rule of thumb to determine whether you have the correct amount of water in your mortar mix: scoop up some mortar on your trowel or putty knife, then quickly turn the trowel upside down. If the mortar drips or slides off, it contains too much water. If it seems stiff and doesn't stick to the trowel, it doesn't contain enough water. If it sticks to the bottom of the trowel, the mixture is just right.

Always soak bricks before laying them in place. If you don't, they will absorb water from the mortar, and weaken it.

To fill cracks in a brick wall, soak the area by brushing it with water; then apply mortar with a narrow, pointed trowel made especially for this purpose.

DECORATIVE BRICK PAVEMENTS

You will need:

> Brick (second-hand, if possible)
> Building sand
> Wood, 2 x 4 inches, about 3 feet long
> Heavy hammer

What to do:

1. Scoop out the area you wish to pave to a uniform depth of about 6 inches. Spread a 4-inch layer of sand on the area. Soak the sand with a garden hose and tamp it by walking on it. For weed-free paving, cover the sand with heavy-duty sheet plastic before laying the bricks. The plastic will keep down the growth of all vegetation.

2. Lay the bricks on the wet sand, placing them close together. Figure 8 shows several brick-laying patterns. Arrange one row of bricks at a time, leveling the row so that all the bricks are the same height. If necessary, adjust the amount of sand under a brick. Tamp the bricks by laying a straight piece of 2 x 4 inch lumber across each row. Strike the wood with a hammer until the surfaces of all bricks are even. Don't strike the bricks directly with the hammer.

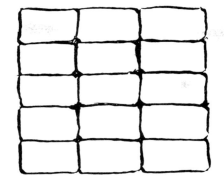

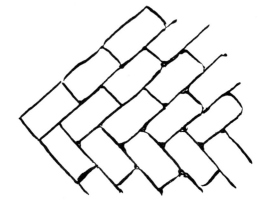

Figure 8. Several paving patterns

3. Scatter dry sand over the bricks. Use a broom to sweep the sand into the cracks. Spray the entire area with a garden hose; this causes more sand to settle into the cracks. Repeat the sanding and watering until all spaces between bricks have been filled.

Hints

Never make a paving bed out of beach sand. Because it is made up of smooth, rounded particles which have been polished by the action of waves and water, this type of sand will not remain firmly packed. Building-sand particles have sharp, irregular edges, so they form a compact mass when wet.

You will occasionally have to remove weeds from between bricks. Do this when the plants are young and the roots have not developed fully. After yanking a weed, fill its place with a little sand, and water it down.

OTHER DECORATIVE PAVEMENTS

You can make a garden path by laying other materials in the same manner as brick paving. For example, try either patio blocks (which look like oversized bricks), slabs of slate, or bluestone.

Or scoop out a 4-inch deep path, and cover it with sheet plastic. Then fill the area with either *gravel*, small *marble chips*, or *screenings*, the fine residue left over after bluestone chips have been passed through special sieves.

Use a garden hose to soak the path, then tamp down the filler material by placing a board over its surface and walking on it. Move the board so that you tamp the entire path.

Soak the path three or four times on successive days to help settle the filler material.

Hints

Don't use large marble chips, stones, redwood-bark chips, or any other large filler material that will not become compacted. Large filler units can make it difficult to walk on a path.

BRICK GARDEN-BED EDGING

Bricks can be used to make attractive edgings for garden beds and patios, and they don't have to be cut. Simply dig a narrow trench, and arrange them in place on their sides. Then

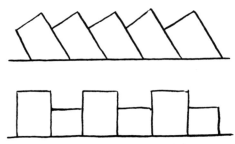

Figure 9. Suggested brick edgings

fill in around the bricks, and tamp the soil firmly with the end of a 2 x 4 inch piece of lumber. Figure 9 shows suggested arrangements.

ATTACHING A MAILBOX

To Wood Siding and Shingles

You will need:
> **Push drill**
> **Screwdriver**
> **Wood screws**

What to do:

1. Use the push drill to make a pilot hole (see page 167). Select screws that will fit through the mounting holes in your mailbox. (Most mailboxes are sold with matching screws.)

2. Lubricate the screws with soap, then drive them into the wood.

To Bricks, Cinder Blocks, or Concrete Blocks

You will need:
> **Electric drill**
> **Masonry drill**
> **Masonry nails or fiber or lead plugs**
> **4⅛ x ¾ inch machine screws**
>   **and nuts**
> **Hammer**
> **2 metal shelf brackets, with arms**
>   **slightly wider than the width of**
>   **the mailbox**
> **Screwdriver**
> **Sheet-metal screws**

Using masonry nails: Masonry nails are made of hardened steel. Some have threaded sides that grip the material into which they are driven. The mailbox will be fastened to the top of two brackets, which are nailed to the wall with masonry nails (Figure 10).

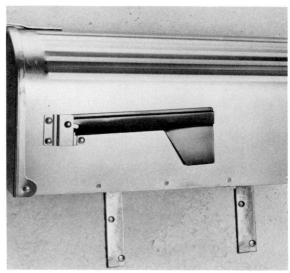

Figure 10. Mailbox on brackets attached to wall with masonry nails

What to do:

1. Place the brackets against the wall, exactly where they will be nailed, and make pencil marks through the mounting holes in the brackets, so you will know where to drill pilot holes.

2. Insert a masonry drill, slightly smaller in diameter than the masonry nails, in the chuck of an electric drill and tighten it.

3. Drill a hole at each pencil mark the same length as the masonry nail. If the holes are too large, the nails will not hold. The reason that the holes should be smaller is that they merely serve as pilots for the nails.

4. Pass nails through the bracket holes; then hammer them into the pilot holes.

5. Place the mailbox on top of the brackets. Mark the underside of the mailbox by making pencil marks through the remaining bracket holes. Drill holes in the bottom of the mailbox.

6. Fasten the mailbox to the brackets with the ¾-inch machine screws and nuts. The heads of the machine screws should be inside the box.

Using fiber or lead plugs: Fiber or lead plugs have one advantage over masonry nails—they receive ordinary wood or sheet-metal screws which can be withdrawn very easily.

What to do:

1. Use a masonry drill to make a hole the same diameter and length as the plug you are using.

2. With a hammer, tap the plug into the hole so that it does not project from the wall.

3. Pass a sheet-metal screw through each mounting hole and drive the screw into the plug; it will cut its own thread. At the same time, it will cause the plug to expand, thus being held securely in the hole.

Hint

If you don't have masonry nails or plugs, you can still attach things to brick or concrete: drill a hole in the wall and plug it solidly by hammering in a piece of scrap wood. Ordinary wood screws driven into the wood will hold.

REPAIRING A LEAKY GUTTER

Gutters catch rainwater as it runs off the roof, and leaders, or downspouts, carry the water away from the gutters. Gutters are made in long sections that are joined together to make up longer lengths. Most leaks occur at these joints.

The simplest way to repair a leaky joint is by sealing it with a special gutter sealing compound.

You will need:

    Caulking gun
    Gutter-sealing compound
    Putty knife
    Whisk broom

What to do:

1. Scrape all dirt from the area to be repaired. Use the whisk broom to brush the joint clean.

2. Squeeze compound into the leaky joint and over all areas which might have pinhole leaks.

Hints

Be sure the joint is clean, or the compound will not stick. Use gutter-sealing compound liberally.

New types of gutters do not have joints. Instead, a long roll of metal is brought to the job and fed through a machine which bends and shapes it into a long, continuous length.

SPLASHBLOCKS

Water pouring from a downspout (or leader) can cause serious erosion. In time, it will wash away topsoil and even weaken your house foundation.

Place a concrete splashblock under each leader wherever it discharges rainwater onto the soil. Splashblocks can be purchased at garden supply stores or building supply yards. Be sure the block is tilted away from the house so water will be carried away and dispersed (Figure 11).

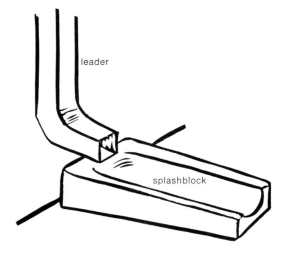

leader

splashblock

Figure 11. Splashblock under leader

EXTENDING A DOWNSPOUT

Some houses have a concrete walk, or apron, next to the foundation walls. As the house settles, the apron breaks away from the foundation, leaving a crack. In addition, the apron is often tilted toward the house, and consequently, rainwater is channeled against the foundation and into the basement.

To direct water away from the house, install downspout extensions.

You will need:

> **Leader, to match the type on your house**
> **Hacksaw, with 32 teeth-per-inch blade**
> **Downspout elbow (if necessary)**
> **Concrete splashblock**
> **Pliers**

What to do:

1. Use the hacksaw to cut a section of leader long enough to extend from the downspout to wherever you are going to install a splashblock (Figure 12).

Figure 12. Cutting section of leader with hacksaw

2. With pliers, bend the edges of one end of the cut section slightly outward, as in Figure 13. Push the flared end of the extension over

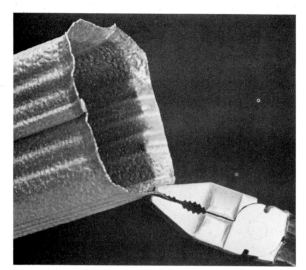

Figure 13. Flaring end of leader with pliers

the elbow on the downspout. If the bottom of the downspout is not equipped with an elbow, install one by simply pushing it on.

Figure 14. Splashblock under leader extension

3. Now place a concrete splashblock under the end of the extension (Figure 14). If necessary, block up the rear end of the splashblock so that it tilts forward. For this, use stones or pieces of brick.

Hints

Gutters and leaders are made of copper, aluminum, plastic, or galvanized iron. When making extensions or adding sections to an existing installation, always use pieces of the same metal. Don't mix two different metals or electrolytic action may cause corrosion.

You can cut gutters and leaders with a saber saw, but you must use a blade with very fine teeth. Coarse teeth will cause the blade to skip on the surface of the metal instead of cutting it.

Gutters must be cleaned periodically. If they are not, the leaders get clogged, and they fill up, overflow, and saturate the wood to which they are nailed. This can cause paint to peel and the wood beneath to rot. Clean gutters with a whisk broom or old paintbrush. If the leader is clogged, try clearing it by discharging the garden hose through it from the top.

THE TERMITE PROBLEM

Termites are more than a nuisance, they're a menace. They cause damage by eating into wood. Should their food supply include parts of your house, you have a serious problem.

Termites can survive only where there is moisture. Although they live in wood, they nest in the ground. They will even build mud tunnels through foundations and stay there to keep out of the sun. Areas most likely to be termite-prone would be moist areas such as those along the East Coast. You would not find them in deserts or drought areas.

One way to tell if you have termites is to examine any creatures that may appear. Termites often swarm in the spring and may arrive in great numbers. If the body of an insect is sharply indented between its thorax (chest) and body, it's probably an ant. If its body is thickish and straight, without sharp indentations, it could be a termite. To be sure, send it to the nearest agricultural or pest control agency, or any firm that specializes in termite extermination.

Because moisture attracts termites, wet basements are their favorite dining grounds. Their nests, however, are always in the ground outside the house.

You may have termites even though you can't see them. They are sneaky. They can eat their way through the supporting beams of a house without ever betraying their presence; they never break through to the outside of a beam, but conduct their affairs inside, leaving a thin shell to fool observers. To outwit them, examine your basement carefully. Go over it inch by inch. Look for accumulations of fine sawdust or wood powder, which are signs of termite acitvity. Probe all exposed beams and wood surfaces with a knitting needle, penknife, or ice pick. An old hatpin is a perfect probing tool. If your tool penetrates more than ½ inch of wood without meeting resistance, you may have encountered a termite-infested area.

Outside, examine the foundations of your home. Search for termite tunnels, which look like mud-covered streaks about ½ inch wide, and extend from the ground to where the siding begins. Destroy the tunnels by scraping them off and spray the area liberally with an approved insecticide. Then call in a professional exterminator.

If you aren't sure whether or not you have termites, it's a good idea to call in a specialist to survey your house and tell you what course of action may be needed.

Before you buy a house, have it inspected for termites by an acknowledged expert. Don't buy unless the house is certified as termite-free.

MENDING A GARDEN HOSE

Don't throw away an otherwise good garden hose, even if it has been cut in two with a lawn mower. Instead, mend it. There are several fasteners on the market which make the job simple. They can be used on either plastic or rubber hoses.

You will need:

    Hose-repair fastener, clincher or clamp type
    Single-edged razor blade in holder or sharp utility knife
    Hammer
    Wood block
    Screwdriver (if you are using a clamp-type fitting)

What to do:

1. Cut out the damaged section of the hose.

2. With a clincher fastener (Figure 15), push one hose end over the tube side of the fastener, using soap as a lubricant.

Figure 15. Clincher-type hose-mending unit

3. Place the hose and fitting on a wood block, and close the fingers on the fastener by hammering them *lightly*. Use just enough force to make them grip the hose. Attach the other hose end to the other side of the fastener.

If you use clamp-type fittings (Figure 16),

Figure 16. Clamp-type hose-mending unit

push the hose end over the end of the fitting, then tighten a clamp around it to hold it securely.

Hints

You can buy special hose connectors that make it possible to hook up or disconnect hoses in a matter of seconds. Instead of screwing and unscrewing them, you merely press them into place.

You can also buy replacement fittings for repairing the male or female ends of a hose.

Store hoses indoors during seasons when they aren't used. If you leave them outdoors, particularly in areas which experience subzero

Figure 17. Hose stored on rotating drum

temperatures, ice may form inside, causing them to crack.

Keep hoses ready for instant use during the growing season. You can coil a hose on a rotating drum (Figure 17), or wind it on a simple rack which can be fastened to the side of the house.

CARE AND MAINTENANCE OF GARDEN POWER TOOLS

Some mowers and edgers are electrically powered, but the vast majority of power garden tools are run by gasoline engines. The same general safety rule applies to both: *never make any repairs or adjustments to a power tool while it is running!*

The most common garden power tool is a lawn mower. There are two types: reel mowers and rotary mowers. No matter what kind of mower you are using, *shut it off* before you adjust its cutting height, install or remove the bag which catches clippings, or refill it with gasoline.

Clean gasoline-powered mowers periodically. Turn off the engine. Pull off the wire (just yank it) that is attached to the spark plug, and bend it sharply so that it can't possibly touch the plug accidentally, but remains a couple of inches away from it. Turn the mower on its side, exposing its bottom. Use a putty knife or other tool to scrape it clean, then spray on a generous coating of silicone lubricant. This will help prevent rust and buildups of grass clippings and leaves. Be sure to reconnect the spark plug before you try to restart the engine.

Consult the manual which came with your mower and follow all recommendations. At the end of the mowing season, prepare the mower for storage by draining off all gasoline in the tank. Your manual will tell you how to do this. Then get it started, and let it run until all the fuel is exhausted. *Never* store a gasoline-powered tool over the winter with fuel in its tank. Old gasoline can become gummy and foul up the carburetor and engine so badly that the mower will not work the next season. This could result in an expensive repair job.

Protecting Tool Handles

The wooden handles of rakes, hoes, cultivators, edgers, forks, spades, and other hand-powered tools will last indefinitely if protected with a coat of either spar varnish or polyurethane varnish before the gardening season begins. If the varnish dries with dull areas, give the entire handle a second coat.

Cleaning Metal Blades

Scrape metal tool blades, removing encrusted mud and rust. Brighten surfaces by rubbing them with either emery cloth or coarse steel wool.

Spray cleaned metal surfaces with silicone to prevent rust.

10

TOOLS, MATERIALS, AND EQUIPMENT

Knowing what tools to use and just how to use them is extremely important for the success of any fix-it job. Familiarity with the materials and additional equipment is equally important.

This chapter is divided into three main sections, the first of which lists the most commonly used tools and gives directions for their use. In the second part, you'll find explanations of the various types of materials and equipment that you may need. Refer to this chapter whenever you are in doubt about what something is or how to use it. The final section provides information on tool maintenance and sharpening techniques. If your tools are kept in good condition, they'll always be ready to use.

Most of the tools and materials that you'll need for household use are readily available at hardware stores. These stores also sell frequently needed plumbing parts and electrical supplies, as well as nails, screws, and other fasteners.

In addition to wood, lumberyards often carry a line of tools and may also sell paints and brushes.

Many neighborhood variety shops carry small items such as rolls of tape and small containers of glue and cement.

You can probably find a source of supply nearby if you check your Yellow Pages for information. If you can't find something you need locally, consult a mail-order catalogue, which usually offers tools and equipment.

Commonly Used Tools

Center punch

A center punch is a rod of hardened steel; one end tapers to a point and its body is

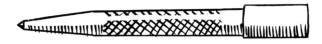

Figure 1. Center punch

generally knurled (Figure 1). Use it to make an indentation in metal before you drill a hole (see Figure 13). This prevents the drill from wandering.

See page 166 for directions on use.

Chisels

Masonry chisel

A masonry chisel (Figure 2) consists of an

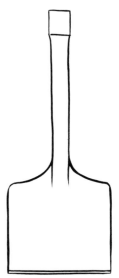

Figure 2. Masonry chisel

octagonally shaped steel bar, one end of which has been flattened to make a wide blade. It is used to remove old mortar from bricks and

other masonry (see Chapter 9, Figure 5), and also to cut bricks, cinder blocks, and concrete blocks.

How it is used

To clean up old masonry, place the blade between the brick and the mortar, and strike the chisel with a hammer. The chisel acts as a wedge, separating the mortar from the brick.

Where mortar and brick are too firmly bonded to be wedged apart, use the chisel as a scraper, holding it against the mortar at an angle and hammering it. Remove the mortar from the brick as though you were a sculptor removing excess stone from a masterpiece!

It is often necessary to shorten a brick so that it will fit into a particular space. Place the brick on the ground and hold the chisel vertically against it, exactly where you want to cut. Strike the chisel sharply with a hammer; the waste piece will fall off. Use the same method to cut cinder and concrete blocks.

Woodworking chisel

A woodworking chisel (Figure 3) consists of

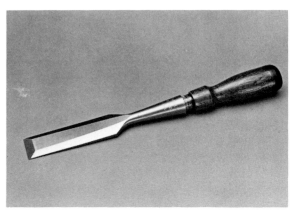

Figure 3. Woodworking chisel

a flat bar of hardened and tempered high-grade steel. One end is ground to a sharp-edged bevel; the other terminates in either a tang (projecting shank) or a socket, fitted to a wooden or plastic handle. Handles are often fitted with metal caps.

Woodworking chisels are available in widths ranging from ½ to 2 inches. You should have one about ¾ inch wide. They are used to cut and smooth wood, primarily in places that can't be reached by other tools. Areas too small to be shaved with a plane can usually be trimmed with a chisel.

There is one simple rule to follow when using a chisel: always cut *with the grain.* Cutting against the grain may split the wood.

Keep your chisel sharp (see page 207). A dull chisel will not cut, but will tear wood fibers, leaving a rough edge.

Use this tool to make a recessed cut. For example, when installing a hinge, it is often necessary to cut out a section from the edge of a piece of wood into which the body of the hinge will fit.

To Make a Recessed Cut

You will need:

> **Woodworking chisel**
> **Hammer**
> **Vise**

What to do:

1. Place the hinge on the edge of the wood, exactly where it is to be installed. Mark the edges with a sharp pencil.

2. Clamp the wood in a vise. Hold the chisel vertically, with its edge exactly on one of the pencil marks and the beveled side facing the inside of the area to be cut out. Strike the chisel lightly with a hammer, driving it into the wood just far enough to accommodate the thickness of the hinge (Figure 4). Make a similar cut on each pencil line.

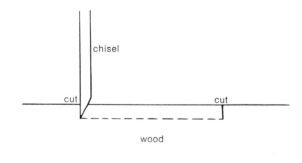

Figure 4. Starting recessed cut

3. Hold the chisel bevel-side down. Tap it *lightly* with the hammer, cleaning out the wood between the vertical cuts. Make light

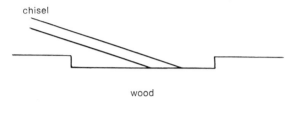

Figure 5. Finishing recessed cut with woodworking chisel

cuts, removing thin shavings (Figure 5). Don't attempt to remove all the wood at once. Finish the cut by hand, pushing the chisel instead of striking it with the hammer.

Clamps

Clamps are essentially sets of wooden or metal jaws, which can be opened or closed by turning a screw thread. They are used to hold things temporarily, such as two pieces of wood that are being glued together. After the glue has hardened, the clamps are removed. Use clamps when regluing shaky furniture.

How they are used

C-clamps, the most common type, are made in many sizes (Figure 6). One jaw is part of the

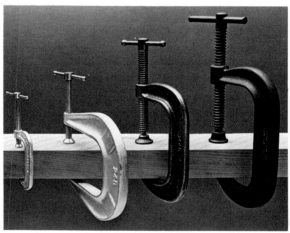

Figure 6. C-clamps

C-frame, and the other is part of the screw thread. To open the jaws, turn the thumbscrew, or screw lever, counterclockwise. Tighten jaws by turning in the opposite direction.

Hand screws are clamps used in fine woodworking. They are made of hardwood, with threaded steel rods attached to the handles

Figure 7. Hand screw

(Figure 7). To open the jaws, turn both handles to the right at the same time. To close the jaws, turn both handles in the opposite direction.

Bar clamps are made in sizes from 12 inches to 8 feet long. One jaw is part of the L-shaped frame. The other jaw is at the end of a screw thread, which passes through a sliding arm (Figure 8). Pull the arm to open the jaws.

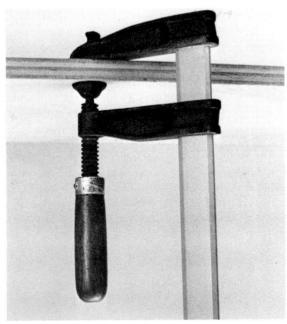

Figure 8. Bar clamp

Then slide it down so that both jaws close around the object being clamped. Twist the screw lever to make everything good and tight.

Spring clothespins, the same ones that are used to hold the laundry on the washline, make dandy little clamps. They are indispensable aids when you are working with thin strips of wood (see Chapter 4, Figure 35).

A *pipe clamp* is an emergency device, used to stop a leak in a pipe. It consists of two metal half-sleeves that you fasten around the pipe with nuts and bolts. The sleeves press a rubber pad against the leak (see Chapter 2, Figure 10).

Drain auger

A drain or clean-out auger looks like a flexible steel cable. One end is equipped with an adjustable handle, and the other end looks like a corkscrew (see Chapter 2, Figure 13). Use it to remove stoppages in sink and toilet drains.

See page 33 for directions on use.

Drills

A drill is a tool that holds a rotating bit; it is used to bore holes in various materials. Some drills are hand-powered, others are electrically operated. There are many types, and many ways to use them. The following are the most commonly used:

Hand drill

A hand drill, used to make holes in wood or metal, looks and works something like an eggbeater. The "business end" of a hand drill has a *chuck,* in which twist drills, or drill bits, can be secured (Figure 9). The size of the

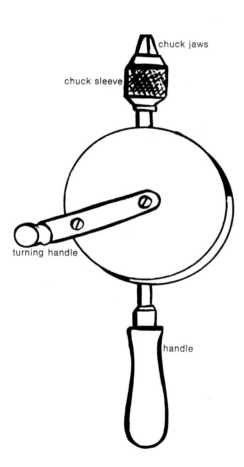

Figure 9. Hand drill

chuck indicates the largest twist-drill size it can hold. For example, a ¼-inch chuck will accept drill bits only up to ¼ inch in diameter. *Carbon-steel drill bits* are suitable only for wood. *High-speed bits* are tougher, and can be used for either wood or metal. You can buy twist drills singly or in sets (Figure 10).

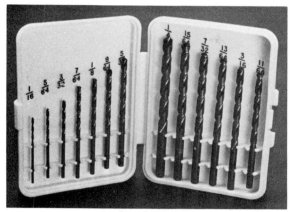

Figure 10. Set of twist drills

Using a hand drill

Select the twist drill you are going to use. Hold the hand drill so that its turning handle can't move. Rotate the chuck sleeve to the left; this opens the chuck jaws. Place the twist drill in the chuck; tighten it in place by turning the chuck sleeve to the right (Figure 11). Using only hand pressure, make it as tight as you can.

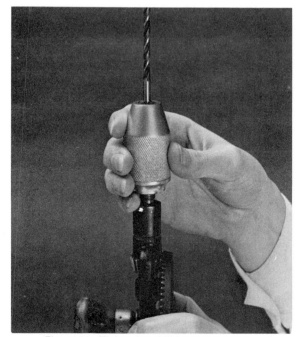

Figure 11. Tightening drill bit in hand drill

Drilling through wood

Small articles to be drilled should be held in a vise or secured to a tabletop with clamps. If you clamp the wood to a tabletop, place a piece of scrap wood under it to protect the surface. Use a hammer and nail to make a shallow nick exactly where you want to drill; this will catch the end of the twist drill and prevent it from wandering as you start to drill. Hold the drill firmly with one hand, and press the end of the bit lightly against the mark you have made. Turn the handle with your other hand using just enough pressure to bite into the wood.

If you turn the drill handle and nothing seems to be happening, you may be turning it backwards; in that case, the drill bit is rotating in the wrong direction and can't cut. If you are right-handed, hold the drill in your left hand, and turn the handle *away* from you (clockwise) with your right hand. If you are a lefty, hold the drill in your right hand, and turn the handle *toward* you with your left hand.

When you have drilled through a piece of wood, don't stop and try to pull the drill free. Keep right on drilling as you slowly withdraw the drill bit; this leaves a clean hole (Figure 12).

Figure 12. Hand drill going through wood

Drilling through metal

First mark the exact spot with a *center punch*, a small, steel tool with a pointed end (see page 162). Hammer it lightly into the metal, making an impression that will engage the drill-bit tip (Figure 13).

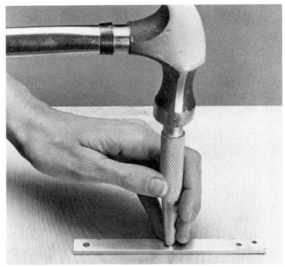

Figure 13. Using center punch on metal

Secure the piece you are drilling in a vise. A thin piece of metal should be backed up with a piece of scrap wood (Figure 14) to keep it

Figure 14. Hand-drilling through thin metal backed by wood

from bending. Press the drill firmly against the punched mark, and turn the drill handle. Use enough pressure to enable the drill bit to cut into the metal, but be careful—too much pressure can snap a thin twist drill. As with wood, keep the drill turning as you withdraw it from the hole.

Push drill

The name of this tool describes it perfectly: it's a drill that operates when you push it. A special set of bits, or *drill points*, is stored in the handle (Figure 15).

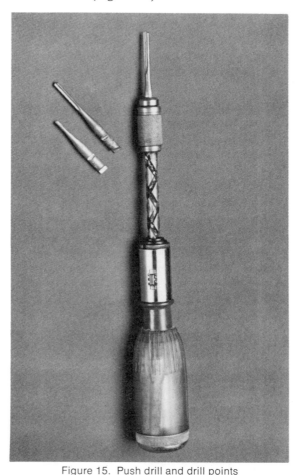

Figure 15. Push drill and drill points

Use a push drill to make *pilot holes* for nails, screws, cup hooks, and other fasteners. Always drill a pilot hole before driving a nail or screw into hardwood, or the wood may split.

How it is used

Select a drill point that is slightly narrower than the nail you are using. (See page 201 for screw pilot holes.) Place the tip of the drill point exactly where you want the pilot hole, and push the handle of the tool forward as far as it will go. As you push, the drill point will rotate.

Release pressure (without dropping the drill), and spring action will snap the handle back to its original position. Keep pushing and releasing pressure on the handle until you have drilled to the depth you want.

Drill points are made to be used on wood; they are too soft to go through metal. You can also use them on plaster or plasterboard walls. Although this may dull their sharp tips, replacements are inexpensive.

Electric drill

An electric drill is one of the most useful tools you can own (Figure 16). Use it not only

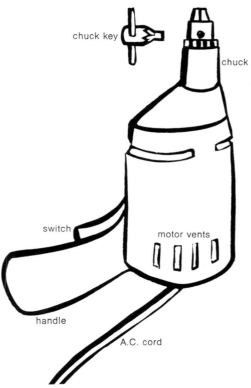

Figure 16. Electric drill

to drill holes, but also for a variety of special purposes.

Drills are classified according to the size of the chuck. A ¼-inch drill has ¼-inch chuck; a ⅜-inch drill has a ⅜-inch chuck. Either is satisfactory for home use.

Using an electric drill
 Tightening a twist drill in the chuck
Turn the outer sleeve of the chuck by hand
until the chuck jaws open wide enough to
admit a twist drill. Tighten the jaws by turning
the sleeve in the opposite direction (Figure 17).

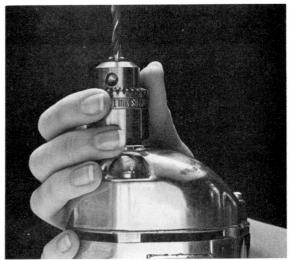

Figure 17. Tightening drill bit in electric-drill chuck by
hand

Now tighten the chuck jaws still more, using
the chuck *key* that is supplied with every
electric drill. Slip the end of the key into one
of the holes at the side of the chuck (Figure
18); the geared teeth of the key should engage
the teeth around the edge of the sleeve.

Figure 18. Key inserted into electric-drill chuck

Drilling a hole in wood
Mark the spot you are going to drill by
tapping a shallow nick with a hammer and nail.
Clamp a wooden piece to a tabletop (with a
piece of scrap wood under it) or secure it in
a vise.

Place the tip of the drill bit against the nick,
press *lightly*, and start the drill. *Don't* start
the drill first.

Keep exerting steady pressure until the drill
has gone through the wood. Let the drill do
all the work; don't force it or it will slow
down. Keep the drill running as you slowly
withdraw it from the hole. Then switch it off.

Drilling a hole in metal
It takes longer to drill a hole in metal, but
it's just as easy as drilling in wood. First use
a *center punch* to mark the spot where you are
going to drill (see page 166). Hammer the
punch lightly into the metal; this leaves an
impression that will engage the tip of the drill
bit and prevent it from skating erratically
all over the metal surface.

To drill through thin metal, first nick it with
a center punch. Then clamp it in a vise with a
piece of scrap wood behind it. That way, it
won't bend while you are drilling. Go through
the metal and into the wood backing
(Figure 19).

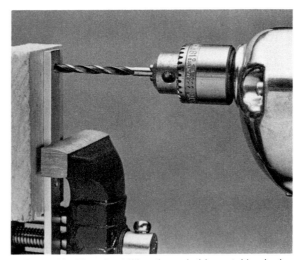

Figure 19. Electric-drilling through thin metal backed
by wood

Special bits for electric drills

The variety of special bits available really expands the range of tasks you can take care of with your electric drill. Twist drills with turned-down shanks (Figure 20) make it

Figure 20. Twist drills with turned-down shanks

possible to drill holes from ⅜ to 1 inch in diameter in either wood or metal, even though the chuck size may be only ¼ inch.

To drill still larger holes in wood, you can use power wood-boring bits (Figure 21). These

Figure 21. Power wood-boring bits

also have turned-down shanks which will fit a ¼-inch drill chuck. Sizes range from ⅜ to 1½ inches in diameter.

Carbide-tipped bits are extremely tough (Figure 22). Use them to drill holes in masonry, brick, ceramics, and interior house walls.

Figure 22. Carbide-tipped bits (masonry drills)

Accessories for electric drills

Many interesting and useful accessories can be powered by your electric drill—for example, a *wire wheel* to clean up garden tools. You can also get attachments to convert your drill into a *sander, paint mixer, hedge trimmer,* or *power screwdriver.* When using these as well as all other attachments, fasten them securely in the drill chuck.

Another handy accessory is a *drill bench stand* which is screwed or bolted to a workbench or tabletop. Clamp the drill to the stand, then tighten the various attachments in the drill chuck. Figure 23 shows a drill

Figure 23. Drill bench stand holds drill with buffing wheel attachment.

bench stand as well as a *buffing wheel,* which you can use with jeweler's rouge to bring up a high polish on badly tarnished silverware.

Important! Whenever you use a revolving accessory, such as a wire wheel, grinding wheel, or buffing wheel, do as the pros do: *wear protective goggles* (Figure 24). They are

Figure 24. Protective goggles

inexpensive, and represent that vital ounce of prevention. Get a pair at any store that sells tools.

Files

Files are bars of hardened steel, the sides and edges of which are covered with fine teeth. One end of the bar tapers so that it can fit into a wooden handle (Figure 25). Some files are flat

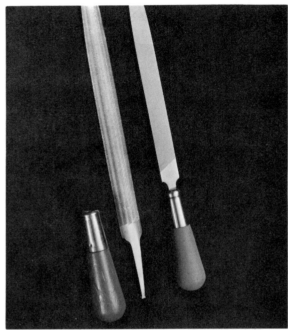

Figure 25. Flat file inserted into handle, half-round file with tang exposed, and unattached wooden handle

on both sides. Others are flat on one side and half-round on the other. Still other files are completely round or triangular.

These tools are available in varying degrees of fineness or coarseness, depending on the size and arrangement of the teeth.

Files are used either to remove or to smooth metal. They do this by cutting tiny shavings. A file with coarse teeth can be used to shape metal quickly. Use a fine-toothed file to smooth metal that has already been shaped by a coarse-toothed file.

How they are used

Metal to be filed should be held in a vise. Hold the file in both hands; place one hand on the handle and the other on the front end of the file. *Put a handle on every file.* If you don't, you run the risk of driving the sharp, tapered end of the file into your hand. File handles may be bought separately. Insert the tang of the file into the opening of the handle. Then, holding the file, strike the handle against a solid surface.

Hold the file horizontally as you work. Press down on it, exerting equal pressure with both hands. Push the file forward so that its full length comes into contact with the object being filed. Release pressure, and bring the file back to its starting point.

Don't press when bringing file back. It cuts only when it is pushed forward because its teeth point forward.

Grouter

A grouter is a hard rubber pad that is cemented to a sheet of metal and fitted with a handle (see Chapter 3, Figure 36). It is used for grouting, or pressing, a waterproof cement into the spaces between the ceramic tiles.

See page 63 for directions on use.

Hammer

A hammer is a common, multipurpose tool with a handle and a head. Good hammers have steel heads, although the handles may be made of wood, reinforced plastic, or steel—all equally good. For general home repair use, any type of handle will do.

Use a hammer to either drive or remove nails. A steel-headed claw hammer with a curved claw will serve both purposes (Figure 26). These are made in different weights; a

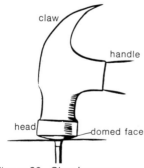

Figure 26. Claw hammer

16-ounce hammer is most commonly used. Try one before you buy it; pick it up and swing it a few times. If a 16-ouncer seems too heavy, try a lighter one. A 12- or 13-ounce hammer may be just right for you.

A good hammer has a slightly domed, or bell face, which makes it possible to drive a nail flush with the surface into which you are nailing without leaving disfiguring dents (see Figure 26).

How it is used

Grasp the hammer firmly near the end of the handle, as though you were shaking hands with it. The handle should be parallel to the surface into which you are nailing. Hold the nail vertically, between thumb and forefinger (Figure 27).

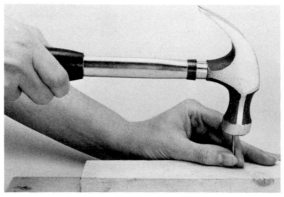

Figure 27. Position of nail

Use a light wrist movement to strike the nail. The hammerhead should meet the nail squarely. Use just enough force to get the nail started in the wood, then let the nail stand alone, and drive it down.

Don't try to drive the nail in with one smashing blow; it won't work. Instead, keep using the same light wrist movement with which you started nailing. If you want to strike with more force—and do this only if you have complete control of the hammer—use a combination movement of wrist and elbow. Control each hammer blow by keeping your elbow close to your body. Also try moving your thumb from the side to the top of the handle.

Removing nails

If you strike a nail at an angle, it will bend. To remove a bent nail, first straighten it as much as you can by tapping it with a hammer. Then slide the hammer claw under the nailhead, and pull the handle to a vertical position (Figure 28).

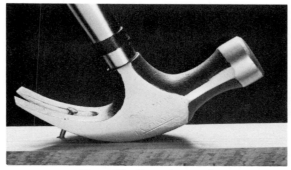

Figure 28. Removing a nail

A long nail may not come all the way out. In this case, slip a block of scrap wood under the hammerhead to increase its leverage, and pull again (Figure 29).

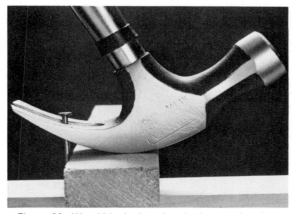

Figure 29. Wood block placed under hammerhead to increase leverage

Magnetic hammers

Magnetic hammers are used to hold and drive tacks that are too small to be held by hand. The hammerheads have one solid end and one split, magnetized end.

How they are used

Pick up a tack with the magnetized end of the hammerhead (the tack will remain in place when you lift the hammer), and spot it in place with a light, careful blow. Reverse the head, and drive the tack all the way in with the solid end.

A straight *tack hammer* will do nicely for light work and occasional use (Figure 30). An

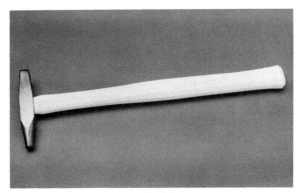

Figure 30. Tack hammer

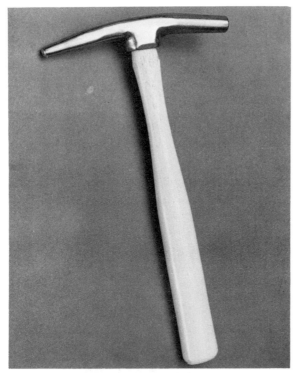

Figure 31. Upholsterer's hammer

upholsterer's hammer is larger and heavier (Figure 31). Use it when working with large tacks or large numbers of tacks.

Insulation stripper

This tool is a "must" if you intend to do any electrical wiring. It looks like a cross between a pair of tin snips and a pair of pliers (see Chapter 1, Figure 16), and is used to remove insulation from the ends of wires without damaging or cutting them.

How it is used

Place an insulated wire in the notch near the end of the tool. Squeeze the handles together and rotate the tool slightly. At the same time, pull the insulation from the end of the wire.

Level

A level is a gauge that works by means of one or more plastic or glass vials containing a liquid and a movable air bubble. The vials are set into wooden or aluminum bodies, which may be anywhere from a few inches to 6 feet long (Figure 32).

Figure 32. Torpedo level

Use a level to check the accuracy, or *levelness*, of horizontal lines or surfaces, and the *plumb*, or verticality, of lines or surfaces. Some levels can also be used to mark off 45-degree angles.

The level is a handy tool to have in order to hang pictures straight, to install brackets and shelves (see Chapter 4, Figure 52), and to check on the proper installation of refrigerators, washing machines, kitchen ranges, and other appliances.

Any inexpensive level with two vials will do for home-repair use (Figure 33).

Figure 33. Two-vial level

How it is used

To check for horizontal exactness: Place the level flat on the surface you are testing, and examine the bubble in the vial. If the bubble is perfectly centered between the two marks, the surface is level. The slightest deviation from this position will cause the bubble to move to the left or right.

To check for vertical exactness: Hold the level vertically against the surface or edge you are checking. The bubble should be centered in the glass.

A combination square is an adjustable square that has a built-in level (Figure 34). It

Figure 34. Combination square on wood

can be used as either a try square (see page 205), or as a level.

Miter box

A miter box is a saw guide. The simplest type consists of three pieces of wood fastened together to form a trough with open ends. Slots cut in the sides can hold a saw blade at angles of 45 or 90 degrees.

More expensive miter boxes have metal saw guides, and can be adjusted to cut at practically any angle.

Use the miter box as a guide when cutting angles in the ends of moldings and other wooden strips.

How it is used

With one hand, hold the wood firmly inside the box, pressing it against the bottom and the far side so that it can't move. The other hand operates a crosscut saw or backsaw, which runs in the slots cut into the sides of the box (Figure 35).

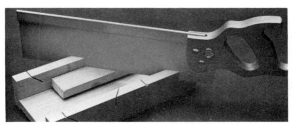

Figure 35. Backsaw and miter box

Long backsaws, known as *miter saws,* are made especially for use in miter boxes. However, you probably can do without one; most modern miter boxes will accept an ordinary crosscut saw.

Nail set

A nail set is a steel rod with a knurled body. One end has a flat head and the other tapers to a small, slightly cupped tip. It is used to drive the head of a finishing nail below the surface of the wood so it can't be seen.

How it is used

First hammer in a finishing nail so that its head is just above the surface. Then, holding the nail set upright, press its small end firmly against the nailhead. Keep your hand steady by pressing your pinky against the wood (Figure 36). The tip of the nail set should be

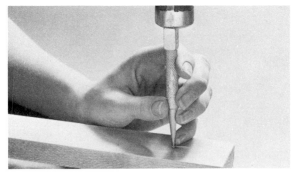

Figure 36. Using a nail set

smaller than the nailhead. Hammer the nail set lightly, and drive the nailhead about ⅛ inch below the wood surface. The hole can be filled with suitable material so that it becomes virtually invisible (see page 53).

Paint remover, electric

An electric paint remover is nothing more than a shielded heating element to which a handle has been attached (see Chapter 8, Figure 1). It is used primarily to soften paint that must be removed from large, flat areas such as ceilings, walls, woodwork, or floors; but it will also soften old, cracked putty so that it can be removed and replaced with fresh glazing compound. Even floor tiles can be softened for easy removal with the paint remover (see page 132).

See page 141 for directions on use.

Plane

A plane is a cutting tool with a sharp, adjustable blade, or *plane iron*, which can be removed for sharpening. The *smooth plane,* usually found in home workshops, is recommended for general use (Figure 37). It is used to smooth wood by slicing away thin shavings.

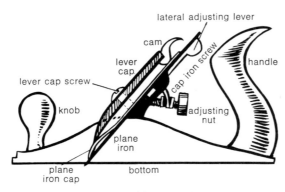

Figure 37. Smooth plane

How it is used

Wood to be planed must be held securely in a vise (see page 190). Determine which way the wood grain runs; *you must cut with the grain* (Figure 38). If you cut against the grain, you will leave a rough finish and may even splinter the wood (Figure 39).

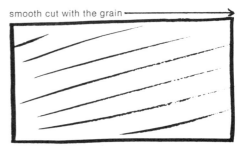

Figure 38. Wood cut by plane with the grain

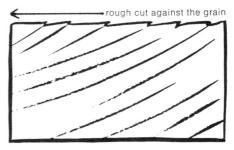

Figure 39. Wood cut by plane against the grain

Hold the plane as in Figure 40. Press down evenly with both hands, and push the plane from one edge of the wood to the other. It should remove a fine, even shaving. If not, the plane iron needs adjustment or sharpening.

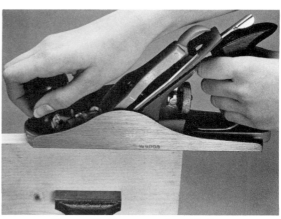

Figure 40. Proper way to hold plane

A few strokes of the plane should be enough to smooth the edge of a board. To make a board slightly narrower, simply keep on planing and removing shavings.

To smooth the *end* of a piece of wood, plane from each edge to the center (Figure 41).

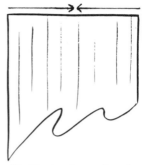

Figure 41. Planing from edges to center

Don't try to cut from one edge to the other or you'll splinter the wood at the far edge (Figure 42).

Figure 42. Planing from edge to edge may splinter the wood.

Cleaning a plane

As you work, wood shavings may become jammed inside the plane, preventing it from operating properly. Or you may want to

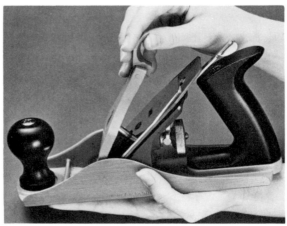

Figure 43. Disengaging lever cap

sharpen the plane iron. In either case, you must take the plane apart. This is easily done by pulling up the *cam*, which is part of the lever cap. Slide it upward to disengage it from the lever-cap screw (Figure 43).

Lift out the plane iron and plane-iron cap, which are held together by a large-headed cap-iron screw (Figure 44); *don't* loosen the screw. That's all there is to it.

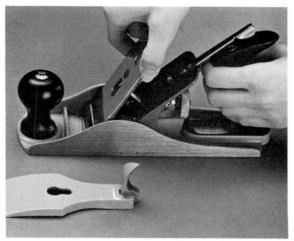

Figure 44. Lifting out plane iron and plane-iron cap

To reassemble a plane

First replace the combined plane iron and plane-iron cap; be sure the head of the cap screw is *underneath*. Next slip the lever cap into place so that the narrow slot in the lever cap slides under the head of the lever-cap screw (Figure 45). Push the cam down, locking the entire assembly into place.

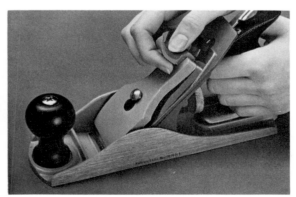

Figure 45. Slipping lever cap into place

To adjust a plane blade

Hold the plane at eye level, bottom-side up, with its front toward you. Sight along the bottom. If the blade doesn't protrude from the bottom of the plane, it can't possibly cut. If it protrudes too much, the shavings will be too thick and the plane will jam.

To adjust the plane iron properly, turn the adjusting nut until the cutting edge of the blade projects from the bottom just about the thickness of a hair. Experiment—you may have to turn the nut either to the right or to the left. If the blade protrudes unevenly, adjust it by moving the lateral-adjusting lever (Figure 46).

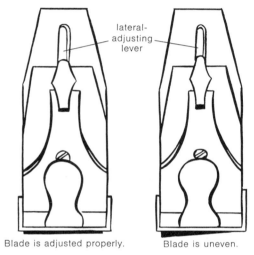

Figure 46. Lateral-lever adjustment

Block plane

This is a small plane, which is simpler in construction than a smooth plane (Figure 47). It is used by carpenters and cabinetmakers for fine wood finishing. You can use a block plane instead of a smooth plane.

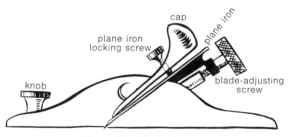

Figure 47. Block plane

Using a block plane

Hold the plane with both hands, as in Figure 48. Press down evenly and firmly against the edge you are planing, and move the plane with the grain, in long, edge-to-edge strokes. Smooth the ends of boards by planing from each edge to the center, just as you would if you were using a smooth plane.

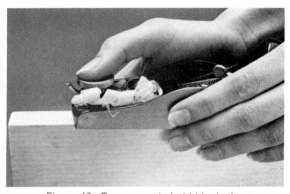

Figure 48. Proper way to hold block plane

To take a block plane apart

Loosen the plane-iron locking screw and remove the cap (Figure 49). Next, lift out the

Figure 49. Loosening block-plane-iron locking screw

plane iron. Turn it over; the underside has notches which fit the plane-iron adjusting mechanism (Figure 50).

Figure 50. Underside of block-plane iron

To reassemble a block plane

Replace the plane iron so that its notches fit snugly into the adjusting mechanism. Slide the cap back into place and tighten the plane-iron locking screw. Leave the screw slightly loose; if it's too tight, you will not be able to adjust the blade.

To adjust a block-plane blade

Hold the plane at eye level, bottom up, with its front facing you. Sight along the bottom, and turn the blade-adjusting screw until the blade protrudes from the bottom about the thickness of a hair. Adjust the blade for evenness by moving it from side to side. Lock everything in place by tightening the plane-iron locking screw.

Rasp plane

The rasp plane, used for smoothing wood, has a flat bottom blade of hard steel, covered with rasplike teeth (Figure 51).

Figure 51. Underside of rasp plane

How it is used

You can use a rasp plane in place of other planes. Grasp it firmly with both hands, press down, and make long strokes. While a smooth or block plane cuts a single, wide shaving, the rasp plane cuts a shaving with each tooth. Holes next to the teeth allow the shavings to ride up into the hollow body. Remove these shavings frequently, or the plane will become packed solidly.

To change a rasp-plane blade

Rasp-plane blades cannot be sharpened; when a blade becomes dull, it must be replaced. Just loosen the screw at the front end of the plane body, remove the dull blade, put in a new one, and tighten the screw.

Pliers

Pliers are metal tools which look something like tongs. They consist of two arms, connected by a pivot screw or rivet. Opening and closing the arms opens and closes a pair of jaws. Jaws may be flat, smooth, serrated, or sharp-edged.

Some pliers are used as gripping tools, others are made for cutting; still others are designed for both gripping and cutting.

How they are used

Hold pliers in one hand. Open the jaws and place them around the object you wish to grip. Squeeze the handles together, closing the jaws. The harder you squeeze, the more leverage is applied to the jaws.

Slip-joint pliers

Slip-joint pliers are used for gripping as well as cutting wire and thin nails.

How to use them

Slip-joint pliers have a double pivot hole. With the pivot screw in one hole, they are limited to gripping small items, such as wires, nails, or nuts and bolts (Figure 52). To change

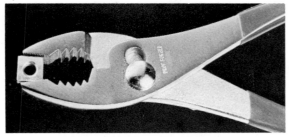

Figure 52. Slip-joint pliers gripping nut

the capacity of the jaws to enable them to grip larger objects, slip the pivot screw from one hole to the other (Figure 53).

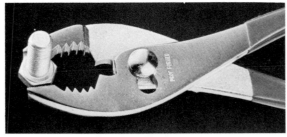

Figure 53. Slip-joint pliers gripping bolt

To use slip-joint pliers as wire cutters, place the wire between the open plier jaws, as in Figure 54. Squeeze the handles together; the shearing action of the two plier halves will cut the wire.

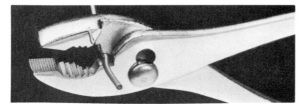

Figure 54. Slip-joint pliers cutting wire

Arc-joint pliers

Use arc-joint pliers to tighten or loosen nuts, bolts, or pipes. They are tough, rugged pliers with either toothed or smooth jaws.

How they are used

Like other pliers, they are grippers. They are also adjustable, with a wider range than slip-joint pliers. Make size adjustments by sliding the pivot screw to different positions in the pivot slot.

You can grip a small bolt (Figure 55) or a 2-inch pipe (Figure 56) with these pliers. They

Figure 55. Arc-joint pliers adjusted to grip a small bolt

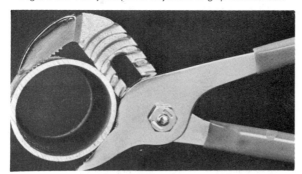

Figure 56. Arc-joint pliers, with wider adjustment, gripping pipe

are available in many sizes, but a pair about 10 inches long is best for all-around home-repair use.

Needle-nose pliers

Use needle-nose pliers for light gripping chores as well as for bending wires into intricate shapes. Their long, narrow jaws make it possible to get into tight spots (see Figure 57).

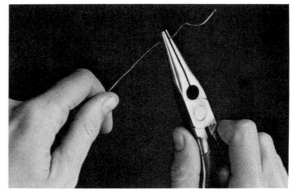

Figure 57. Needle-nose pliers bending wire

How they are used

Needle-nose pliers are not made for heavy work. To shape a wire, grasp it firmly with the pliers and turn the pliers to make bends. Form large shapes by holding the wire near the crotch of the jaws. For smaller, more delicate shapes, use the plier tips (Figure 57).

Diagonal-cutting pliers

Use diagonals (Figure 58) to cut soft thin nails, and copper, brass, iron, or other soft wire. Never use them on hard steel wire or nails.

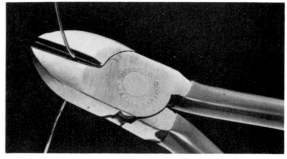

Figure 58. Diagonal-cutting pliers cutting wire

How they are used

Open the cutting jaws and place them around the material to be cut. Squeeze the handles together; the cutting blades will sever the wire.

End-cutting pliers

These are made especially for cutting wire and nails. You can remove small nails with them.

How they are used

Use end-cutting pliers as you would other cutting pliers. Place the jaws around the material you wish to cut, and squeeze. To remove a nail, grip the head just hard enough to hold it firmly (Figure 59); if you grip too

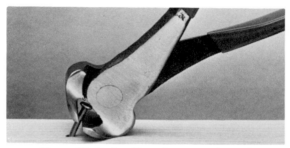

Figure 59. End-cutting pliers removing nail

hard, you'll cut through it. Roll the pliers on their end, and the nail will come out. To avoid damaging a finished wood surface, place a piece of thin wood or cardboard between the pliers and the wood.

Pry bar

A pry bar is a rod or bar made of tough, hardened steel. One end is usually flattened; the other is curved, with a forked tip which can be used to remove nails. Use it to separate ceiling (see Chapter 4, Figure 20) or baseboard moldings from walls, to take apart nailed wooden structures, or to pry up large nails.

How it is used

Use the bar as a lever. To remove molding, insert the thin end between the molding and the wall. Place a strip of scrap wood under the bar, near the thin end; this acts as a fulcrum. Push down on the other end of the bar, and the thin end will be lifted with tremendous force.

You can use a pry bar as a temporary lifter-upper, too. For example, you can lift one end of a door that has settled out of place. Or pry up a large appliance while you insert wedges underneath to level it.

Putty knife

See Scraper, page 185.

Rasp

A rasp is like a file, but it has coarser teeth (Figure 60). It may be flat, half-round, or round. Use it to shape and smooth wood. (Files are used on metal.)

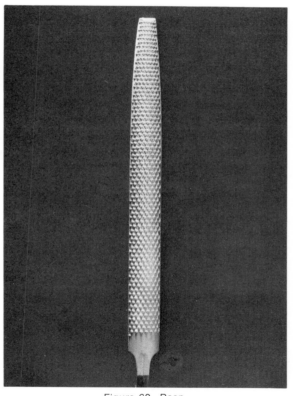

Figure 60. Rasp

How it is used

You can use a rasp in places that can't be reached with a plane or chisel. For example, use a rasp to shape a small opening in a piece of wood. *Always* fit a handle to a rasp before you use it; otherwise, the pointed tang at the end of the tool may injure the palm of your hand.

Sander, electric

A flat-bed electric sander (Figure 61), the type recommended for general home use, is actually a power-driven sandpaper block used to clean and smooth wood surfaces, and to refinish and polish furniture.

Figure 61. Heavy-duty sander and vibration sander

Types of flat-bed electric sanders

The least expensive electric sander you can buy is a *vibration sander,* also known as a magnetic-impulse sander. It's perfectly adequate for light-duty use around the house. Use it to put a supersmooth finish on bare wood or, with silicon carbide paper and water, to obtain a satin finish on varnished or lacquered surfaces. Or attach a lamb's wool pad to buff the furniture.

Don't expect a vibration sander to remove old paint from that old chest you are going to restore, or to smooth down a really rough wooden surface. It's not meant for rough work, and should be regarded as a fine finishing tool.

Heavier flat-bed sanders have powerful motors, and can be used for both rough and fine work. You can use this type of sander to do a tough job like removing paint and wood from the edge of a door to make it fit, or for a delicate job like fine furniture polishing. All you have to do is change the abrasive paper.

When buying one of these sanders, be sure to get the tool that suits your needs. An *orbital sander* (the sanding pad moves in tiny circles) is great for rough work and quick removal of surplus wood. A *straight-line sander* (the sanding pad moves in a straight line) is unequalled for fine finishing. Some sanders can be converted to perform either type of action by simply moving a lever.

To use an electric sander

First install in it a sheet of abrasive paper. You can buy papers of every type cut to fit your sander, or you can prepare your own from large sheets.

Although clamping systems vary with different makes, spring clamps usually hold the abrasive sheet to the bed of the sander. Use finger pressure to loosen one clamp. Insert the end of a paper, then release the clamp so that it grips the paper. Fold the paper flat against the bed, and clamp the other end in place (Figure 62). Be sure the abrasive side of the paper faces *away* from the bed.

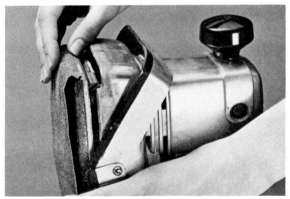

Figure 62. Clamping abrasive paper to bed of electric sander

Note: When you use an electric sander with abrasive paper, be sure to wear a respirator (Figure 116).

Rest the sander against the wood you wish to smooth, then turn on the motor. Hold the sander firmly; if necessary, use both hands. Go over the entire surface with overlapping strokes. For rough work, it doesn't matter in which direction you move the sander. As a general rule, however, keep the long dimension of the tool parallel to the grain of the wood (Figure 63). If you move it across the grain, you may leave scratches.

Figure 63. Electric sander held parallel to wood grain

For a very smooth finish on bare wood, begin with a medium-grade abrasive paper, then use progressively finer grades, ending with a very fine paper.

Use wet-or-dry silicon carbide papers to obtain supersmooth finishes on thoroughly dry, hard, lacquered or varnished surfaces. Clamp a sheet of 400-grit paper in your sander. Wet the surface you are smoothing with water (add a few drops of liquid soap or household detergent to the water). The water acts as a lubricant, preventing the spaces between the individual grits from becoming clogged. *Never* wet the paper by dipping the sander into the sink basin or a container of water. *Always* wet the paper separately.

Hold the sander firmly and move it over the water-wet surface (Figure 64). Work over a

Figure 64. Electric sander on tabletop with water-wet paper

small area at a time until the entire surface to be refinished loses its high gloss.

Sanders make fine polishers as well. Instead of abrasive papers, use a polishing pad made of lamb's wool (Figure 65). Buff your furniture and other woodwork to a high gloss after applying the proper wax.

Figure 65. Electric sander with lamb's-wool buff used as polisher

Saws

Hand saw

A handsaw has a wooden handle and a steel blade, one edge of which has teeth cut into it (Figure 66). Use it only to make straight cuts

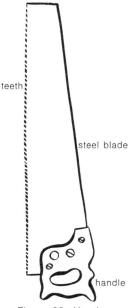

teeth

steel blade

handle

Figure 66. Handsaw

in wood, composition board, or other materials that will not dull its teeth.

There are two types: *crosscut* saws, which are used to cut *across* the grain of a piece of wood, and *ripsaws*, which cut *with* the grain. Crosscut-saw teeth are like tiny knives, which slice across the wood-grain fibers (Figure 67).

Figure 67. Top view of crosscut-saw teeth

Ripsaw teeth are shaped like chisels, which punch out tiny chips of wood when the saw is pushed (Figure 68).

Figure 68. Top view of ripsaw teeth

Saws are marked to show the number of *points*, or teeth, per inch. The greater the number of points, the smoother the saw cut will be. A 10-point crosscut saw can take care of all your home-repair needs. It can be used for occasional ripping, but progress will be slow.

How it is used

To cut across a board, use a *try square* as a marking guide; a try square is used for marking right angles. Press the handle against the edge of the board, and run a pencil point against the blade (Figure 69) to mark the board.

Figure 69. Try square in use

Use the saw the way a carpenter would. Rest the wood on a low table or bench—the section of the wood with the sawing line on it should protrude over the edge. Kneel on the board to prevent it from moving. Hold the saw at an angle of about 45 degrees, and rest it on the marked line. To steady the saw, grasp the edge of the wood with your hand, resting your thumb or knuckle against the blade, well above the teeth. Draw the saw back and forth a few times, moving it just a few inches at a time, so that you begin to make a cut (Figure 70).

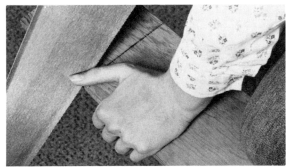

Figure 70. Beginning stroke with the handsaw

Remove your thumb from the saw blade, and make full cuts. Use the entire length of the saw. The only pressure you need on the downstroke is the weight of the saw itself. Since it cuts only on the downstroke, there should be no pressure at all on the return, or upstroke. Try to keep the saw at about the same 45-degree angle as you work (Figure 71).

Hold small pieces of wood in a vise, maintaining the same cutting angle.

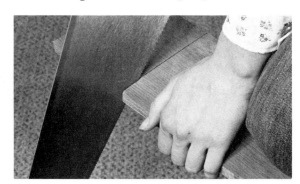

Figure 71. Hold saw at 45-degree angle.

Coping saw

A coping saw is used to make curved cuts in thin wood. It consists of a metal frame with a wooden handle and a thin, narrow blade.

How it is used

Mark your cutting design in pencil, and place the wood in a vise. Hold the saw horizontally, and move it back and forth (Figure 72). Exert very little pressure—just

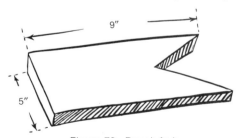

Figure 72. Using coping saw

enough to cut into the wood. The saw cuts only when you *pull*, not when you push it forward.

Or make a *bench fork* from scrap wood, as in Figure 73. (Dimensions shown are not absolute; vary them as much as you like.)

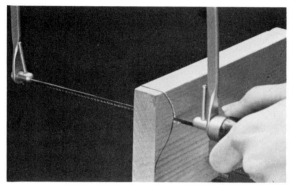

Figure 73. Bench fork

Clamp the bench fork to the edge of a table or bench. Place your wood on the fork. Steady it with your hand or clamp it to the fork. Cut with an up-and-down movement, with the saw handle *beneath* the fork. In this position, the saw cuts only on the downstroke (Figure 74). Move the wood you are cutting so that the saw blade is always in the notched opening of the bench fork.

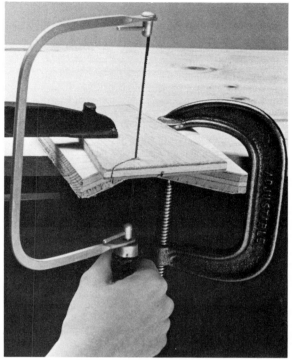

Figure 74. Bench fork, coping saw in use

To change coping-saw blades

Blades are available in different degrees of fineness or coarseness to enable them to cut either wood or metal.

Holding the frame and lower adjusting pin, turn the handle counterclockwise to loosen the blade (Figure 75).

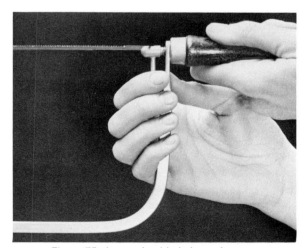

Figure 75. Loosening blade in coping saw

Insert a new blade with its teeth pointing down, toward the handle. Again, take hold of the lower adjusting pin and frame, and turn the handle to the right. Just before it is fully tightened, align the adjusting pins with the frame so that the blade teeth face outward and the blade is not twisted. Tighten the handle.

Hacksaw

A hacksaw consists of a metal frame into which a narrow saw blade is clamped (Figure 76). The frame can be adjusted to accommodate

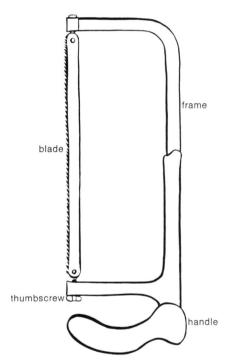

blade

frame

thumbscrew

handle

Figure 76. Hacksaw

blades of various lengths. Use a hacksaw to make straight cuts in metal (see Chapter 9, Figure 12). Cut rods, tubes, or firm sheet-metal structures.

How it is used

Metal to be cut must be held firmly or clamped in a vise. As with other saws, the teeth of a hacksaw blade point forward; therefore the saw cuts only when it is pushed forward. Don't press down when drawing the blade back.

Hacksaw blades are classed according to the number of teeth per inch. The thicker the metal, the coarser the blade; the thinner the metal, the finer the blade.

MATERIAL TO BE CUT	TEETH PER INCH
Brass, copper, steel, bars, ¼ inch to 1 inch	18
Thick tubing, iron pipe, ⅛ inch to ¼ inch thick	24
Thin tubing, sheet metal	32

Keyhole saw

A keyhole saw consists of a handle and flat, tapered steel blade with a row of teeth along one edge (Figure 77). It is used to cut shapes out of the center of a piece of wood.

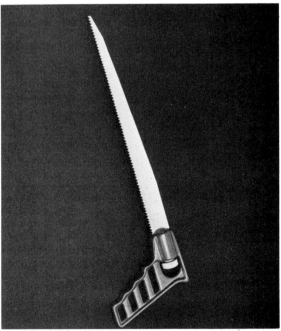

Figure 77. Keyhole saw

How it is used

First draw the shape to be cut directly on the back of the wood you are using. Drill one or more holes at the edges of the part to be cut out. Insert the thin, narrow keyhole-saw blade, and cut out the piece you have marked.

Saber saw

A saber saw is a portable, electrically operated saw (see Chapter 6, Figure 7). It uses thin blades which can easily be interchanged. Use a saber saw to make straight or curved cuts in wood, metal, or plastics.

How it is used

Edge cut: Start from the edge of a piece of wood. Hold the saw down firmly, and follow any line you have marked on the wood.

Pocket cut: This cut removes a section of wood. For example, to cut a rectangle from a wall panel to expose a wall box, you would have to make a pocket cut. Mark the rectangle you wish to cut and draw an oval inside the rectangle (Figure 78). Rest the base of the saw

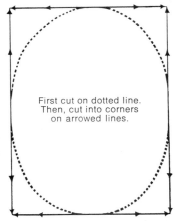

First cut on dotted line. Then, cut into corners on arrowed lines.

Figure 78. Oval drawn on wood before making pocket cut

on the wood, leaning the saw forward as in Figure 79. Keep the blade well clear of the

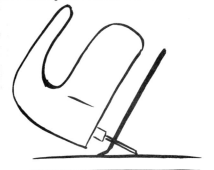

Figure 79. Proper position of saber saw for starting pocket cut

surface. Turn on the saw and lower it slowly so that the blade makes contact with the wood very gradually. Keep lowering the saw until its base is almost flat against the wood (Figure 80). The saw blade will penetrate the wood.

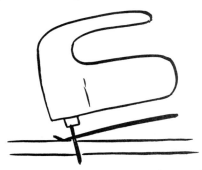

Figure 80. Saber saw penetrating wood

Once the saw has penetrated the wood, saw around the marked oval line until you have completed the cut; the oval section will fall out. Then cut out the corners of the rectangle (see Figure 78).

Scraper

A paint scraper is like a broad knife with a straight end. It consists of a wooden or plastic handle and a flat, steel blade. Blades vary from 3 to 7 inches wide (Figure 81).

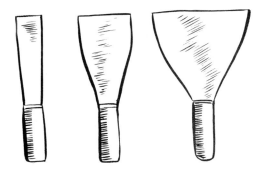

Figure 81. Paint scrapers

This tool, also called a painter's knife, is used to remove old wallpaper, clean wood and plaster surfaces before they are painted, apply patching compounds to walls and ceilings, scrape away loose paint and blisters from house exteriors, and remove old furniture finishes that have been softened by paint remover (see Chapter 3, Figure 4).

How it is used

Push a scraper against the area to be cleaned so that its sharp front edge cuts away unwanted material.

Other types of scrapers

A *putty knife* is a narrow paint knife, about 1½ inches wide. Use it for applying putty to windows, patching small areas on walls and ceilings, and scraping narrow places that can't be reached with a painter's knife.

A *wood scraper* has a wooden handle and a replaceable steel blade, slightly hooked at its end (Figure 82). Wood scrapers are made with

Figure 82. Wood scraper

blades from 1 to 4 inches wide. Use a wood scraper to remove paint or varnish from woodwork. This tool is *pulled*, not pushed.

Other scrapers use razor blades, and are mostly used to clean paint from windows.

Screwdrivers

A screwdriver is a metal rod (it may be round, square, or octagonal) with a handle at one end and a flat blade with a square tip at the other. Flat-bladed screwdrivers fit screws with slotted heads, while Phillips screwdrivers fit screws with cross-slotted heads (Figure 83).

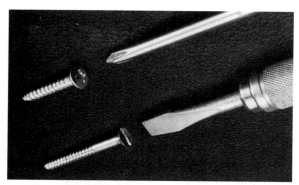

Figure 83. Phillips cross-slotted screw and driver; flat-bladed screwdriver and slotted screw

Use a screwdriver to turn, or *drive*, screws into wood or other materials, and to *draw*, or remove, them. Don't use good screwdrivers for any other purpose. An *old* screwdriver, however, may be used as an all-purpose tool. There's scarcely a home in the country that doesn't have one sitting in the kitchen drawer. Use it to pry covers from paint cans, and as a general pusher, poker, and all-purpose utility tool.

How it is used

Be sure to select a screwdriver that fits the screw you are using or else both screw and driver may become mutilated. A screwdriver that is too small is just as bad as one that is too large. The correct size fits the screw slot snugly, with little or no play. As a rule, the width of the screwdriver tip should be about the same as that of the screw slot (Figure 84).

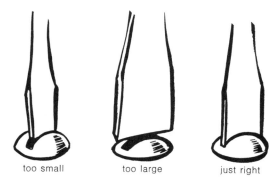

too small   too large   just right

Figure 84. Screwdriver tips in screw slots

Before driving a screw into wood, drill a *pilot hole* (see page 167). Next lubricate the screw threads by scraping them across a bar of soft soap. Push the end of the screw into the pilot hole, and get it started with a few turns to the right.

Hold the butt of the handle snugly in the heel of your hand. With your other hand, hold the blade near its tip, and guide it into the screw slot (Figure 85). Turn to the right, and exert pressure. At the same time, hold the screwdriver firmly, to prevent it from slipping out of the slot.

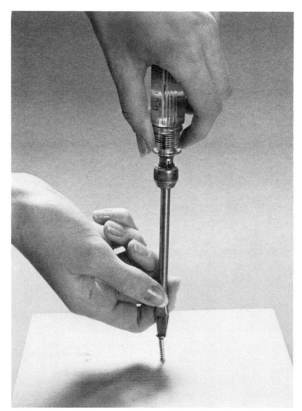

Figure 85. Using screwdriver with one hand guiding tip

Screw-holding driver

This is simply a screwdriver with an attachment that holds the screw to the driver, enabling you to start and drive it with one hand.

One type has two spring-steel fingers which hold the screw (Figure 86). Another has

Figure 86. Spring-steel fingers holding screw

a double blade. Pushing a sleeve toward the top will cause the blades to twist, locking screw and driver together with a wedge action (Figure 87).

Figure 87. Wedge-type screw-holding driver

Automatic-return ratchet screwdriver

This screwdriver, made in two sizes, has an interchangeable tip. When you push the tool against a screw, an internal spiral mechanism causes the tip to rotate.

How it is used

Hold the handle in one hand; with the other, hold the knurled collar near the tip. Guide the tip into the screw slot and push the handle down (Figure 88). The blade will turn and drive the screw.

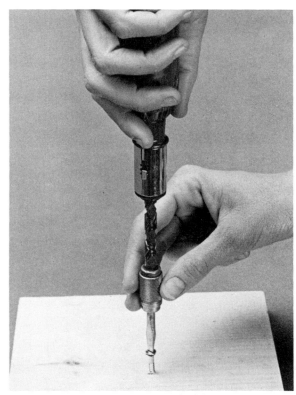

Figure 88. Using a ratchet screwdriver

When you have pushed the handle as far as it will go, ease up just enough to allow the tool's built-in spring to return the handle to its starting position. Don't relax completely; if you do, the screwdriver will slip out of the screw slot. Also, be sure to hold the screwdriver firmly, or it may flip right out of your hand. Because a simple adjustment will reverse the direction in which the tool turns, you can use it to draw, or remove, screws.

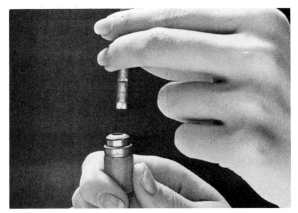

Figure 89. Changing an automatic-screwdriver bit

To change bits, hold the handle firmly against your body or a tabletop. Pull the knurled sleeve down, away from the tip. Pull out the blade—you may have to jiggle it a bit in order to free it—and insert another (Figure 89).

Offset screwdriver

The tip of this screwdriver is bent at a sharp right angle and can therefore be used when you don't have enough space to manipulate a conventional screwdriver. It is made to fit either slotted or cross-slotted screws.

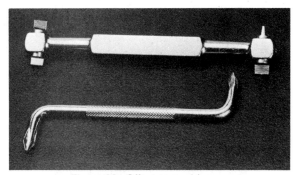

Figure 90. Offset screwdrivers

How it is used

Figure 90 shows two typical offset screwdrivers. They are held with the handle parallel to the surface on which you are working. Fit the screwdriver tip into the screw head, then rotate the handle either right or left to tighten or loosen the screw.

When you just don't have enough room to turn the screwdriver very much, use a ratchet

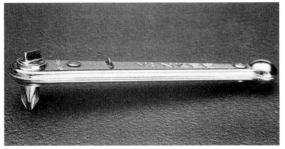

Figure 91. Ratchet offset screwdriver

offset screwdriver (Figure 91). These are made for both slotted and Phillips (cross-slotted) screws. Flip a small lever on the handle to reverse the ratchet action.

Staple tacker

A staple tacker, or staple gun, is a hand-held tool that drives staples (see Chapter 5, Figure 14). Staples are used to fasten all kinds of things to wood: you can staple carpeting to floors, runners to stairs, and chicken wire to fence posts. In many cases, staples take the place of nails and tacks.

How it is used

To load the stapler, first remove the rear spring. Staplers may have slightly different loading systems, but they all operate on the same principle. Insert a strip of staples (Figure 92) and replace the spring by pushing

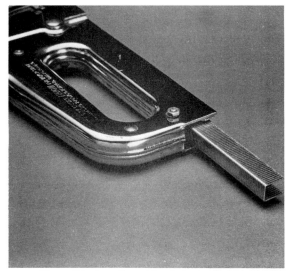

Figure 92. Inserting strip of staples in tacker

it in until it clicks into place. If it does not go in far enough, there are probably too many staples in the gun; remove some, and try again.

As an illustration of how to use a stapler, suppose you are tacking down a corner of loose carpeting. Hold the staple tacker *flat* against the carpet, and exert *firm* pressure downward. Squeeze the trigger without letting up on the downward pressure; a powerful spring will drive a staple through the carpet and into the floor.

Examine the staple; it should be close to the floor. If it stands away from the floor, one of three things may be wrong: (1) you have not exerted enough downward pressure; (2) you have been holding the tacker loosely; or (3) the staples you are using are too long.

Use staples of the size and type recommended for your particular make of stapler. *They are not interchangeable.* Staples comes in different sizes, in boxes of 1000. Figure 93 shows some uses to which they can be put.

SUGGESTED USES	LENGTH OF STAPLE LEG:
Bulletin boards, window screening, closet linings, shelf paper, window shades, display signs, party decorations	¼ inch
Weatherstripping, upholstery materials, applying heavy shelf coverings	⁵⁄₁₆ inch
Tacking down insulating bats (fiberglass, rockwool, etc.); securing wire mesh, netting, carpeting, roofing paper, felt weatherstripping, window screening	⅜ inch and ½ inch
Heavy carpeting, wire mesh around garden areas, general heavy-duty use around farm and home	⁹⁄₁₆ inch

Figure 93. Suggested uses for staples

Rust-proof staples for outdoor use are available in bronze and monel metal. These are especially recommended for window screening and other places where they will be exposed to the weather.

Tile nippers

Tile nippers, special end-cutting pliers made of hardened steel (Chapter 7, Figure 7), are used to cut tiles. They are particularly useful where irregular shapes or curves must be cut.

See page 133 for directions on use.

Tin snips

Tin snips are like heavy-duty scissors. They have long handles and short, powerful jaws. Use them to cut sheet metal, but don't use them on wire or metal bars. Snips are made for either right- or left-handed people.

Aviation tin snips are made in three styles: right-cut for the right-handed, left-cut for the left-handed, and straight-cut for either (Figure 94).

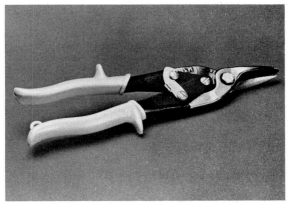

Figure 94. Straight-cut aviation snips

How they are used

Use tin snips as though they were scissors. Regular tin snips are best for straight cuts; for curves, use aviation snips.

Trowel

A trowel is a rigid, flat plate, fitted with a handle. It may be made of wood or metal. Metal trowels may have smooth or notched edges (see Chapter 3, Figure 35). A straight-edged trowel is used to smooth plaster or cement. A notched trowel is used to apply the correct amount of adhesive before laying tiles.

See page 63 for directions on use.

Utility knife

A utility knife is simply a metal handle that

holds a sharp blade (Figure 95). Blades can be

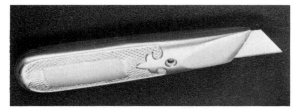

Figure 95. Utility knife

replaced as necessary. Figure 96 shows several other types of utility knives.

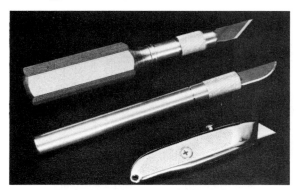

Figure 96. Other types of utility knives

Use the knife for cutting or scoring resilient floor tiles, shaving wood, cutting carpeting, stripping insulation from wires, or any other tasks which call for a sharp, heavy-duty blade.

How it is used

Cut with the sharp point of a blade. When cutting a shape out of cardboard or other material, place the piece you are cutting on a backing of heavy scrap cardboard or soft wood. If possible, cut through with a single stroke, going into the backing underneath; this insures a clean cut. Otherwise, make several light strokes.

Vise

A vise is a holding device used to grip things as you work on them. It is usually made of heavy steel, and has two jaws. The space between the jaws can be adjusted by turning a handle, which is attached to a heavy screw. The jaw at the front of the vise moves back and forth as the handle is turned in either direction.

How it is used

There are two general types of vises. The jaws of a *woodworker's vise* are lined with wood (Figure 97) to keep them from leaving

Figure 97. Woodworker's vise

marks on anything they grip. A *machinist's vise* has metal jaws, often with sharp, serrated teeth. To avoid damaging delicate objects, special lead or plastic inserts can be used to line the jaws. You can also use a machinist's vise for woodwork by simply sandwiching your work between two pieces of scrap wood, as in Figure 98.

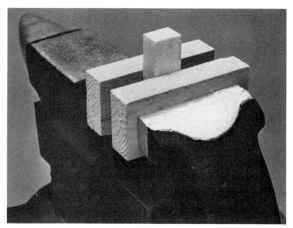

Figure 98. Using machinist's vise with two pieces of scrap wood inserted

To use a vise, first fasten it in place so that it can't move. Clamp small vises to the edge of a table or workbench (Figure 99). Large vises may be screwed or bolted to a bench top. Some vises are the vacuum-action type. Flipping a lever causes a rubber base to adhere to almost any smooth, hard surface, except unfinished wood.

Figure 99. Small vise clamped to table edge

Open the jaws of a vise by turning the handle to the left. Insert the piece on which you are working, and close the jaws by turning the handle in the opposite direction.

Wrench

A wrench is a gripping tool. It is usually made of tough steel, and may have either fixed or adjustable jaws. Figure 100 shows an adjustable-end wrench in two different sizes.

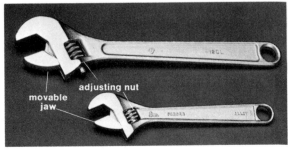

Figure 100. Two adjustable-end wrenches

A wrench is used to tighten or loosen threaded objects, such as nuts, bolts, pipes, and plumbing fittings.

How it is used
Adjustable-end wrenches are the type you are most likely to need for home repairs. They have smooth jaws, which may be used on plumbing fittings without causing any damage. You should own one 8-inch wrench and one 12-inch wrench (see Figure 100).

Fit the jaws of the wrench around the object you wish to tighten or loosen. Do this by turning the adjusting nut. Don't make the jaws too tight; you should be able to slide them on and off the object easily.

Most threaded objects have right-hand threads; turning them to the right will tighten them. To loosen them, turn them in the opposite direction.

Wherever possible, pull the wrench toward you as you work; this gives you greater control than if you were to push it.

Open-end wrench

An open-end wrench is a flat steel bar, with a smooth, U-shaped opening at each end. The openings are designed to fit standard-sized nuts, from ¼ to 1½ inches in diameter. You can buy wrenches singly or in sets of different sizes (Figure 101).

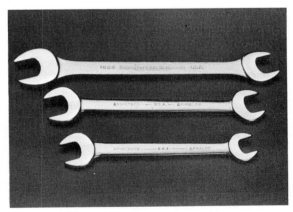

Figure 101. Open-end wrenches

Box wrench

A box wrench has a notched opening at each end (Figure 102). When placed over a

Figure 102. Box wrench

nut, the notches engage its corners. As with other wrenches, you must use one that fits the nut exactly.

Pipe wrench

This is a rough, tough wrench, used mainly for turning pipes and other plumbing fittings where scratches and gouges won't matter (Figure 103). *Don't* use a pipe wrench on plated

Figure 103. Pipe wrench

fittings, even if you protect them by wrapping tape around them. The teeth of the wrench will cut through the tape, leaving marks.

Hexagonal wrench

Hex, or hexagonal, wrenches (also known as hex keys), are needed to loosen or tighten *Allen screws*, screws with hexagonal holes in their heads.

Hex keys come in sets and range in size from $1/16$ to 1 inch. Some sets consist of loose pieces, while others are swung out of a holder, as needed (Figure 104).

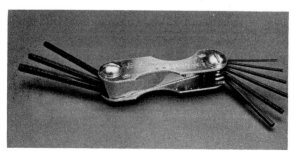

Figure 104. Hex keys

Materials and Equipment

Abrasives

Abrasives are fine, hard particles, or *grits*. Abrasive papers and cloths consist of grits glued to paper or cloth backings. When rubbed against wood or metal, the grit wears away tiny bits of the surface, leaving it smooth and clean.

How they are used

Abrasive papers and cloths are usually torn into quarters or other convenient sizes. *Do not cut them;* the hard grits will ruin sharp scissors and knives. Instead, place the paper or cloth on a flat surface. Lay a strip of wood or a ruler along the line you wish to tear. Press down on the wood, and with a firm pull, tear the paper or cloth along its edge (Figure 105).

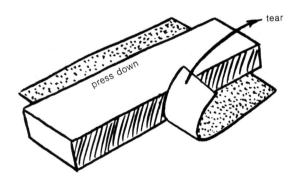

Figure 105. Tearing abrasive paper

Next make a *sanding block*, which is nothing more than a small piece of wood around which you wrap the paper or cloth you have just torn (Figure 106). Rub the area you wish to smooth, using overlapping strokes and firm pressure. On wood, sand with the grain to avoid disfiguring scratches.

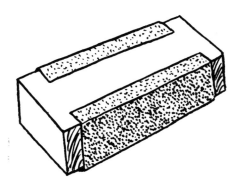

Figure 106. Sanding block

When the abrasive becomes dull and worn, shift the paper around the block so that a new surface is available for rubbing.

Tear abrasive cloth into narrow strips if you want to polish a piece of metal that can be held in a vise. Use it as though you were shining shoes.

Types of abrasive papers and cloths

Sandpaper, also known as *flint paper,* is composed of sharp bits of quartz glued to heavy paper. Depending on the size of the abrasive grits, papers may be graded as very fine, fine, medium, coarse, or very coarse. Or they may have numbers stamped on the back.

You can translate the numbers into degrees of fineness or coarseness by using the table shown in Figure 107 which applies *only* to sandpaper.

VERY FINE	FINE	MEDIUM	COARSE	VERY COARSE
4/0 to 6/0	2/0 to 3/0	1/0 to 1/2	1-2	2½-3½

Figure 107. Sandpaper grades

Garnet paper cuts faster than sandpaper, lasts longer, and is available in a greater variety of grit sizes. Abrasive grits are made of crushed garnet.

Aluminum oxide is a man-made abrasive that is tougher than garnet.

Emery is aluminum oxide in its natural state.

Silicon carbide is the toughest of all abrasive papers. It is made with silicon carbide, a synthetic material. Silicon carbide papers may be used wet or dry. With water as a lubricant, a fine-grit paper can smooth out tiny irregularities on varnished and lacquered surfaces, leaving a satin finish.

Crocus cloth is one of the finest abrasives, used for polishing metal. It is made in only one grade.

Steel wool needs no introduction to anyone who has ever washed pots and pans. Unlike the household product, the type used for home repairs does not contain soap. Grades range from No. 0000 (very fine) to No. 3 (coarse). It is used with paint remover to remove old finishes. It is also useful as a general metal scourer and polisher.

ABRASIVE	USED FOR
Sandpaper	Light wood sanding; removing paint and varnish from wood.
Garnet paper	All wood sanding; removing paint and varnish from wood; can be used with electric sander.
Aluminum oxide paper and cloth	All wood sanding; light metal sanding; removing rust; polishing metal; removing rust from metal; can be used in an electric sander.
Emery cloth	Polishing and scouring metal; removing paint, varnish, and rust from metal.
Crocus cloth	Polishing metal.
Silicon carbide	Wet sanding of varnish, enamels, and lacquers; used dry to polish metal.

Figure 108. Uses for abrasive papers and cloths

Grit sizes

The degree of fineness or coarseness is stamped on the back of every sheet of abrasive paper. Some manufacturers show grit sizes, while others use a numbering system. The table in Figure 109 gives equivalents of numbers and grit sizes. See Figure 107 for sandpaper grades.

	GRIT SIZES	NUMBERS
Superfine	400	10/0
Extra fine	320	9/0
	280	8/0
	240	7/0
	220	6/0
Fine	180	5/0
	150	4/0
	120	3/0
Medium	100	2/0
	80	1/0
	60	½
Coarse	50	1
	40	1½
	36	2
Very coarse	30	2½
	24	3
	20	3½

Figure 109. Comparison of grit sizes and numbers

Oilstone

An oilstone is a block of synthetic, abrasive material. It is usually made of either aluminum oxide or silicon carbide molded into a rectangular shape. Most oilstones have a coarse and a fine side.

Oilstones are used for sharpening tools (see page 206).

Adhesives

Glues, cements, and other substances used to hold things together are generally known as adhesives. There are hundreds of different ones on the market, most of which you will never be called on to use or need to know about. However, you should know about the basic types and how they are used (see Figure 110).

Contact cement

Use contact cement to bond any two flat surfaces together.

Apply a coat to both of the surfaces to be bonded. Wait until the cement is not quite dry, but still a bit tacky. Align both surfaces, and press them together. You must be accurate, as you can't make any adjustments after they make contact.

Epoxy

This is a two-part adhesive. One container holds *resin*; the other holds *hardener*. Mix them in equal proportions—squeezing the same amount from each tube—then stir them together with a nail, toothpick, or wood sliver. Working fast, glue your two pieces together; once the two parts have been mixed, the adhesive sets very rapidly.

Epoxies will hold most things together, but shouldn't be used on flexible surfaces or porous materials.

Latex glue

This contains rubber, and is used to cement fabrics together. It is particularly useful when making a repair where flexibility is important.

Mastics

Mastics have the consistency of toothpaste. There are dozens of different kinds, sold in tubes, cartridges, or large cans. They have a limited use, mostly on large surfaces such as floors, walls, or large wood panels.

Rubber cements

Paper cement is one type of rubber cement which will stick to most surfaces. Use it to make decorative, paper-covered articles. *Heavy-duty rubber cement* is stronger, and can be used to repair rubber articles as well as other materials.

Silicone cements

Silicone cements, sold in squeeze tubes, are too thick to flow like liquids, yet thin enough to be squeezed out of the tube. Use them to permanently bond two dissimilar materials. When dry, they form a tough, flexible, waterproof, rubbery substance.

Waterproof wood glues

Some glues are sold in powder form to be mixed with water. Others have a resin which must be mixed with a powder. With either type, apply the glue, then clamp the work until the glue sets. Work either indoors or, on a warm day, outdoors. Use waterproof glues for repairing outdoor furniture.

White glues

These are mostly plastic compounds, sold in squeeze-bottle containers for easy application. They will take care of most household gluing jobs.

Here is a quick reference table to help you choose the right glue for each job.

SUGGESTED USES	CONTACT CEMENT	EPOXY	LATEX	MASTIC	PAPER CEMENT	HEAVY-DUTY RUBBER CEMENT	SILICONE	WATER-PROOF WOOD GLUE	WHITE GLUE
To fasten paper to almost any surface	●				●				
Gluing cardboard, cork, fabric, leather to each other or to flat wood or metal surfaces	●		●			●			●
Gluing stones into jewelry settings; repairing tool handles		●							
Patching fabrics—carpets, seat covers, upholstery	●		●			●			
Resetting loose brick, resilient tile, ceramic tile; installing wall panels	●			●			●		
Repairing glass, ceramics, ceramic tile		●					●		
Repairing wooden outdoor furniture		●						●	
General wood repairs		●						●	●
Joining metals	●	●		●			●		
Joining glass to glass, glass to wood, glass to metal		●					●		
Installing ceramic tile				●					
Installing resilient floor tile				●					

Figure 110. Types of adhesives and their uses

Brushes

Brushes may have either natural or nylon bristles. Use nylon brushes for both oil- and water-base paints, but don't use natural-bristle brushes for water-base paints; they soak up water and become limp. Also, don't use nylon brushes with shellac.

Buy good brushes. You can tell a good brush from a poor one by feeling it. Squeeze the bristles where they emerge from the handle. The brush should feel full. If there is a hollow space inside, don't buy that brush. Examine the ends of the bristles as well. Natural bristles and good nylon bristles have flagged, or split, tips. A good brush also holds its shape—the bristles come together at the end, forming a solid, even tip.

You will need more than one brush. It's not a good idea to use the same brush for enamel, varnish, water-base paints, and lacquer. Keep a brush for each different type of paint you use; don't interchange them.

Brushes may be flat, oval, or round. Flat brushes are used for most paint jobs.

Below is a list of suggested types and sizes of brushes to be used for specific jobs:

For woodwork	use a 2 or 3 inch flat brush
For window sash	use a 1 inch flat or oval brush
For walls, ceilings, and other large areas	use a 4 inch flat brush
For furniture finishing	use a 2 or 3 inch flat varnish brush

After you have cleaned a brush you have used, replace it in its original cardboard packing. Or wrap it in paper, as on page 46.

Chemical drain cleaner

Many chemical drain cleaners contain lye, a strong corrosive. It combines with grease and organic material to form a soluble soap that can be flushed down the drain. Use lye cleaners only if some drainage is present, never where there is a complete stoppage.

Circuit tester

This is a simple device consisting of a neon lamp bulb in a plastic housing, and two wires which lead from it (see Chapter 1, Figure 6). It is used to determine whether current is flowing in a circuit.

How it is used
Plug the leads into the openings of an electrical outlet. If the outlet is "live," the neon bulb will light up.

Expansion fastener

Used to attach things to hollow walls or ceilings, an expansion fastener consists of a bolt and a special nut with expanding legs (see Chapter 4, Figure 33).

How it is used
Drill a hole large enough so that you can pass the expansion fastener through it. Turn the head of the bolt clockwise, until it is tight. As you turn, the nut on the other side of the hollow wall becomes compressed, and expands.

Now turn the bolt head counterclockwise, and remove it from the nut, which is now attached to the wall. Pass the bolt through the object you wish to hang, then screw it into the nut until it is tight.

Extension wire

Extension wires for light-duty use are usually made of a 2-conductor lamp cord with a male plug at one end and a female receptacle at the other. Heavy-duty extension cords may be made of 2-conductor or 3-conductor wire. You can buy extension wires in lengths up to 100 feet or make your own (see page 12).

Female receptacle

This is the fitting at the end of an extension cord to which an appliance can be connected.

Force cup

See Rubber plunger

Friction spring

Friction springs are made of thin steel, bent into a curved V-shape. They are used to replace broken sash cords in double-hung sashes (see Chapter 5, Figure 21).

Fuses

A fuse is a safety device containing a strip of low-melting-point alloy (see Chapter 1, Figure 1). Excessive current drawn through a circuit will cause the strip to melt, breaking the circuit. Fuses which screw into a control panel are rated from 10 to 30 amperes.

Kerosene

Kerosene is a petroleum distillate used as a fuel in some heating units or as a cleaner and solvent. Use it to remove paint and caulking compound from tools, and to rub lightly rusted areas.

Ladders

A *stepladder* has two legs, which open to form a letter A; it also has a platform that can be folded down to hold tools or containers of paint. A 6-foot ladder is best for all-around house use.

An *extension ladder* is more convenient for outdoor use, when painting siding or trim, or cleaning gutters. It has two straight sections which slide against each other, thus making it possible to adjust the ladder to a variety of lengths.

Stepladders and extensions ladders are made in both wood and aluminum.

Lintless cloths

Use a lintless cloth when cleaning a surface before applying varnish. You can buy lintless cloth or use a piece of worn but well-laundered sheet. Sprinkle a cloth with varnish to make a *tack rag* with which you can wipe up tiny particles of dust on a surface that is to be given a fine finish.

Machine oil

This is a light-bodied, free-flowing oil (such as sewing machine oil) used for general lubricating purposes around the house. Use it sparingly on hinges, small motors, and places where two metal pieces rub together.

Male plug

One end of an appliance cord or extension wire has a male plug attached to it (see Chapter 1, Figure 17). Depending on the number of conductors in the cord, the plug may have two or three prongs. A male plug fits into a wall outlet.

Metal triangle

A triangle made of sheet metal is an invaluable aid when cutting and trimming wallpaper that is next to a ceiling or baseboard. Buy one at a paint or artist's supply store.

Mirror clips

Mirror clips may be made of either plastic or metal. They can be screwed to a door or wall to support a mirror and prevent it from slipping (see Chapter 4, Figure 43).

Nails

Nails are fasteners that look like pieces of stiff wire; one end is pointed, the other has a head. Ordinary nails are made of iron. Specialized nails may be made of copper, brass, bronze, aluminum, hard steel, stainless steel, or monel metal.

Use nails to hold pieces of wood together, either temporarily or permanently. They can also be used to fasten things to masonry.

Nails most often used

Unless you need a specific type nail for a special purpose, use *wire nails*, available at any hardware store. Buy them by the pound, either loose or packaged. It's a good idea to buy a package of *assorted nails*, which contains many different sizes and types.

Common nails, with flat, disklike tops, or heads, are used for rough work. *Finishing nails* have small heads, and are mostly used indoors for fine work (Figure 111).

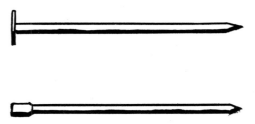

Figure 111. Common nail and finishing nail

Nail sizes

Nail sizes are indicated by the symbol *d*, which stands for *penny.* Its exact meaning has been lost, but nails are still bought and sold according to this ancient system. Sizes of nails range from 2d to 60d, as in Figure 112. Finishing nails less than 1 inch long are called *brads*, and are classed according to their length.

NAIL SIZE	LENGTH IN INCHES
2d	1
3d	1¼
4d	1½
6d	2
8d	2½
10d	3
12d	3¼
16d	3½
20d	4
30d	4½
40d	5
60d	6

Figure 112. Nail sizes

Masonry nails

Masonry nails are used to fasten things to brick, cinder block, concrete block, or concrete walls. They are made of hardened steel, and generally have fluted sides to hold them in place after being driven (Figure 113).

Figure 113. Masonry nail

How they are used

Using a carbide-tipped bit in an electric drill, drill a hole slightly smaller in diameter than the nail you are using. Pass the nail through the object you are fastening to the wall, and hammer it into the hole.

Nuts and bolts

A bolt is simply a threaded rod with a head at one end. If its entire length is threaded, it is usually known as a *machine screw.* The head of a bolt may be flat, round, or square, and is usually slotted so that it can be turned with a screwdriver (Figure 114).

Figure 114. Nut and bolt

A nut is a small block of metal with an internal thread that allows it to be turned on a bolt. It may be square or hexagonal.

Used to fasten metal pieces together, nuts and bolts may be made of steel, brass, bronze, stainless steel, or aluminum. Some are galvanized—that is, plated with zinc. Others are chrome-plated.

How they are used

Drill a hole through both pieces of metal. Pass the bolt through the holes. Turn the nut on the bolt by hand as far as you can, then tighten it with a wrench. If the head turns as you turn the wrench, hold it steady with a screwdriver.

Oilstone

See pages 194 and 206.

Packing

Packing for faucets and valves may be made of either graphite-impregnated cord, solid graphite, or teflon. A single winding of packing is applied under a packing nut (see Chapter 2, Figure 6). As the nut is turned down, the packing is compressed, forming a solid, waterproof washer.

Paint, or brush, pad

Paint pads are flat rectangles of carpetlike material about ½ inch thick. A pad fits into a frame to which a handle is attached (see Chapter 8, Figure 9). The pad is dipped into paint, then used to paint shingles or siding.

Paint remover

Made in liquid or paste form, paint remover softens old paint so that it can be scraped off. It should be used in a well-ventilated area. Wear rubber gloves. There are two general types of paint remover. After use, traces of paint remover left by one type must be washed off with paint thinner. The other can be cleaned off with water.

(See electric paint remover, page 174)

Paint roller

A paint roller consists of a cylindrical frame over which a sleeve is slipped (see Chapter 8, Figure 2). Sleeves are made in various textures to suit the surface you are painting. Some sleeves are disposable: use them once, then throw them away. Most are made to be cleaned and reused.

Paint thinner

Paint thinner is also known as mineral spirits. Use it to dilute oil-base paints, and for cleaning brushes. You can buy it by the gallon, in sealed cans.

Picture hooks

Picture hooks, or hangers, are secured to a wall by a finishing nail that goes through the hanger and enters the wall at an angle (see Chapter 4, Figure 46). Hooks, made to hold different weights, come in a variety of sizes.

Picture wire

Picture wire, usually sold in 15-foot coils, is made for hanging pictures and mirrors. Since it is composed of many thin strands of steel twisted together, it is both strong and flexible.

Pipe insulation

Pipe insulation is sold in strips, about 2 inches wide. It may be made of cork glued to paper or cloth, plastic foam, or any other substance that has many air cells. Insulation prevents cold-water pipes from sweating during hot, muggy weather.

Plumber's joint compound and tape

A leak may occur wherever a pipe is screwed into a fitting. To prevent this, coat the pipe threads with joint compound, a thick, paintlike substance that seals the spaces between the threads of the pipe and fitting. Teflon joint tape serves the same purpose; wrap one winding around pipe threads before screwing the pipe into a fitting.

Plumb line

A plumb line is an invaluable tool if you intend to hang wallpaper or put up wall panels. It is simply a string with a weight attached to the bottom. The upper, free end of the string is tacked to the wall, and held until the bottom weight comes to rest. The string is now *plumb*, or perfectly vertical.

Razor blade holder

This is a simple clamp, sometimes equipped with a handle, which holds a single-edged razor blade . There are two types: one uses a razor blade as a cutting tool (see Chapter 3, Figure 50), and the other uses it as a scraper (Figure 115).

Figure 115. Razor blade in holder to be used as scraper

Use a razor blade in a holder for any job that requires a sharp cutting edge. It can easily cut through fabrics and various types of window screening. Used as a scraper, a razor blade can remove dried paint from windows and ceramic tiles.

The holder is a protective device which makes it possible to use a razor blade without cutting yourself. You can change blades easily; in most cases, simply slide them out of the holder. *Never* use a double-edged blade.

Respirator

A respirator is simply a mask that fits over the nose and mouth (Figure 116). It consists of a frame and a filter. Filters, made of gauze or foam plastic, are replaceable. Use a respirator when spraying paint or sanding wood.

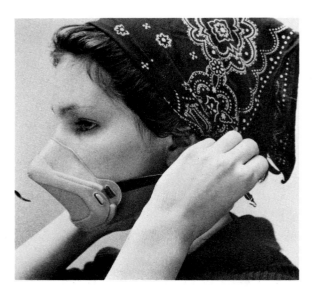

Figure 116. Face mask, or respirator

Rubber gloves

Protect your hands with rubber gloves whenever you use paint remover or any other substance that might irritate your skin. Dust the insides of gloves with talcum powder to make them easy to slip on.

Rubber plunger, or force cup

Also known as a plumber's friend, this is a rubber cup which is attached to a wooden handle (see Chapter 2, Figure 12). Place it over a clogged drain and push the handle down repeatedly. This builds up air pressure in the drain, which can often force out the obstruction.

Screen roller

This is a special tool, used only when replacing screening on an aluminum screen frame. It consists of a handle with a roller at each end. The convex roller at one end is used to press the screening into the slot in the screen frame. The other, concave end is used to roll the plastic strip into the slot to hold the screening (see Chapter 5, Figures 19 and 20).

Screw plugs

Plugs may be made of lead, plastic, or wood. They are inserted into holes drilled in brick or masonry walls. Pass a screw through the object to be hung on the wall, then drive it into the plug. The screw will cause the plug to expand so that it fits tightly in the hole.

Screws

Screws are fasteners made of threaded metal. One end has a sharp, pointed *tip*. The other end, the *head*, may be either slotted or cross-slotted. Wood screws (designed to be driven into wood) may have flat, round, or oval heads (Figure 117).

Figure 117. Wood screws

They are made in many sizes of various metals—steel, brass, bronze, aluminum, stainless steel, and monel—each suited to a particular purpose. Screws may be plated with nickel, cadmium, brass, or chromium; some are galvanized, or coated with zinc, to make them rust-resistant.

Screws are used to fasten things either temporarily or permanently. Use them to hang a bulletin board, toothbrush holder, towel rack, or a small cabinet. Fittings such as cabinet-door catches, knobs, hinges, and wall-bracket supports are also held in place with screws.

How they are used

Outdoors

For all outdoor work, screws and fittings should be made of the same metal, otherwise electrolytic action will take place, resulting in corrosion. For example, when installing or replacing screws in a galvanized gate latch, you should use galvanized screws. For the same reason, a brass door knocker should be fastened in place with brass screws.

However, like all rules, this one can be broken. You can use stainless-steel screws almost anywhere, as they resist corrosion. Since aluminum screws are relatively soft, it's better to use stainless steel screws to hold aluminum storm doors and screen frames.

Indoors

For indoor work, it doesn't matter too much what kind of screws you use—just match their color and finish to the object you are fastening.

Pilot holes

Before driving a screw, drill a pilot hole—a narrow hole placed exactly where the screw is to be driven. It should be about the width of the inner thread diameter, and narrower than the outer thread (Figure 118). If the hole is too

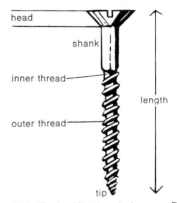

Figure 118. Typical flat-headed screw. Drill pilot hole according to size of screw threads.

large, the screw will not hold because the threads will not grip the wood.

A pilot hole makes it easy to start and drive a screw; it also prevents the screw from acting as a wedge and splitting the wood.

WOOD SCREW BODY SIZE	DRILL SIZE FOR PILOT HOLE (inches)	DRILL SIZE FOR BODY HOLE (inches)
2	1/16	5/64
4	1/16	7/64
6	5/64	9/64
8	3/32	11/64
10	7/64	3/16
12	7/64	7/32

Figure 119. Pilot-hole drill sizes

Fastening two boards with screws

Select a screw long enough to go all the way through one board and about three-quarters of the way through the other.

Consult the table in Figure 119 to determine the size of the pilot hole needed for your screw size.

Drill a pilot hole all the way through the top board and about three-quarters of the way through the bottom board (Figure 120).

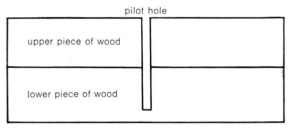

Figure 120. Pilot hole through two boards

Drill a *body hole* (Figure 121) through the top board. The body of the screw should pass through this hole without difficulty.

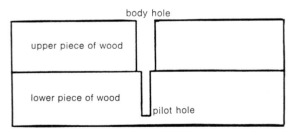

Figure 121. Body hole in top piece of wood

If you are using a round-headed screw, push it through the body hole so that its tip engages the pilot hole in the bottom board. Drive it until its head rests snugly against the wood. The entire head should show.

When using flat- or oval-headed screws, *countersink* the body hole before driving the screw. A countersink is a wedge-shaped cutter used in either a hand drill or an electric drill. It shapes the top of the body hole so that the screw head fits in perfectly (Figure 122).

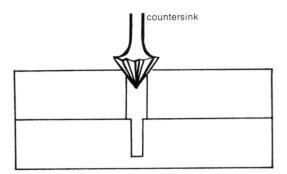

Figure 122. Countersinking body hole

Drive the screw until the head is seated firmly inside the countersunk area. The head of the screw should be even with, or slightly below the wood surface. Figure 123 shows how

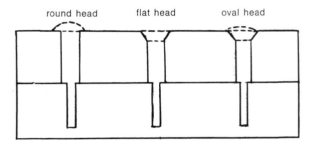

Figure 123. Profiles of round-, flat-, and oval-headed screws in holes

round-, flat-, and oval-headed screws should be driven.

You can save a lot of fuss by using a *wood-screw pilot bit*. This clever little tool, which can be used in a hand or electric drill, drills a pilot hole and a body hole, and

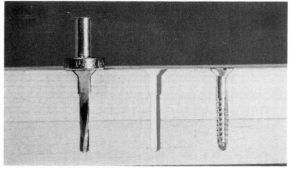

Figure 124. Cutaway showing wood-screw pilot bit; pilot hole and countersunk body hole; screw in place

countersinks the body hole—all in one operation (Figure 124). Bits come in sizes to match screw sizes.

Sheet-metal screws

Sheet-metal screws are generally used to fasten metal to metal, plastics to metal, or plastic to plastic. They are made of hard steel and have sharp threads which cover the entire length of the screw. They may have oval, flat, round, or binding heads, either slotted or cross-slotted (Figure 125).

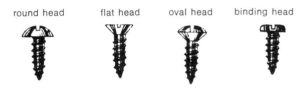

Figure 125. Sheet-metal screws

How they are used

To fasten two pieces together, drill a body hole in the top piece and a pilot hole in the bottom piece. The pilot hole must be slightly smaller than the outside screw-thread diameter. The screw should pass easily through the body hole (Figure 126).

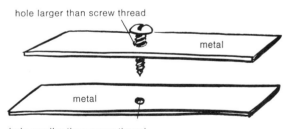

Figure 126. Body hole with sheet-metal screw inserted, and smaller pilot hole for screw tip

To drive a sheet-metal screw, first slip it through the body hole. Then fit the screw tip against the pilot hole, and turn the screw with *firm pressure* so that it cuts its own thread in the bottom piece. These are also called *self-tapping* screws.

A typical example of the use for sheet-metal screws would be fastening an outdoor thermometer bracket to an aluminum storm-sash frame. The body hole is drilled in the bracket, and the pilot hole in the aluminum frame.

Other screw devices

Screw hooks, screw eyes, cup hooks, and L-hooks are all designed to be screwed into wood (Figure 127).

Figure 127. Screw hook, screw eye, cup hook, and L-hook

Hook-and-eye combinations are often used as latches on doors and gates. Figure 128

Figure 128. Hook-and-eye combination on shutter

shows a hook that closes to engage a screw head, for use on an interior window shutter.

Always drill a *pilot hole* before installing a hook or eye. You needn't be too fussy about the exact drill size; just select one that looks thinner than the screw thread. Drill a hole in a piece of scrap wood to try it out. If the thread holds securely in the wood, the pilot hole is satisfactory. If the hook or eye pulls out easily, you need a thinner drill with which to make the pilot hole.

Lubricate screw threads before you drive them into place. Do this by scraping them across a piece of beeswax or a bar of soft soap. Lubrication is particularly important when working with hardwoods; unlubricated screws

may snap off when only partly driven into place.

How can you tell hardwood from softwood? Easy. If you can nick it with your thumbnail, it's softwood.

Seam roller

This is a small wooden roller used to roll down the edges of freshly hung wallpaper so that they won't curl up as the paper dries.

Silicone

Silicone is a synthetic lubricant that will practically eliminate friction and enable drawers to slide smoothly.

Solderless connectors

Solderless connectors are used to make connections between two or more wires. Connectors are made of plastic or ceramic material. Sometimes they have coiled wire inserts. Bare the wire ends to be connected, push them into a connector, then turn the connector clockwise (see Chapter 1, Figure 11). It will twist the wire ends, while at the same time gripping them firmly.

Solderless plugs

These are also known as quick-connecting plugs. No tools are needed in order to connect lamp cord to a plug of this type. Simply raise a lever at the top or side of the plug, insert the end of the lamp cord, and snap the lever down (see Chapter 1, Figures 13 and 14).

You can buy quick-connecting male plugs, female receptacles, and line-cord switches.

Sponges

Most sponges on the market are made of nylon or some similar plastic. Get the largest size you can for washing wallpaper after it is hung, or for cleaning up walls before you paint them. After use, clean a sponge by rubbing it with soap, then squeezing it repeatedly under running water.

Steel rule

Steel rules are made of metal about 1/16 inch thick. They may be bought in lengths ranging from 1 to 3 feet. Use a steel rule as a measuring device as well as a guide when cutting straight lines with a utility knife or razor blade.

Steel tape

A steel tape is a thin strip of flexible steel coiled within a metal case. The strip (Figure 129) is marked so that it can be used as a ruler to measure such things as heights and widths of furniture, rug dimensions, sizes of boards, and practically anything else around the house that needs measuring.

Figure 129. Steel tapes

Some tapes have to be pushed back into the case when you have finished using them. Others are self-retracting; a built-in spring pulls the tape back at the touch of a button.

How it is used

An *outside* measurement is one that gives you the dimensions of an *object*. For example, to measure the width of a board, pull out a length of tape. Hook the end of the tape over

Figure 130. Tape measuring width of board

one edge of the board. Pull the tape past the other edge, and read the width directly from the tape. Figure 130 shows a tape and a 2⅝–inch-wide board.

An *inside* measurement gives you the dimension of a *space,* such as a door opening, the inside of a drawer, or the distance between any two things.

To measure the distance between two boards, stretch the tape so that the hooked end touches one board, and the case touches the other. The case on most steel tapes is 2 inches wide. Read the last number visible on the tape, and add two inches to compensate for the width of the case. Figure 131 shows a tape measuring 4⅝ inches between boards.

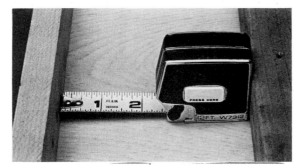

Figure 131. Tape measuring distance between boards

Straightedge

Commercially made straightedges are lengths of hardwood, often with brass edges along one side. You can use any straight piece of wood as a straightedge; it is simply a guide.

Stud finder

A stud finder is a simple device which holds a freely swinging magnet (see Chapter 4, Figures 38 and 39). It is used to locate the positions of nails in a wall, to show where a stud would be.

See page 92 for a directions on use.

Tape

Cellophane tape can be used to make temporary repairs to paper and cardboard articles. Buy it in dispensing rolls.

Colored plastic tape, which ranges from ½ to 2 inches in width, is primarily a decorative tape.

Duct tape is a wide cloth tape with an aluminized back. It is generally used when installing air ducts, for it will not permit air to escape. This makes it perfect for repairing slits in vacuum-cleaner hoses.

Electrician's tape is made of tough black plastic. A couple of turns around an electrical wire joint will insulate the wire. Use it also to prevent insulation from fraying at the end of a wire.

Package wrapping tape is a 2-inch wide paper tape with a pressure-sensitive adhesive backing. It is used primarily for temporary repairs.

Seaming tape is used to repair carpets. You can buy self-adhesive tape or the kind that is cemented down with latex. Even though you may only need a short length of tape, you will have to buy a whole roll because that's the only way it is sold.

Special masking tape is made for use by house painters. Tape around window panes to avoid smearing them. Also tape the edges of freshly painted walls so that you don't get paint on them when you are doing the woodwork in a different paint or color.

Toggle bolt

A toggle bolt is a threaded pin, or rod, with a head at one end. The head is usually round. A winglike nut is threaded on the bolt (see Chapter 4, Figure 32). Use a toggle bolt when fastening things to hollow walls or ceilings.

How it is used

First drill a hole large enough so that the winged nut, when folded, can pass through. Unscrew the nut from the bolt. Pass the bolt through the object you are going to hang, then rethread the nut.

Fold the nut and push it through the drilled hole. The wings on the nut will expand on the other side of the hollow wall, permitting you to draw the bolt up tight.

Toggle switch

Most wall switches make use of a lever, or toggle, which is flipped up to turn lights on, and down to turn them off. Some work mechanically. Better, silent types use mercury to make and break contact. A mercury switch can last indefinitely.

Transformer

A transformer is a device which can change the voltage that is fed into it. Most homes use a transformer to convert 115-volt current to the 10 or 15 volts needed to operate bells or chimes.

Try square

A try square has a metal blade and a wooden or metal handle. The blade is always at a perfect right angle to the handle. When the handle is pressed against the edge of a piece of wood, the blade will show you where to mark a perfectly square line across it (see Figure 69).

Valve-seat reamer

A valve-seat reamer looks like a threaded steel bar. One end has a hole through which a removable handle can be passed and the other end has a sharp, cutting face (see Chapter 2, Figure 3). Use it to smooth a rough valve seat in a faucet.

See pages 25-26 for directions on use.

Wall plate

Every wall switch and electrical outlet is covered by a wall plate which not only hides the outlet box in the wall, but also protects against electric shock. Decorative wall plates are made of wood, plastic, metal, or ceramics.

Washers

A washer is a flat disk with a hole in its center. It is usually made of metal. Sometimes a washer is used to separate different parts of a mechanism. Faucets use rubber or fiber washers. A leather washer is part of a flush-tank mechanism.

A *packing washer* made of fiber or brass is located on a faucet stem, just below the stem packing.

Some faucets use an *O-ring* instead of packing. This is a rubber ring, which fits into a slot and forms a waterproof joint. A worn O-ring can be easily pried out and replaced (see Chapter 2, Figure 5).

Tool Maintenance

Keep all your tools sharp and shiny. If they are clean and in working order, your tools will always be ready to use and will work efficiently when you need them. You wouldn't use a rusty knife to slice a roast, so why use a rusty tool on a piece of wood?

Rust

Clean lightly rusted tools by rubbing them with either steel wool, emery cloth, or aluminum-oxide paper or cloth.

Use a special rust remover (available at any hardware store) to clean up badly rusted tools. Brush it on, allow it to remain for the recommended time, then flush it off with water. Be sure to wear plastic or rubber gloves when using rust removers, as they usually contain acids.

To prevent rust from forming on metal surfaces, coat them with a thin film of oil applied with a rag. Use any light machine oil, such as sewing-machine oil. Don't use salad oil! Or spray tools with a rust-preventing silicone compound. Dispose of oily rags as soon as possible, placing them in a covered metal rubbish can.

Loose Tool Handles

During the winter when the heat goes on, humidity drops and wood shrinks. You'll find drawers easier to open and close; you may also find that hammer handles have shrunk, resulting in loose hammerheads. A loose hammerhead is not only awkward, but it can be dangerous.

To tighten a hammer handle, strike the bottom sharply to drive the handle further into the head. Do this with another hammer or by simply hitting it against a smooth, hard surface, such as a heavy vise or the top of a worktable.

To tighten the head further, stand the hammer on your workbench, with its head up. Locate the *wedge*, a small metal piece that is driven into the top of every wooden-handled tool; this spreads the wood so that the head stays on. Use a hammer and large nail set to drive the wedge down into the handle as far as it will go.

Cut or file off any wood that protrudes from the head; it should be even with the top of the head.

Next seal the wood that can be seen at the top of the hammerhead. Use two coats of any paint, varnish, shellac, or lacquer, or brush on a couple of coats of nail polish.

You can also tighten handles the easy way—by applying a prepared solution that swells and seals the wood.

Sharpening

Whether you are carving a turkey or shaving down a sticking drawer, you'll find it's easier and safer to work with a sharp tool. A sharp tool requires less force, and consequently allows you to maintain better control.

Since an oilstone is used for most sharpening jobs, you should know how to prepare it.

You will need:
> Oilstone
> Scrap plywood
> Wood strips
> Light machine oil or oil and kerosene (half and half)

What to do:

1. *Before using an oilstone,* mount it on a piece of plywood about 3 inches wider than the stone. Place the stone in the center of the wood, and nail narrow strips of wood around it, as in Figure 132. This holds the stone in place.

Figure 132. Oilstone with wooden support

2. Prepare the stone for use by saturating it with light machine oil or a mixture of half machine oil and half kerosene.

3. Place a few drops of light machine oil on the stone before you use it to sharpen a tool. This floats away metal particles which might clog the stone. Wipe the stone clean after using it.

Sharpening knives

Hold the knife with its blade almost flat against the stone. Grasp the handle with one hand. Push down against the tip of the knife with your other hand. Raise the back edge of the knife.

Starting at one end of the stone, push the cutting edge of the knife *against* the stone; at the same time draw the blade sideways so that by the time you have reached the other end, the entire knife edge has come into contact with the stone (Figure 133). Turn the knife over, and repeat the procedure on the other side.

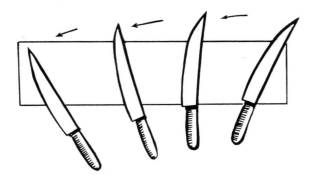

Figure 133. Movement of knife across stone

If the knife is very dull, give each side four or five strokes on the coarse side of the stone, then the same number of strokes on the fine side. To test for sharpness, hold up a piece of paper and try to slice through it.

You can use an electric knife sharpener as well, although it cannot be used on a knife with a serrated edge.

Sharpening a woodworking chisel

You will need:

Oilstone
Light machine oil or kerosene

What to do:

1. Apply a few drops of oil or kerosene to the oilstone. Place the chisel against the fine side of the oilstone so that the beveled end makes full contact. Hold the handle with one hand; with the other, press down on the bevel (Figure 134).

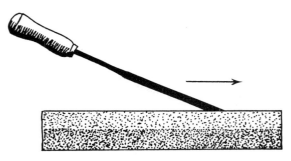

Figure 134. Sharpening a chisel

2. Push against the cutting end of the chisel along the full length of the stone. Be careful not to change the angle at which it rests against the stone. Lift the chisel and make as many strokes as needed until the end is sharp. Unless the chisel is badly nicked, three or four strokes should be sufficient to sharpen it.

3. Turn the chisel over and lay it *flat* on the stone with its beveled side up. Make a *light* stroke, the length of the stone. This will remove the rough wire edge that is formed when the chisel is sharpened on the beveled side.

4. For a superfine edge, strop the chisel on a piece of leather until it is sharp enough to cut a piece of paper. Any leather will do—try an old belt or purse.

Sharpening a plane iron

Follow the same procedure as you would if sharpening a chisel. Sharpen it by rubbing *across* the stone (Figure 135).

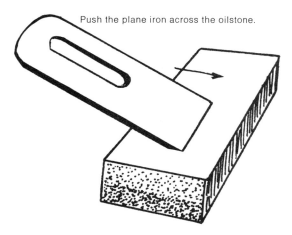

Push the plane iron across the oilstone.

Figure 135. Sharpening a plane iron

Sharpening scissors

Dull scissors can be just as exasperating as a dull knife, but you can easily restore a pair to useful service.

Examine a pair of scissors; you will find that the shearing edge is ground at right angles to the inner face of the blade. Place this edge flat against the oilstone; the inner face of the blade will be vertical. If you keep the blade vertical while you are working, you will not change the angle of the edge.

Make four or five zigzag strokes on the fine side of the oilstone; at the same time, move the blade from one end of the oilstone to the other (Figure 136).

Zig-zag scissors across the oilstone

Figure 136. Sharpening scissors

INDEX